THE JAPAN-US ALLIANCE OF HOPE

JAPAN LIBRARY

THE JAPAN-US ALLIANCE OF HOPE

Asia-Pacific Maritime Security

EDITED BY
Nakasone Peace Institute

SUPERVISED BY
Shinichi Kitaoka and Fumiaki Kubo

Japan Publishing Industry Foundation for Culture

Note to Readers
This book follows the Hepburn system of romanization. Long vowels are indicated by macrons. Japanese names are given in Western order, surname last.

The Japan-US Alliance of Hope: Asia-Pacific Maritime Security
Edited by Nakasone Peace Institute.
Supervised by Shinichi Kitaoka and Fumiaki Kubo.
Translated by Charles Stewart and Ikuo Anai.

Published by
Japan Publishing Industry Foundation for Culture (JPIC)
2-2-30 Kanda-Jinbocho, Chiyoda-ku, Tokyo 101-0051, Japan

First English edition: March 2020

© 2016 Nakasone Peace Institute
English translation © 2020 Japan Publishing Industry Foundation for Culture
All rights reserved

This book is a translation of *Kibō no Nichi-Bei dōmei: Ajia Taiheiyō no kaiyō anzen hoshō* (Chuokoron-Shinsha Inc., 2016).

English publishing rights arranged with Nakasone Peace Institute.

Book design: Kazuhiko Miki, Ampersand Works

Printed in Japan
ISBN 978-4-86658-138-5
https://japanlibrary.jpic.or.jp/

FOREWORD TO THE ENGLISH EDITION

The original Japanese version of *The Japan-US Alliance of Hope*, edited and published by the Nakasone Peace Institute, was based on the results of a research project conducted by the Institute. I am truly delighted that this book is now being published in English.

The Japanese edition was released in 2016. Since that time, the maritime security situation in the Asia-Pacific region has become considerably more tense, reflecting the overall worsening of the region's security environment. Japan has made numerous efforts to respond to the changing situation over this period, but there have been some concerns regarding the direction of the United States, Japan's ally. That does not by any means imply that the value of the Japan-US alliance is being diminished, however. And while there are some signs of improvement in Japan-China relations, we cannot be overly optimistic. Please see the addendum at the end of this English edition for an account of the major changes on the regional security scene since the original Japanese version was compiled.

I am very pleased at the unexpected possibility that the work of the Nakasone Peace Institute will reach readers worldwide through this English translation. I will be truly grateful if this book deepens people's understanding of Japan, particularly its security policy and security environment, and leads to progress in this area.

I can only express my hope that Japan's security environment becomes more favorable in the near future.

Yasuhiro Nakasone

Note: Former prime minister Nakasone wrote the above foreword for this English edition in the autumn of 2019, when the work was being translated. Unfortunately, he passed away in late November, before the project was completed. He was 101 years old. May he rest in peace. (Fumiaki Kubo)

FOREWORD TO THE JAPANESE EDITION

The maintenance of the maritime security order is essential for the development of the Asia-Pacific region. However, China's assertive maritime advance and the relative decline in the US presence are destabilizing the maritime security environment in this region.

For Japan, which has scarce natural resources and must depend on international trade for its prosperity, maintaining the stability of the maritime security environment is a vital issue.

After the Second World War, under the Japan-US alliance, Japan had the good fortune of being able to pursue economic prosperity while remaining lightly armed. Times are changing, however, and in the current international situation, Japan cannot ensure its own security through a one-sided alliance and the pacifism of a single nation. For Japan to sustain freedom and prosperity under the international order of democracy and the rule of law into the future, it must be prepared to take on a suitable burden for the preservation of order.

Recognizing that Japan is also expected to fulfill its appropriate roles and responsibilities under these conditions, the governments of Japan and the United States formulated new Guidelines for Japan-US Defense Cooperation in 2015. These guidelines reinforce the peace and security of Japan, and also strengthen the Japan-US alliance in the Asia-Pacific region and on a global scale.

In addition, the Japanese government decided to authorize limited use of the right of collective self-defense in 2014, and passed legislation for peace and security in 2015. With these developments, Japan's security policy reached a turning point, and it became possible for Japan to bear greater responsibility under the Japan-US alliance. As a consequence, policy decisions concerning security will become even more important in the future.

In a democratic nation, the understanding and support of the people constitute the foundation of national security policy. For that reason, the government must provide highly detailed explanations of security policy to the nation. Moreover, the security policies of a given country are closely related to international and regional conditions, so it is necessary for the Japanese people to share a correct understanding of the current conditions surrounding Japan.

This book is an easy-to-understand compilation of diverse essays written by experts on the topic of maritime security in the Asia-Pacific region and the Japan-US alliance. I hope that it will enable readers to deepen their understanding of the international situation centered on the Asia-Pacific, as well as Japan's new security policy and the Japan-US alliance.

I strongly recommend that people with an interest in Japan's security policy, including those who may not entirely agree with the direction being taken by the government, take the time to read this book. I sincerely hope that it will help to spark more active national discussions regarding the direction of the Japan-US alliance and Japanese security policy.

> *Yasuhiro Nakasone*
> Prime Minister of Japan 1982–1987
> Chairman, Nakasone Peace Institute

CONTENTS

PREFACE

Fumiaki Kubo

Professor, Graduate School for Law and Politics, University of Tokyo; Executive Director of Research, Maritime Security in the Asia-Pacific Region and the Japan-US Alliance Project, Nakasone Peace Institute

The title of this book, *The Japan-US Alliance of Hope*, comes from Prime Minister Shinzō Abe's April 2015 address to the US Congress, "Toward an Alliance of Hope." In that speech, Abe spoke about the past relations between Japan and the United States, which fought each other in the Second World War, as well as the present robust Japan-US alliance and the hope for a future in which Japan and the United States make a better world.

The Japan-US alliance has continued to deepen and develop for some sixty years in accordance with the changing security environment of the times, but we are now at a critical turning point which will determine the security order of the Asia-Pacific region. China's activities at sea are continuously intensifying, and the regional maritime security environment is becoming increasingly unstable. At a time when the existing order of the Asia-Pacific region, centered on the seas, is being threatened in this way, the Japan-US alliance is an "alliance of hope" for peace and prosperity.

This book analyzes the current conditions of the Japan-US alliance from the perspective of maintaining the maritime security order of the Asia-Pacific region, and examines the future direction of the partnership. It incorporates research on the diplomatic and security policies not only of Japan, the US, and China, but also of India, Australia, South Korea, Russia, and the countries of Southeast Asia as major players in the seas of the region, and offers important suggestions for the Japan-US alliance.

This book presents, in revised form, the results of the "Maritime Security in the Asia-Pacific Region and the Japan-US Alliance" research project implemented by the Institute for International Policy Studies (the current Nakasone Peace Institute) over a period of around one year from November 2014.

That project was implemented with assistance from the United States–Japan Foundation, and I would like to express my deepest gratitude for their support.

Authors' Note to the English Edition

This book was originally published in Japanese in April 2016. Since then we have seen major developments affecting the various situations and relationships that the book examined. In preparing this English edition we have not rewritten our respective chapters to reflect the new developments; instead we have attached an addendum that summarizes them. (Authors' professional titles and affiliations are given as of March 27, 2020.)

Meanwhile, we wish to express our sorrow at the passing of former prime minister Yasuhiro Nakasone in late November 2019, not long after he wrote a new foreword for this English edition. We can only hope that the Japan-US alliance—which he worked for many decades to strengthen—will progress in the positive direction for which he aimed.

Security and the "Defense of the Constitution" Debate

Shinichi Kitaoka

President, Japan International Cooperation Agency (JICA); Professor Emeritus, University of Tokyo; Chief Research Adviser, Nakasone Peace Institute

When a nation embarks on formulating security policies, the process should involve analyzing the security environment surrounding it and studying what is essential to prepare for potential threats to its security. It goes without saying that, in the process, due consideration should be given to internal conditions, including fiscal affordability, as well as to external factors, including not only the military balance with other nations but also diplomatic relations with them.

That said, national-security-related discussions in Japan to date have quite often been focused first and foremost on whether or not defense activities are constitutional. Discussions on the security environment surrounding the nation and relevant security policies have been held far less frequently. Since December 2012, when Shinzō Abe launched his second term as prime minister, his administration has carried out a series of reforms to Japan's security policies. Needless to say, the Abe administration has encountered various forms of opposition to the reform initiatives—the fiercest of which was seen when a new package of security bills was debated in the National Diet from May to September 2015. What happened during that period highlighted the typical peculiarity of security-related discussions in Japan. Parliamentary debates went on and on about the constitutionality of the proposed legislation rather than looking at the security environment surrounding the nation and considering necessary measures. The above-mentioned peculiarity became particularly conspicuous during deliberations on the package of security bills in the ordinary session of the Diet in 2015.

Prime Minister Abe Reforms Japan's Security Systems

Since its launch in December 2012, the second Abe administration has made a series of reforms in the fields of security and foreign affairs. The following is a brief overview of what the administration has achieved thus far:

First, the Abe administration secured passage of the Act on the Protection of Specially Designated Secrets in December 2013. Japan has had much leakage of secret information, and this has hindered the deepening of its relations with friends and allies. The new law established a set of rules to prevent leaks of sensitive security-related secrets. However, its passage caused the administration to suffer a sharp fall of as much as about 10 points in approval ratings in public opinion polls conducted by various news outlets. Despite the fact that it was only adopting what should have been implemented much earlier, the administration was accused of trying to restrict people's right to know. Some opponents of the new legislation were upset enough to liken it to the prewar Maintenance of Public Order Act. A few months later, however, the public approval ratings of the Abe administration bounced back.

In December 2013, the administration also made history by inaugurating the National Security Council and implementing the nation's first National Security Strategy, clarifying its pledge to make a more proactive contribution to international peace. The NSC and the NSS serve as a highly important mechanism and a fundamental code, respectively, to allow the nation to deal with its diplomatic and security challenges strategically and comprehensively while overcoming the notorious shortcomings of its vertically segmented administrative system. As for the pledge to contribute more proactively to international peace, some people criticized it as a way of enabling the government to easily dispatch Japan's Self-Defense Forces (SDF) overseas. Nonetheless, generally speaking, opposition did not gather momentum, an outcome that might be attributed to the fact that the Democratic Party of Japan (DPJ), which governed the nation from September 2009 to December 2012, had at that time promoted plans to set up an NSC on its own.

In December 2013, the government set out the "National Defense Program Guidelines for FY 2014 and Beyond" (NDPG 2013), as new guidelines for Japan's national defense, based on the National Security Strategy. NDPG 2013 was a rewritten version of the "National Defense Program Guidelines for FY 2011 and Beyond" (NDPG 2010), which was adopted when the DPJ was governing the nation. The guidelines drew attention for their "Dynamic Joint Defense Force" concept; NDPG 2010, in contrast, had envisaged developing a "Dynamic Defense Force" that would possess "readiness, mobility, flexibility, sustainability, and versatility." The 2013 concept added a new goal of "developing advanced technology and information, command, and communications capabilities" on top of the 2010 version's goal. However, the "Dynamic Defense Force" concept itself was a rewritten version of the "Basic Defense Force" concept, which had been originally adopted in the midst of the Cold War with a focus on strengthening self-defense capabilities in northern Japan. The conceptual shift to the "Dynamic Joint Defense Force," therefore did not necessarily mean a significant transformation of the Basic Defense Force concept in practice. In a nutshell, there was not much of a difference between the security policies adopted by the second Abe administration after December 2012 and those adopted under the DPJ government that preceded it. It was therefore natural that criticism of the Abe administration did not get out of hand.

In April 2014, the government introduced the "Three Principles on Defense Equipment Transfers," superseding the decades-old "Three Principles on Arms Exports." While the earlier self-imposed ban very strictly prohibited arms exports, the new Three Principles allow the nation, on the basis of the National Security Strategy, to take a flexible approach to exporting defense equipment in order to ensure the peace, stability, and prosperity of the international community. For example, Japan may be able to contribute more effectively to peace in the world by agreeing to a request for the provision of defense equipment from a small country that is being threatened by a large one.

Such an approach is clearly in line with the Development Cooperation Charter adopted by the government in February 2015. Development cooperation can be part of a broadly defined security policy. While pledging to continue contributing to the international community by extending development cooperation for non-military purposes as in the past, the charter states: "In case the armed forces or members of the armed forces in recipient countries are involved in development cooperation for non-military purposes such as . . . disaster-relief purposes, such cases will be considered on a case-by-case basis in light of their substantive relevance."[1] This is in conformity with one of the purposes of the NSS—strategic utilization of official development assistance. As a result, it is now possible to provide military personnel from certain recipient countries with education on international relations without restraints. When this approach to military personnel in recipient countries was adopted, various groups of people raised their voices against the plan, but again, there was no widespread criticism.

In April 2015, Tokyo and Washington agreed on a new set of "Guidelines for Japan-U.S. Defense Cooperation." The new guidelines clarify the roles and missions as well as the policy direction of both sides for improved bilateral security cooperation and coordination. In other words, the relevance of the Japan-US alliance has been enhanced to the extent that it now can deal better with the new security environment.

As explained above, the Abe administration has achieved a number of diplomatic and security policy reforms—all of which have been important—in a relatively short time. In the past, it would have taken many years even for just one of Abe's reform initiatives to be realized. Indeed, it can be said that Japan has witnessed a series of major changes in diplomatic and security policies under the second Abe administration. I think that there are external and internal factors that have accelerated the aforementioned changes. The external factors include changes in the international situation, such as China's fast-rising military power. The domestic factor to note is the fact that the Democratic Party of Japan was in power for more than three years before Abe's Liberal Democratic Party took back the reins.

However, in 2015, when a package of bills named "Legislation for Peace and Security" was before the Diet, changes did not take place smoothly. Both Japanese news media and opposition parties strongly opposed the package, especially the parts concerning reinterpretation of the Constitution.

The Debate on "Reconstruction of the Legal Basis for Security"

Now, let me look back on what was discussed in the government's Advisory Panel on Reconstruction of the Legal Basis for Security in 2013 and 2014. The panel's recommendations became a theoretical basis for the government's security-related bills. The chairperson of the panel was Shunji Yanai, a former ambassador to the United States; I served as deputy chairperson.

The advisory panel pointed out that, first of all, the Constitution of Japan expresses various values, the most fundamental of which is the safety of the country. Without safety, the panel went on to say, the values of popular sovereignty, basic human rights, and the pursuit of happiness cannot be realized. As such, paragraph 2 of Article 9 of the Constitution—"Land, sea, and air forces, as well as other war potential, will never be maintained. The right of belligerency of the state will not be recognized"—should be seen as a stipulation that defines a means of achieving peace, not as something like a supreme principle.

The second point at issue raised by the advisory panel was that, while there are those who argue that it is not permissible to change interpretation of the Constitution, the panel's conclusion was that it should be viable to do so.

For example, paragraph 2 of Article 66 of the Constitution states, "The Prime Minister and other Ministers of State must be civilians." This became a point of contention even in the years immediately after the Constitution was introduced—some questioned who "civilians" (i.e., non-military personnel) were in Japan, where no armed forces existed in the wake of the country's 1945 defeat in the Second World War. The definition of the term "civilian" consequently changed a few times. Later on, a conclusive interpretation emerged that "civilians" are those who are not members of the SDF. It is compatible with the global interpretation of the term. This is a definite example of a change in interpretation of the Constitution.

Likewise, we have Article 89 of the Constitution, which states, "No public money or other property shall be expended or appropriated for the use, benefit or maintenance of any religious institution or association, or for any charitable, educational or benevolent enterprises not under the control of public authority." If this article is strictly interpreted, there cannot be any way for the government to provide public subsidies to private universities and schools under the existing Constitution. In reality, as everyone knows, they do receive public subsidies—an example of a de facto revision of part of the Constitution. As is clear from all these cases, it can be possible to effectively revise the Constitution by changing its interpretation.

The third point at issue raised by the Advisory Panel on Reconstruction of the Legal Basis for Security was the possibility of changing the interpretation of the Constitution regarding a particularly pressing issue—the security of Japan.

Shigeru Yoshida, who was prime minister when the Constitution was promulgated in November 1946, interpreted the new basic and supreme law as prohibiting both war and armed forces. Nevertheless, in 1954, Yoshida's constitutional interpretation was modified by the government. On December 22 of that year, Seiichi Ōmura, then director-general of the Defense Agency, speaking of the Self-Defense Forces established in July of the same year, said in answer to a question in the Budget Committee of the House of Representatives: "The Constitution, while renouncing war, has not renounced fighting for self-defense. . . . To repel an armed attack in the event of such an attack from other countries is self-defense itself, and is essentially different from settling international disputes. Hence, the use of force as an instrument for defending national territory when an armed attack has been launched against the nation does not violate the Constitution. . . . It is not a violation of the Constitution for Japan to set up an armed force such as the SDF having a mission for self-defense and to possess military force to the extent that is necessary for that purpose."

In December 1959, the grand bench of the Supreme Court issued the following ruling on the so-called Sunagawa case:

> Article [9] renounces the so-called war and prohibits the maintenance of the so-called war potential prescribed in the article, but certainly there is nothing in it which would deny the right of self-defense of Japan inherent in our nation as a sovereign power. The pacifism advocated in our Constitution was never intended to mean defenselessness or nonresistance.
>
> As it is clear from the Preamble of the Constitution, we, the Japanese people, desire to occupy an honored place in international society, which is striving for the preservation of peace and the banishment of tyranny and slavery, oppression and intolerance for all time from the earth, and affirm that we have the right, along with and in the same manner as all the people of the world, to live in peace, free from fear and want.
>
> In view of this, it is only natural for our country, in the exercise of powers inherent in a state, to maintain peace and security, to take whatever measures may be necessary for self-defense, and to preserve its very existence.[2]

As for the 1954 modification of the interpretation of the Constitution that followed the establishment of the SDF, members of the Diet should have extensively discussed whether to approve or disapprove of this. If the opposition parties insist that they have not agreed to any modification, it has to be said that the SDF continues to exist in violation of the Constitution. Considering that the presence of the SDF is actually supported and appreciated by a great majority of people in Japan, the opposition camp is likely to continue to put itself in a difficult position in terms of its relations with the electorate if it declares that it does not consent to this 1954 reinterpretation. If, on the other hand, the opposition camp says that it has already given its consent to the modification of the government's constitutional interpretation, it is tantamount to acknowledging that (1) changing constitutional interpretations is permitted and that (2) "use of force" to the minimum extent necessary for the purpose of self-defense is constitutional. Needless to say, those two points were different from the position of the DPJ and other opposition parties in 2015.

The fourth important point at issue is who is responsible for deciding what the "minimum necessary" requirements are for the purpose of self-defense.

The "minimum necessary" level of Japan's self-defense force naturally varies from time to time. One of the challenging aspects of security is the difficulty of foreseeing what kinds of events will actually happen in the future. For instance, only about twenty years after the Russo-Japanese War, three sea changes occurred to the security environment surrounding Japan: the use of oil as a mainstay fuel in the military sphere; the emergence of aircraft; and the development of submarines. These changes made it clear that Japan, which has virtually no oil reserves to exploit, had to import oil from areas far away from it; that the nation was highly vulnerable to air raids; and that imports might come to a halt once the sea transportation lanes used by it were disrupted by foreign submarines. The nation became aware of this new security environment during the First World War. Nevertheless, it entered the Second World War without modifying its overall maritime policy. What is clear from the nation's aforementioned experiences is that its safety can only be jeopardized if it opts to keep its security policies unchanged even in light of a change in its security environment.

As explained above, the Advisory Panel on Reconstruction of the Legal Basis for Security squarely declared that there was nothing wrong with amending the interpretation of the Constitution—a clear message that criticized those who advocated preserving it strictly intact.

The Advisory Panel Report and the Subsequent Cabinet Decision

The Advisory Panel on Reconstruction of the Legal Basis for Security issued its report on May 15, 2014, and a cabinet decision was adopted on July 1 of the same year. Despite news reports that the latter was based on the advisory panel's recommendations, there were in fact considerable differences between the two.

As detailed above, the advisory panel recommended (1) that the nation restart its debate on the Constitution from the points clarified in the 1954 statement of the then Defense Agency chief that reinterpreted the Constitution and the Supreme Court's ruling of 1959 on the so-called Sunagawa case; and (2) that "international disputes" mentioned in paragraph 1 of Article

9 of the Constitution—which renounces "use of force as means of settling international disputes"—be reconsidered.

However, in its July 1, 2014, decision, the cabinet made a move on its own to reinterpret the document the government submitted to the Diet in 1972, which stated that "use of force . . . is permitted only when an armed attack against Japan occurs." The new cabinet decision said:

> The government has reached a conclusion that not only when an armed attack against Japan occurs but also when an armed attack against a foreign country that is in a close relationship with Japan occurs and as a result threatens Japan's survival and poses a clear danger to fundamentally overturn people's right to life, liberty and pursuit of happiness, and when there is no other appropriate means available to repel the attack and ensure Japan's survival and protect its people, use of force to the minimum extent necessary should be interpreted to be permitted under the Constitution as measures for self-defense in accordance with the basic logic of the government's view to date.[3]

For its part, the advisory panel's recommendation said:

> The provision of paragraph 1 of Article 9 of the Constitution ("Aspiring sincerely to an international peace based on justice and order, the Japanese people forever renounce war as a sovereign right of the nation and the threat or use of force as means of settling international disputes.") should be interpreted as prohibiting the threat or the use of force as means of settling international disputes to which Japan is a party. The provisions should be interpreted as not prohibiting the use of force for the purpose of self-defense nor imposing any constitutional restrictions on activities that are consistent with international law, such as participation in United Nations peacekeeping operations (PKOs) and the like or collective security measures.[4]

The cabinet decision of July 2014 made no mention of this part of the advisory panel's recommendation. In essence, the advisory panel recommended that the existing constitutional interpretation prohibiting Japan from exercising the right of collective self-defense be completely reconsidered; i.e., that it should be permitted for this right to be exercised, but that the government should be as prudent as possible in actually choosing to exercise the right.

Instead of accepting this recommendation, the cabinet asserted that exercising the right of collective self-defense was "permitted on a limited basis." I think this represented a victory for the Cabinet Legislation Bureau and Kōmeitō, the junior coalition partner of the ruling Liberal Democratic Party.

What Will Eventually Change?

The Diet finally voted the Legislation for Peace and Security into law in 2015. What will happen next?

The first thing we need to know is what will happen within the territorial land, sea, and air of Japan under the new legislation. In the past, a set of different security responses, including "defense operations" by members of the SDF under the Self-Defense Forces Law, has been in place to deal with an armed attack on the nation. In the event of an infringement from a foreign nation that does not amount to an armed attack, known as a "gray-zone case," police will be primarily responsible for dealing with it. If it is deemed that the infringement exceeds ordinary police capabilities to control and maintain public safety, the SDF will be ordered to undertake "public security operations." The Maritime Self-Defense Force will be ordered to take "maritime security action" when special measures are deemed necessary to protect lives and property or maintain order at sea.

It has been pointed out for many years that SDF troops ordered to undertake "public security operations" and "maritime security action" might not be able to carry out their duties properly because the criteria for use of weapons in such operations are different from those for "defense operations." Nonetheless, the 2015 Legislation for Peace and Security did not include any revisions pertaining to "gray-zone" situations. In other words, the government chose to uphold the long-standing principle of responding to an external armed attack against Japan only with "defense operations."

Second, we need to scrutinize measures to protect Japanese nationals overseas. SDF troops now can carry out operations to rescue Japanese nationals overseas in the event of an emergency in their host countries. Considering the transportation and intelligence-gathering capabilities that would be required, it is thought that such missions will hardly ever be undertaken. That said, the presence of SDF troops abroad could become necessary and even effective for the protection of Japanese nationals under some circumstances. The new principle also means that armed forces abroad that pose threats to Japanese nationals must be aware that they will have to bear the extra burden of preparing for a situation in which SDF personnel may actually come to the rescue of Japanese nationals.

The third point is related to crises that occur outside of Japan but will inevitably result in threatening Japan's own survival if it opts to do nothing in support of foreign countries with close ties to Japan when they (or, in many possible cases, their vessels) are under attack. This issue turned out be the most contentious in the process of discussing the Legislation for Peace and Security. The new legislation has opened the way for Japan to make a new approach to the above-mentioned situations outside of the country. Japan is now able to exercise the right of collective self-defense to join forces with others for repelling such attacks. The new legislation thus permits Japan to partially exercise the right of collective self-defense. This essentially means that the SDF can now cooperate more closely in areas around Japan with the armed forces of the United States and other countries that have close ties with our country.

With the adoption of the new comprehensive legislation, what was previously known as the "Act Concerning Measures to Ensure the Peace and Security of Japan in Perilous Situations in Areas Surrounding Japan" has been replaced by the "Act Concerning Measures to Ensure the Peace and Security of Japan in Situations That Will Have an Important Influence on Japan's Peace and Security." This revision now enables Japan to more flexibly provide logistical support to the armed forces of the United States and other countries that have close relations with Japan.

As stated above, Japan is now permitted to exercise the right of collective self-defense on a limited basis. So Japan can now engage in security cooperation with not only the United States but also other countries that have close relations with our nation. Further, such cooperation can now be reciprocal, albeit on a limited scale, with geographical restraints eased to some extent. Those changes are certain to make SDF operations increasingly flexible, enhancing deterrence to some extent.

Fourth, as mentioned above, these changes may help ensure the safety of maritime transportation. As is often pointed out in the Diet, Japan has already dispatched Maritime Self-Defense Force vessels to the seas off the coast of Somalia and the Gulf of Aden to take part in a multilateral anti-piracy task force aimed at enhancing the safety of maritime transportation. In the 2000s, the MSDF carried out refueling activities for vessels from a number of countries in the Indian Ocean as part of the international fight against terrorism. So even if Japan has an opportunity to engage in patrol activities in the Indian Ocean—a new development that will surely contribute to the enhancement of deterrence—there will be little practical change from what Japan has already done.

After all, as observed above, the Legislation for Peace and Security is unlikely to bring any major change in superficial terms. Nonetheless, it will help Japan enhance deterrence, a function that is usually invisible. There is no question at all about the possibility that the new legislation will contribute to the long-term stabilization of the security environment around Japan. It is widely thought that the legislation tacitly focuses on China. But, as history shows, China has been cautious about military clashes with other countries. Therefore, though there may be an escalation in military tensions between Japan and China, it is unlikely that a military clash will take place between the two countries. The new legislation is exactly what was hoped for as a security-related framework, since it is not provocative to other countries but still enhances Japan's deterrence. As mentioned earlier, it will also increase deterrence in the context of maritime transportation.

I have to mention one thing in connection with the new legislation that causes me regret. It is about international peacekeeping operations, an area that is likely to change drastically in the years to come. Many countries in the world get actively involved in international cooperation activities, such as peacekeeping operations, contributing to the peace of other countries or regions, despite dangerous circumstances surrounding their PKO personnel. Only one country—Japan—tends to evade such circumstances. When the Diet debated the Legislation for Peace and Security, it should have seriously taken up this shameful aspect of Japan's PKO activities. The fact that it spent almost no time meaningfully discussing this issue was a disgrace to the Japanese parliament.

Instead, certain lawmakers expressed opinions that only revealed their surprising lack of understanding about the latest in the military sphere. They characterized the new legislation as a "conscription law" or a "war law"—both of which were far different from the contents of the new legislation—thereby leading the public astray. As for the current security environment, we are now living in an age in which outer space and cyberspace are rapidly gaining prominence as new realms in the theater of war. It is undeniable that Japan is at least one lap behind other major countries in terms of developing space and cyber warfare capabilities. Despite the adoption of the Legislation for Peace and Security, Japan's policies and activities in the security sphere are still far short of the international norm, and most foreign governments recognize that the security policies pursued by the Abe administration are not excessive.

Conclusion

Throughout their debates, members of the Advisory Panel on Reconstruction of the Legal Basis for Security shared a common understanding—an utterly common-sense view in the rest of the world—that security issues and issues related to the Constitution should be discussed separately.

In reality, there is no guarantee that an effort to preserve a constitution itself can guarantee the security of a nation. For example, in 1939 and 1940—the early years of the Second World War—France, Belgium, Denmark, Norway, and Poland kept preserving their respective constitutions. It is well known that all of them were unable to guarantee their security against the invading Germans. Meanwhile, if Japan had opted to abide strictly by the Constitution of the Empire of Japan, also known as the Meiji Constitution, to the very end, it would not have been able to surrender in August 1945. Under the Meiji Constitution, sovereignty rested with the emperor. This Constitution ruled out any possibility of the absolute imperial sovereignty being either delegated to anyone else or any institution or placed under certain restrictions. This prospect was exactly what the Allied Powers told Japan to accept in July 1945 with the Potsdam Declaration (Proclamation Defining Terms for Japanese Surrender), which stated, "The authority of the Emperor and the Japanese government to rule the state shall be subject to the Supreme Commander for the Allied Powers."

In the Diet debate on the Legislation for Peace and Security, some advocates of preserving the Constitution argued that doing so would preserve the security of the nation. Their arguments were groundless in both theoretical and empirical terms. It must be emphasized that the Constitution, international law, and the military balance with other nations are all essential in order to ensure Japan's security.

The debate in the Advisory Panel on Reconstruction of the Legal Basis for Security left an important lesson to be learned by people in the future. The Legislation for Peace and Security may take root in the Japanese political landscape, as happened in the case of the constitutional reinterpretation of 1954 and that of the International Peace Cooperation Act of 1992. Even so, it should be remembered that the advisory panel concluded that the right of collective self-defense is fully constitutional and that, at the same time, the government should be fully prudent in actually exercising the right. But the Abe administration decided to only partially remove the ban on exercising this right of collective self-defense. Someday in the future, the Japanese government may reach the limits of what it is allowed to do in terms of collective security or the like under this decision. And now that Prime Minister Abe has told the Diet that the Constitution allows nothing beyond these limits, the only possible response to such an eventuality would be to amend the Constitution. In the meantime, if the new security-related legislation does not take a firm hold, measures taken to ensure the security of Japan will likely continue to be insufficient. In any case, the issue of reconciling the existing Constitution and the nation's security policies will have to be dealt with anew in the future, because the recommendations of the advisory panel were not fully accepted by the government. What to do with paragraph 2 of Article 9 of the Constitution—the cornerstone on which those who advocate preserving the Constitution rely to continue their campaigns—is expected to remain the core agenda for Japan's debate on its security in the future.

1   English translation from the Ministry of Foreign Affairs, "Cabinet Decision on the Development Cooperation Charter," February 10, 2015, https://www.mofa.go.jp/files/000067701.pdf.

2   English translation from the Supreme Court of Japan, "Judgment upon case of the so-called Sunakawa Case," http://www.courts.go.jp/app/hanrei_en/detail?id=13.

3   English translation from the Ministry of Foreign Affairs, "Cabinet Decision on Development of Seamless Security Legislation to Ensure Japan's Survival and Protect its People," July 1, 2014, https://www.mofa.go.jp/fp/nsp/page23e_000273.html.

4   English translation from "Report of the Advisory Panel on Reconstruction of the Legal Basis for Security," May 15, 2014, https://www.kantei.go.jp/jp/singi/anzenhosyou2/dai7/houkoku_en.pdf.

CHAPTER 1

Asymmetry in the Rights and Obligations under the Japan-US Security Treaty

Fumiaki Kubo

Professor, Graduate School for Law and Politics, University of Tokyo; Executive Director of Research, Maritime Security in the Asia-Pacific Region and the Japan-US Alliance Project, Nakasone Peace Institute

Introduction

In this chapter, I would like to examine the asymmetry in the rights and obligations under the Japan-US Security Treaty.

As used here, "asymmetry" does not refer to asymmetry in military power or wide-ranging national strength. The Japan-US alliance is obviously asymmetrical in military terms, because US military power is predominant. In that sense, all alliances concluded by the United States are asymmetrical.

Here, asymmetry refers to the rights and obligations specified by the treaty. The examinations in this chapter are limited to the Japan-US Security Treaty (Treaty of Mutual Cooperation and Security between Japan and the United States) as revised in 1960.

Under the Japan-US Security Treaty, the US has the right to use bases in Japan and the obligation to defend Japan in return. Japan, conversely, has the obligation to allow the US to use military bases in Japan and the right to be defended by the US. The point that should be noted here is that under this treaty, Japan has no obligation to defend the US unless US government facilities are attacked at a location where Japan has administrative authority. Because an attack on US government facilities inside Japan is considered virtually the same as an attack on Japan (and attacking US government facilities inside Japan without attacking Japan itself is virtually impossible), in real terms Japan is exempt from any obligation to defend the US.

In alliances throughout the world and throughout history, it is usual for both parties to promise one another rights and obligations that are basically identical. For example, in an alliance between country A and country B, if country A is attacked, country B agrees to protect country A, and if country B is attacked, country A likewise agrees to provide support to country B. Under the definitions used in this chapter, alliances structured in this way are deemed to be symmetrical in terms of rights and obligations, because the rights and obligations of country A are the same as those of country B.

In this chapter, I will consider the strengths and weaknesses of the Japan-US alliance, which is asymmetrical in this sense.

Benefits for the US

Why is it that the US undertook the obligation to defend Japan under the Japan-US Security Treaty, even though that places the lives of American troops at risk? The answer lies in the rights secured by the US under the treaty. Under Article 6, the US is granted the right to use military bases in Japan for the purpose of contributing to the peace and security of the Far East. In other words, in exchange for undertaking the obligation to defend Japan, the US gained the right to use bases in Japan for purposes other than the defense of Japan. This is precisely at the heart of the national interests secured by the US under the Japan-US Security Treaty.

There is not enough space here for a detailed account explaining why such an asymmetrical alliance was formed, so I will limit the discussion to presenting the following points.

When the original Japan-US Security Treaty was signed in 1951, Japan had already adopted its postwar Constitution, including Article 9, which renounces war as a sovereign right. The country had been completely disarmed after the Second World War, and did not even have the Self-Defense Forces (SDF), which were established in 1954. At the same time, the US had overwhelming military strength, with no real need to rely on Japan for the defense of the US mainland. But with the outbreak of the Korean War in 1950, Japan came under direct threat as well, and the US judged that it needed to continue making use of Japan's military bases for its own efforts to counter the military threat from the Communist camp.

Many analysts use the term "unilateral" when describing the Japan-US Security Treaty from 1960 up to the present. Strictly speaking, however, that is not correct. Because the US is obliged to defend Japan, and Japan is obliged to allow the US to use military bases in Japan for purposes other than the defense of Japan, the US and Japan both have obligations under the treaty. In that sense, the treaty is certainly bilateral. Nevertheless, as explained above, because the rights and obligations on the two sides are not the same, the treaty is asymmetrical.

Incidentally, under the original treaty signed in 1951, the US gained the rights to station its military on bases within Japan, but its obligations did not include the duty to defend Japan, so the treaty was truly one-sided. Naturally, this original treaty was heavily criticized, especially within Japan.

When the Japan-US Security Treaty is compared with other US alliances, definite differences become apparent. The Mutual Defense Treaty between the United States and the Republic of Korea (South Korea) signed in 1953 specifies mutual defense obligations, and the defense obligations among the member countries in the North Atlantic Treaty Organization (NATO), which was founded in 1949, are also mutual. Beyond those obligations, however, the stationing of US armed forces in South Korea and in some NATO countries in Europe is specified as an addition.[1]

In the following sections, I would like to consider the strengths and merits of the Japan-US Security Treaty, as well as its weaknesses and drawbacks, in the context of this unusual structure of rights and obligations. I would like to conduct this discussion keeping in mind the comparison with alliances that are symmetrical in terms of their rights and obligations.

Weaknesses of the Asymmetrical Alliance

To begin with, I will enumerate the weaknesses and drawbacks of the asymmetrical alliance.

First, one may note that this alliance is extremely difficult for nonspecialists to understand. In a country that is a partner in an alliance, the public perception of the alliance generally emphasizes the burdens undertaken by that country, as this is what catches the attention of citizens and the media. As a result, public understanding and support of the alliance does not grow stronger; rather, people voice criticism of it that is uninformed and often off the mark.

In Japan, the burdens that the US military bases impose on local residents tend to be perceived as problematic; this perception is particularly strong in Okinawa. Meanwhile, in the US, the Japan-US alliance is often characterized as a one-sided and unfair alliance whereby the US is obliged to defend Japan while Japan bears no obligations whatsoever. When Japan-US trade friction intensified from the 1980s through the 1990s, such arguments were frequently voiced in the US. Pundits questioned why it was necessary to allow American blood to be spilled to defend a powerful country like Japan, which was threatening the US economically. Recently, in the primary battle within the Republican Party prior to the 2016 US presidential election, leading candidate Donald Trump frequently voiced such a position. It is easy to elicit this kind of dissatisfaction from Americans who have only a superficial understanding of the Japan-US alliance.

Second, it is easy to generate opposition to the bases within Japan, where the burdens they impose are felt most keenly. This opposition may be directed not just at the presence of these foreign military facilities but also at the presence of their foreign personnel. Friction with local residents is frequently noted. (Crimes by US military personnel sometimes become a serious issue, but according to the US authorities, the crime rate among this group is lower than the overall average in Okinawa. This is an area that requires more thorough investigation). Of course, even if the Japan-US Security Treaty did not exist, Self-Defense Forces bases would likely be concentrated in Okinawa to some extent because of that region's importance as a strategic point for Japanese security. Nevertheless, there is certainly a difference in scale between the level of military force required solely for the defense of Japan and the level of military force required for other defense in addition to Japan's—especially defending the peace and security of the Far East. It goes without saying that the latter is far greater. In that sense, the burden of large bases is one drawback of the asymmetrical alliance.

Third is the fact that some Japanese view the stationing of US forces as a continuation of the US occupation of Japan (1945–1952). For Japanese with a nationalistic viewpoint, the stationing of foreign troops inside Japan is itself humiliating, and a violation of Japanese sovereignty.

Fourth, from the Japanese perspective, I would like to point out the possibility that Japan may have lost some of its will to defend its own security. Because US forces are permanently stationed inside Japan, reliance on the US has tended to grow stronger. As a result, even in the midst of the Cold War, the relationship between the US and Japan was rarely perceived as an alliance of partners who fight together. (In contrast, the US–South Korea alliance was established after the Korean War was fought, and was in fact formed as a result of the two countries' troops fighting together in that conflict).

Fifth, within Japan there are problems besides those related to the stationing of US forces. Japan and the US have concluded a status of forces agreement; this can easily become a point of contention or a cause of dispute pertaining to issues such as the rights of the US armed forces stationed in Japan, environmental pollution, and the obligations of the Japanese side and so-called host-nation support.

Strengths of the Asymmetrical Alliance

Next I will point out some strengths and advantages of the asymmetrical alliance.

First, having US troops stationed in Japan is a powerful and credible deterrent to attack. Having US armed forces stationed in Japan is clearly a stronger deterrent than the prospect of rushing troops from the distant US mainland when some incident occurs. It certainly leaves no room for doubt regarding US military support, as attacking Japan becomes virtually the same as attacking the US. It may even function as deterrence against a nuclear attack.

Second, the ability of US armed forces to respond to disasters should be acknowledged. This was witnessed by local residents after the Tōhoku earthquake and tsunami of March 11, 2011. The assistance rendered by US forces under Operation Tomodachi in response to the disaster was on a very large scale, and was highly effective. This operation involved 24,000 US service members and cost $80 million. This was a case where the benefits of having US forces nearby were manifest. There is no small value in having a fully equipped aircraft carrier and other resources manned by well-trained troops that can respond very quickly.

Third, one can generally note the contributions of the bases to the local communities, starting with the economic benefits. Fundamentally, it can be said that the contributions to local economies are substantial.

For many years, the US Department of Defense has struggled with its inability to close unnecessary bases within the US. This is because the congressional representatives of the areas where these bases are located work hard to keep them open. Such efforts, of course, represent the will of their constituents. These bases also function as a countermeasure against depopulation. However, there is also a logical argument that the existence of bases may serve as an obstacle to economic growth; careful case-by-case analysis is required to determine whether this is happening.

At any rate, US military bases in Japan have been shown to strengthen communities and bring greater vitality to depopulated areas. The same effect has been recognized for Self-Defense Forces bases.

Fourth, the US military bases in Japan are a venue for cultural exchange. Japanese people come into contact with American culture, while US military personnel are given an opportunity to become familiar with Japanese culture and possibly even become fans of Japan. With some skillful arranging, this can facilitate substantial cultural exchange. Moreover, after they return to the US, the Americans are likely to feel positive toward Japan. It may be necessary for Japanese to keep this in mind as they interact with US bases and military personnel while they are in Japan.

A fifth advantage is the US forces' contribution to regional security in areas near Japan. This can be said to be a direct consequence of the asymmetrical character of the Japan-US security alliance. The US has the right to use its troops stationed in Japan for purposes other than the defense of Japan. As a result of Japan's hosting of US military bases, the US can extend its military influence beyond the Korean Peninsula and the Taiwan Strait to the Philippines, the South China Sea, and all the way to the Middle East. All of this is supported by the Japan-US alliance. Furthermore, Article 6 of the Japan-US Security Treaty supports the foundations of maritime security in the Asia-Pacific region, which is the main topic of this book.

A sixth advantage is the broader economic benefits that the presence of US armed forces brings to Japan. Because the US troops stationed here act as such a powerful deterrent, Japan has been able to keep its defense expenditures minimal (they have long been less than 1 percent of its GDP). This has allowed Japan to devote itself largely to economic development while remaining lightly armed. Furthermore, this minimal military buildup means that other countries do not view Japan as much of a threat.

Some Additional Observations

Former prime minister Yukio Hatoyama firmly believed in a Japan-US Security Treaty that did not involve the stationing of US troops. His idea was that the US military should not be stationed in Japan during peacetime, but should rather come to Japan's aid and defend Japan in case of a crisis. Hatoyama says that though he did not raise this idea while he was in office, that does not mean he abandoned it as incorrect. In any case, the US would benefit very little from the Japan-US alliance if such a proposal were adopted.

Democratic Party of Japan leader Ichirō Ozawa has said that stationing only the US Seventh Fleet would be sufficient for Japan. However, this view takes only the defense of Japan into account, and ignores US rights under Article 6 of the Japan-US Security Treaty. Many Japanese question whether the presence of the US Marine Corps is really necessary for the defense of Okinawa or the defense of Japan. This question, like the statements of Hatoyama and others, is rather one-sided. The US Marine Corps is useful for the defense of Japan in many ways, but even if that were not the case, Article 6 allows the US to station Marines in Japan as long as is deemed necessary.

These assertions are just two examples of many showing the lack of understanding that a great many people in Japan, including a prime minister, have demonstrated regarding the fundamentals of the Japan-US Security Treaty.

Conclusion

In the above sections, I have examined the strengths and weaknesses of the structure of the Japan-US Security Treaty, focusing on the asymmetry in the rights and obligations that it specifies. My intent, however, is not to suggest or propose that this asymmetry be eliminated.

The above discussion has confirmed that, while the asymmetry in rights and obligations under the alliance has rather serious drawbacks, it also has certain advantages. Given these circumstances, priority should be given in the future to consideration of how to maintain or increase the above-noted advantages, while also working to address and compensate for the shortcomings of the alliance.

The fact that the Japanese government revised its interpretation of the Constitution regarding the right of collective self-defense, securing the enactment of new national security legislation in 2015 to redefine the parameters, may also be deemed revolutionary and historic in terms of this asymmetrical alliance structure. The government's revised interpretation of the right to collective self-defense, while still subject to various restrictions, has greatly expanded the extent to which the Japanese side can contribute to US military actions. The addition of the exercise of collective self-defense not as a treaty obligation, but as a right held by Japan, has shored up the weakest aspects of the asymmetrical alliance structure. This change means that when certain conditions are met, Japan can fight for its own security together with the US military.

The administration of an alliance is never easy, regardless of the terms specified. When the rights and obligations are asymmetrical, as under the Japan-US alliance, it becomes even more difficult. From this perspective, the recent enactment of Japan's new security legislation can be expected to ease this difficulty over the medium to long term.

1   For a more detailed comparison, see Fumiaki Kubo, "Amerika gaikō ni totte no dōmei to Nichi-Bei dōmei: Hitotsu no mitorizu" [Alliances for American diplomacy and the Japan-US alliance: One sketch] in *Amerika ni totte dōmei to wa nanika?* [What are alliances for America?], edited by Fumiaki Kubo and supervised by the Japan Institute of International Affairs, Chuokoron-Shinsha, 2013, 3–30.

CHAPTER 2

Japan's National Security Strategy and the Japan-US Alliance

Yūichi Hosoya
Professor, Keiō University; Senior Researcher, Institute for International Policy Studies

Introduction

Japan's security policy is evolving significantly under the administration of Shinzō Abe, who took office on December 26, 2012. At the same time, the Japan-US alliance is also being transformed in response to a new era and a new security environment. Just how, then, is Japan's security policy evolving and changing? And how is the Japan-US security alliance being transformed?

There have been four main developments in Japanese security policy under the Abe administration. The first was the establishment of the National Security Council of Japan. A bill to partially revise the act establishing the previous security council passed the Diet on November 27, 2013, and came into force on December 4 that year. Then, on January 7, 2014, the National Security Secretariat was established inside the Cabinet Secretariat. Conceived for the smooth operation of the National Security Council (NSC), this secretariat is expected to facilitate comprehensive and rapid response to security crises as the "control tower" for Japan's national security.

The establishment of the Japanese version of the NSC changed the policy-making process for security policy considerably. Shōtarō Yachi, the former administrative vice-minister for foreign affairs and a confidant of Prime Minister Abe, was appointed as the first secretary general of the National Security Secretariat. Nobukatsu Kanehara, former director-general of the Ministry of Foreign Affairs International Legal Affairs Bureau, and Nobushige Takamizawa, former director general of the Ministry of Defense Bureau of Defense

Policy, were appointed as deputy secretaries general. These two also served as assistant chief cabinet secretaries, linking the Prime Minister's Office with the National Security Secretariat, and they were responsible for planning, designing, and adjusting national security policy at the center of government. Along with Secretary General Yachi, they formed the core of the National Security Secretariat, and the three together constituted a powerful team to support Prime Minister Abe and Chief Cabinet Secretary Yoshihide Suga.

The second development was the formulation of the National Security Strategy, which was adopted by Cabinet decision on December 17, 2013. The National Security Strategy, the first such strategy ever formulated by Japan, sets Japan's basic national security policy, and stands above the National Defense Program Guidelines. The National Defense Program Guidelines have always been centered on the Ministry of Defense, and are no more than a medium-term plan for the development of defense capabilities. In contrast, the National Security Strategy integrates foreign policy with defense policy and presents Japan's long-term strategic vision as a nation. In formal terms, the National Security Strategy was a revision of the 1957 Basic Policy on National Defense, and has a purview of around ten years.

The third development was the passage of a package of security-related legislation. Based on the report of the Advisory Panel on Reconstruction of the Legal Basis for Security submitted on May 15, 2014, and following consultations between the ruling parties—the Liberal Democratic Party (LDP) and the Kōmeitō—the Cabinet Decision on the Development of Seamless Security Legislation to Ensure Japan's Survival and Protect Its People was adopted on July 1, 2014. This Cabinet decision incorporated a number of different policies, including approving partial exercise of the right of collective self-defense, which had previously been deemed as not allowed under the Constitution, and was directed at upgrading Japan's international peace cooperation activities and rear-area support activities. Then the actual legal revisions and new laws were prepared as security-related legislation; 11 bills were passed and adopted as a package on September 17, 2015 (House of Councillors special committee), and passed by the Diet (House of Councillors plenary session, September 19). These security-related laws, which came into force on March 29, 2016, revised the foundations of Japan's security policy.

The fourth development was the agreement on the new Guidelines for Japan-US Security Cooperation reached at the Japan-US Security Consultative Committee (two-plus-two) on April 27, 2015, in order to reinforce the Japan-US alliance and make it "seamless." This was the third revision of the

Guidelines (prior revisions were made in 1978 and 1998), and the changes made shifted the alliance to reflect the new security environment.

These four new interrelated developments show that Japan's security policy is steadily evolving. The most important of the four is the National Security Strategy. This document clearly states how Japan will secure its own safety while contributing to establishing peace in the international community. Consequently, it conveys the basic direction of Japan's present security policy. Regarding the significance of the formulation of the National Security Strategy, International University of Japan President Shinichi Kitaoka, who played a central role in its preparation, said that it was prepared "not only to gain the understanding of the Japanese people, but also to avoid unnecessary misunderstandings by neighboring countries."[1]

In this chapter, based on the context given above, I would like to discuss the evolution of Japan's security policy under the Abe administration, and the National Security Strategy in particular. I will also clarify how the National Security Strategy is linked to the reinforcement of the Japan-US alliance.

Shinzō Abe's Diplomatic Vision

The major evolution of Japan's security policy under the Abe administration is tied to the fact that Prime Minister Shinzō Abe himself has long had a keen interest in diplomatic and security issues and is well versed in that realm. During his first term (2006–2007), Prime Minister Abe established the Advisory Panel on Reconstruction of the Legal Basis for Security, as well as the Council to Strengthen the Function of the Prime Minister's Office regarding National Security, clearly intending for the Prime Minister's Office to act as the "control tower" in leading foreign policy and security policy.

Prior to this, the Jun'ichirō Koizumi administration (2001–2006) had strengthened the functions of the Prime Minister's Office in 2001, following the administrative reforms achieved under the Ryutarō Hashimoto administration (1996–1998).[2] The latter included policies intended to strengthen the functions of the Cabinet, clarify the leadership of the prime minister toward that end, and reinforce the system of assistance and support to the Cabinet and the prime minister. The scope of authority of the Cabinet Secretariat was expanded to include "Planning, drafting and comprehensive coordination of basic principles concerning important Cabinet policies," which made it possible for the Prime Minister's Office to take the lead in conducting diplomacy.[3]

The Koizumi administration made the greatest possible use of this broadened function of the Cabinet Secretariat to formulate economic and fiscal policy via the Council on Economic and Fiscal Policy, and drafted the 2001 Anti-Terrorism Special Measures Law and the 2003 Act on Special Measures concerning Humanitarian Relief and Reconstruction Work and Security Assistance in Iraq.

Shinzō Abe, who was serving as the deputy chief cabinet secretary for government affairs at that time, was actively involved in developing these policies with support from Shōtarō Yachi, then assistant chief cabinet secretary (Yachi was the director-general of the Ministry of Foreign Affairs Foreign Policy Bureau through October 2002). The second Abe administration has made use of this experience in foreign policy and security policy leadership by the Prime Minister's Office, which achieved some measure of success during the Koizumi administration, and developed it further.

It goes without saying that Prime Minister Abe's own views on foreign policy have strongly influenced the diplomatic and security policy directed by the Prime Minister's Office. Abe spoke about his own vision for foreign policy and security policy at a press conference on December 26, 2012, just after he took office.

"We must also restore proactive diplomacy that defends our national interests. . . . More than anything else, it is imperative that we rebuild the relationship of trust we enjoy under the Japan-US alliance. The other day, I had a telephone conversation with President Obama . . . I recognize that the first step in turning Japan's foreign and security policy around is reinforcing our *kizuna*—our bonds of friendship—once more under the Japan-US alliance, which is the cornerstone of Japanese diplomacy."[4]

Similarly, on January 28, 2013, Prime Minister Abe spoke about his diplomatic vision as follows in his general policy speech to the Diet. "There is also a pressing need for us to undertake a drastic reshaping in the areas of diplomacy and security. Above all, we must further reinforce the Japan-US alliance, which is the cornerstone of Japanese diplomacy and security, and fully restore the bonds of friendship between Japan and the United States. At the Japan-US summit meeting scheduled for the third week of February, I am determined to demonstrate to both the people of Japan and people around the world that the close ties of the Japan-US alliance have been restored."[5]

By focusing on rebuilding the Japan-US alliance, Prime Minister Abe is setting the restoration of proactive diplomacy and the reinforcement of the Japan-US alliance as the highest-priority issues. In fact, the Abe administration has centered its foreign policy on reinforcing ties with the US, boosting the reliability of the alliance, and preparing a framework to realize these objectives. The idea was that by reinforcing ties with the US and boosting Japan's influence in the international community at the same time, Japan would be able to assert its positions with greater clarity.

Furthermore, in an essay entitled "Asia's Democratic Security Diamond," which was published on December 27, 2012, Abe wrote, "I envisage a strategy whereby Australia, India, Japan, and the US state of Hawaii form a diamond to safeguard the maritime commons stretching from the Indian Ocean region to the western Pacific."[6] A map showing this "security diamond" concept reveals Abe's foreign policy vision quite clearly. This basic strategy of reinforcing relations between Japan and Australia and between Japan and India, with the US alliance as the foundation, is a hallmark of the Abe administration's foreign policy.

What is the logic that leads Prime Minister Abe to consider the Japan-US alliance so important? Abe revised his 2006 book *Towards a Beautiful Country* and renamed it *Towards a New Country* (published in 2013). In this work, he made the following comment regarding the Japan-US alliance.

> It goes without saying that the spirit of making the greatest possible efforts to help oneself and defend one's own country by oneself is necessary, but considering nuclear deterrence and the stability of the Far East region, the alliance with the US is essential. Furthermore, considering America's influence on the international community, its economic strength, and the strength of its military force, the Japan-US alliance is the best option. . . . What must be confirmed is that today Japan and the US share the fundamental values of freedom and democracy, human rights, the rule of law, and free competition in a market economy. These are the common understandings shared among the free nations of the world.[7]

This demonstrates how, in addition to the ideological reasons for sharing democracy and other fundamental values, Abe strongly grasps the practical importance of the Japan-US alliance from the standpoint of nuclear deterrence and the stability of the Far East region. This is a shift from the diplomatic policy of the Yukio Hatoyama administration (2009–2010) formed by the Democratic Party of Japan (DPJ), which attempted to transcend differences in political systems to form stronger bonds with China than with the US.

This shows the exceptional clarity and consistency of Abe's foreign policy vision. Abe also clearly presented his foreign policy vision in his speech "Japan Is Back" presented at the Center for Strategic and International Studies (CSIS), a US think tank, on February 22, 2013.[8] In that speech, Abe noted three roles that should be fulfilled by Japanese diplomacy.

First, he stated, "Japan must remain a leading promoter of rules" in the Asia-Pacific and Indo-Pacific regions. His message here was that establishing a rules-based international order is the most important priority for Japanese diplomacy. Also, by saying both "the Asia-Pacific region" and the "Indo-Pacific region," he demonstrated that his view incorporates a wide-ranging regional order. Emphasizing cooperation between Japan and China and between Japan and South Korea would limit the framework of cooperation to Northeast Asia. In contrast, Abe takes a wider regional viewpoint, relativizing criticism of Japan by China and South Korea and focusing on friendly relations with Australia and India, which seek to reinforce their cooperative relations with Japan.

Second, he said, "Japan must continue to be a guardian of the global commons, like the maritime commons, open enough to benefit everyone." This means having strong political will to oppose threats to maritime commons, which are global commons. Abe was conveying how Japan, which was a challenger to the prewar international order, is now defending the international order.

Pointing out the third role, Abe said, "Japan must work even more closely with the US, [the Republic of] Korea, Australia, and other like-minded democracies throughout the region." This stance promotes the "values-oriented diplomacy" that was also emphasized in the first Abe administration. It shows how Japanese diplomacy, which must often seek pragmatic interests out of necessity, is emphasizing norms and values.

Viewing these three roles together reveals the framework of Abe's foreign policy vision. It also shows how Abe intended to transform Japan's basic security policy, security legislation, and security culture to implement this type of diplomatic strategy. To those ends, he worked toward drafting the new National Defense Program Guidelines and preparing Japan's first National Security Strategy. Putting these developments in context makes the direction of the current administration's foreign policy clear.

The Path to the National Security Strategy

Since Japan's Basic Policy on National Defense was established in 1957, more than half a century has passed without any revision to that fundamental document. Since 1976, the National Defense Program Guidelines, which fall under the basic policy, have set the direction of Japan's fundamental defense strategy.

To date, Japan has formulated four sets of National Defense Program Guidelines: in 1976, 1995, 2004, and 2010. The 1957 Basic Policy on National Defense was just a brief document, less than one page long, with no mention of guiding principles for specific policies or strategies. Understanding the National Defense Program Guidelines is vital to grasping the postwar history of Japanese defense strategy.

All four National Defense Program Guidelines were adopted as government documents after they were decided on by the Security Council and the Cabinet. These Guidelines were limited to defense readiness, and were centered on the Defense Agency (now the Ministry of Defense). Japan did not normally publish clear information on Self-Defense Forces operations and its defense strategy during the Cold War.

The process of preparing the Guidelines changed along with Japan's administrative structure. While the 1976 Guidelines and the 1995 Guidelines were prepared inside the Defense Agency, the 2004 Guidelines mostly originated from the Cabinet Secretariat. The 2004 Guidelines were formulated under the Koizumi administration after the functions of the Prime Minister's Office had been strengthened in the 2001 administrative reforms mentioned earlier. Consequently, the Prime Minister's Office initiated the formulation of these Guidelines, as it did the development of other policies.

In contrast, the formulation of the 2010 Guidelines under the DPJ administration was led by Diet members, with the Four-Minister Meeting (chief cabinet secretary, minister for foreign affairs, minister of defense, and minister of finance) at its center. The DPJ administration aimed to switch from the bureaucratic initiative used in the past to political initiative; as a result, the DPJ, rather than the Ministry of Defense and Cabinet Secretariat, took the lead in drafting the new National Defense Program Guidelines, and was to some extent successful.

Also, in the process of forming these policies, councils were established to collect opinions from a wide range of private-sector experts. This was probably an effort to demonstrate that the administration was willing to listen to the opinions of authorities outside the government in a manner that was open to the Japanese public. At the same time, having the leading scholars of international politics and security policy experts from each area participate in the discussion presented a conceptual framework suitable for the times.

In preparing the 1976 Guidelines, the Committee for Consideration of Japan's Defense was established and held wide-ranging discussions regarding the role of Japan's defense forces.[9] Led by renowned international political scientist Masataka Kōsaka of Kyoto University, the Committee produced the "Concept of Basic Defense Capability" (*kibanteki bōeiryoku kōsō*), which Administrative Vice-Minister for Defense Takuya Kubo then incorporated into actual defense policy. This served as the basis of Japan's defense strategy for thirty-four years until the new "Dynamic Defense Force" concept was introduced in the 2010 Guidelines under the DPJ administration.

During the preparation of the 1995 Guidelines, an Advisory Group on Defense Issues was established, chaired by Hirotarō Higuchi. The formulation of its report was led by Administrative Vice-Minister of Defense Seiki Nishihiro and Aoyama Gakuin University professor Akio Watanabe, who was close with Nishihiro.[10] The report proposed orienting the new defense policy around "multilateral security cooperation" in the post–Cold War era. This set off some alarm bells within the US government due to its relativization of the Japan-US alliance, which had been deemed all-important up until that time.

As the 2004 Guidelines were being drafted, a Council on Security and Defense Capabilities was established, chaired by Hiroshi Araki. Its task was to consider the direction of defense policy in the post-9/11 "war on terror" era. The defense policy proposed by the Council was based on three pillars: Japan's own efforts; cooperation with allies; and cooperation with the international community. Kobe University Professor Makoto Iokibe—known as the "brains" behind Prime Minister Koizumi's foreign policy—and University of Tokyo Professor Akihiko Tanaka put forward the basic framework for the 2004 Guidelines.

The 2010 Guidelines drafted under the DPJ administration made a monumental change by discarding the prior "Concept of Basic Defense Capability" and replacing it with the new "Dynamic Defense Force" concept. Maritime security to the southwest of Japan was also a focus, as demonstrated by the tension in Japan-China relations following the September 2010 incident where a Chinese fishing trawler collided with Japanese Coast Guard patrol boats offshore the Senkaku Islands.

As mentioned previously, in these new National Defense Program Guidelines the DPJ was attempting to clearly demonstrate political leadership.[11] Analyzing this effort, the international political scientist International University Professor Tomohito Shinoda writes, "In the diplomacy and security fields, the greatest manifestation of political initiative was in the formulation of the new National Defense Program Guidelines."[12] Specifically, he argues that three groups had a major impact on the formulation of the new National Defense Program Guidelines: the DPJ Research Committee on Foreign Affairs and Security; a private advisory group to Chief Cabinet Secretary Yoshito Sengoku led by University of Tokyo Professor Shinichi Kitaoka; and the Social Democratic Party.

Professor Kitaoka, who contributed to the drafting of the Guidelines, makes the following comments regarding their formulation: "At that time, the process of preparing the Guidelines changed. Up until then, the Ministry of Defense had been responsible for adopting or rejecting advisory committee proposals, and the contents tended to only concern the Ministry of Defense and the Self-Defense Forces, barely touching on cooperation with the Ministry of Foreign Affairs, Japan Coast Guard, and other pertinent ministries and agencies. Now the direction shifted toward consulting with experts and concerned Cabinet ministers to draft Guidelines with a more comprehensive viewpoint in a manner that would limit the involvement of bureaucrats."[13] According to Kitaoka, this broader approach was considered necessary because of the heightened tension surrounding Japanese national security. "The background to this was regret over the lack of comprehensive preparations across ministries and agencies [that became evident] during the confusion surrounding the September 2010 collision with a Chinese fishing vessel in the waters off Okinawa and the Senkaku Islands."[14]

Thus, there have been major changes in the content and drafting process of the past four National Defense Program Guidelines, reflecting the times in which they were created. What process, then, was used to draft the 2013 Guidelines under the second Abe administration? As seen above, the Abe administration aimed to significantly change the very structure of the political process of drafting new defense guidelines. As a result, in addition to the prior research prepared by the Ministry of Defense, Diet members, and members of the advisory panel, a new body, the National Security Council of Japan, was established on December 4, 2013, to prepare new defense strategy.

So how were the 2013 National Defense Program Guidelines decided on by the Cabinet in December 2013 actually drafted?[15] First, the Defense Posture Review Commission, established inside the Ministry of Defense with Parliamentary Senior Vice-Minister of Defense Akinori Eto as chairman, released its Defense Posture Review Interim Report on July 25, 2013, in the run-up to preparation of the new Guidelines.[16] As part of that process, three new developments were noted as being relevant to the role of the defense forces. First among these was China's intensification of activities intruding into Japanese territorial waters and violating Japan's airspace; second was North Korea's defiant ballistic missile launches and nuclear tests; and third was the importance of preparing for large-scale disasters. The report notes that these considerations should direct the conduct of joint operations and the enhancement of defense posture.

The report also stresses the importance of "responding to attacks on remote islets" in pursuing the buildup of new defenses, and states that "command of the sea and air superiority must be maintained" to achieve this, which will require "mobile deployment capability" and "amphibious capability." Amphibious capability was to be newly established within the Ground Self-Defense Force; an Amphibious Rapid Deployment Brigade has been established in the Western Army as an important pillar for the defense of remote islets.

Meanwhile, in September 2013, after the House of Councillors election, Prime Minister Abe decided to establish the Advisory Panel on National Security and Defense Capabilities as a private advisory council to the prime minister. This panel held its first meeting at the Prime Minister's Office on September 12, 2013. The members were expected to utilize their expertise to contribute to the work of drafting Japan's first National Security Strategy and the new National Defense Program Guidelines. International University of Japan President Shinichi Kitaoka served as chairman.

In his opening remarks at the first meeting of this Advisory Panel on National Security and Defense Capabilities, Prime Minister Abe said, "In today's international community, no country can maintain its peace and safety by itself. The Abe administration will proactively contribute to securing the peace, stability and prosperity of the world under the banner of proactive contribution to peace, based on a belief in international cooperation."[17] Furthermore, panel chairman Shinichi Kitaoka said, "This is a decisive step toward formulating a comprehensive national security strategy with diplomatic and defense policy as its core for the first time."[18]

This Advisory Panel on National Security and Defense Capabilities met seven times over three months through December 11, 2013; the National Security Strategy and 2013 National Defense Program Guidelines were adopted by Cabinet resolution on December 17.[19] Even prior to that, the National Security Council of Japan, which had already been established, decided to adopt the two documents. The National Security Strategy, which is the overriding document, lays out Japan's medium- to long-term national security strategy integrating foreign policy and defense policy, while the 2013 National Defense Program Guidelines provide the basic direction for defense policy focusing on defense forces readiness, as in the past.

Eight experts participated in the Advisory Panel on National Security and Defense Capabilities. Among them were former administrative vice-minister for foreign affairs Shōtarō Yachi and former Japanese ambassador to the United Kingdom Shin Ebihara from the Ministry of Foreign Affairs, and former administrative vice-minister of defense Kimito Nakae and former chief of staff Ryōichi Oriki from the Ministry of Defense. The other four were academics specializing in international politics and diplomatic history. This panel differed from prior similar advisory bodies in several respects. First, in previous advisory panels, participating experts prepared the reports that served as a reference for the drafting of the National Defense Program Guidelines, which was done mostly by Ministry of Defense bureaucrats. This advisory panel did not prepare a report; rather, it deliberated on the outlines to be incorporated into the actual national security strategy and national defense program guidelines, and also held discussions regarding the specific wording.

Secondly, the period from the establishment of this advisory panel to the Cabinet decision on the National Security Strategy and the 2013 National Defense Program Guidelines was just three months. The core of the 2013 National Defense Program Guidelines was inherited from the 2010 National Defense Program Guidelines decided on under the DPJ administration, and while the term "dynamic defense force" was changed to "dynamic joint defense force," the basic spirit of the 2010 Guidelines was retained. Important new initiatives concerning emphasis on the southwestern region and defense of remote islands put forth under the DPJ administration were also carried forward in a nonpartisan manner. The novelty and significance of the 2013 Guidelines lay in the measures taken to facilitate the actual implementation of such new initiatives. It was possible to prepare the 2013 Guidelines in such a short period of time for two main reasons: for one, preparatory work had taken place beforehand within the Ministry of Defense and an interim report had been released; also, the core concepts were retained from the 2010 Guidelines.

"Proactive Contribution to Peace Based on the Principle of International Cooperation"

What are the characteristics of Japan's first National Security Strategy? And what principles determined the fundamental direction of Japan's security strategy?

First, the National Security Strategy places a strong emphasis on international cooperation. As discussed above, this is a consistent principle throughout Prime Minister Abe's foreign policy. The strategy also takes a more proactive stance toward conducting security activities than in the past. Shinichi Kitaoka, who was involved with drafting this document, says, "What Prime Minister Abe put forth this time as the fundamental principle of the National Security Strategy was proactive contribution to peace based on the principle of international cooperation."[20] Kitaoka notes that "this was a shift from the passive pacifism to date . . . [which] was the belief that the more Japan is demilitarized, the better it is for international peace."

To make this sort of proactive contribution to peace, Japan needs to maintain its international position as a major power. This is mentioned in the National Security Strategy as follows.

> Under the evolving security environment, Japan will continue to adhere to the course that it has taken to date as a peace-loving nation, and as a major player in world politics and economy, contribute even more proactively to secure the peace, stability, and prosperity of the international community, while achieving its own security as well as peace and stability in the Asia-Pacific region as a "proactive contributor to peace" based on the principle of international cooperation. This is the fundamental principle of national security that Japan should stand to hold.[21]

Prior to this, the bipartisan policy proposal known as the Nye-Armitage Report (*The US-Japan Alliance: Anchoring Stability in Asia*) was published in 2012. Its compilation was led by former US deputy secretary of state Richard Armitage, a Republican, and former assistant secretary of defense (and Harvard University professor emeritus) Joseph Nye, a Democrat. This report posed a somewhat provocative question regarding Japan, perhaps referencing its perceived decline and downfall: "Does Japan desire to continue to be a tier-one nation, or is she content to drift into tier-two status?"[22] The National Security Strategy created under the Abe administration the following year clearly answered this question: "Japan should play an even more proactive role as a major global player in the international community. . . . As a major player in world politics and economy [it aims to achieve] its own security as well as peace and stability in the Asia-Pacific region." The Abe administration is clearly determined to ensure that Japan will not become a "tier-two" country.

In response to the question of what sort of security policy Japan should adopt as a "major player in world politics and economy," the National Security Strategy states,

> To overcome national security challenges and achieve national security objectives, as well as to proactively contribute to peace in cooperation with the international community, Japan needs to expand and deepen cooperative relations with other countries with the Japan-US Alliance as the cornerstone. At the same time, Japan needs to make effective use of its diverse resources and promote comprehensive policies.

In this way, the National Security Strategy supports proactive contribution to peace based on international cooperation; it puts forth the Japan-US alliance as the platform for realizing this goal, and appeals to the importance of that alliance. At a time when China is rapidly enhancing its military forces and disturbing the balance of power in East Asia, the Abe administration is seeking to contribute to regional stability by strengthening the Japan-US alliance, which fell into disarray over the issue of the relocation of the Futenma US Marine Corps base during the DPJ administration.

Japan's Identity as a Maritime State

Another characteristic of the National Security Strategy is its clear presentation of Japan's national identity as a maritime state. Many members of the Advisory Panel on National Security and Defense Capabilities had supported the doctrine of Japan's national identity as a maritime state from the beginning. As a maritime state, Japan has formed alliances with the UK and the US, which are also maritime states; it has emphasized the value of freedom as a maritime state and the value of the rule of law, and made defending freedom of navigation an important goal.

The National Security Strategy presents Japan's principles as a maritime state. "Surrounded by the sea on all sides and blessed with an immense exclusive economic zone and an extensive coastline, Japan as a maritime state has achieved economic growth through maritime trade and development of marine resources, and has pursued 'Open and Stable Seas.'" This shows that Japan's National Security Strategy not only prioritizes the defense of Japan's own territory, but also considers it important to defend "open and stable seas" as a global commons. This can be seen as a significant evolution, considering Japan's security policies up until that time.

The National Security Strategy explains the importance of guaranteeing maritime security as follows: "As a maritime state, Japan will play a leading role, through close cooperation with other countries, in maintaining and developing 'Open and Stable Seas,' which are upheld by maritime order based upon such fundamental principles as the rule of law, ensuring the freedom and safety of navigation and overflight, and peaceful settlement of disputes in accordance with relevant international law."

Here, once again, maritime security is emphasized as a core element of Japan's National Security Strategy. The Strategy adds, "Japan will provide assistance to those coastal states alongside the sea lanes of communication and other states in enhancing their maritime law enforcement capabilities, and strengthen cooperation with partners on the sea lanes who share strategic interests with Japan." This shows Japan's policy of providing capacity-building assistance to establish and maintain open and stable seas. Japan has in fact provided capacity-building assistance to Southeast Asian nations during the Abe administration, and is continuing efforts to maintain the openness and stability of the South China Sea as well. Such efforts are raising Southeast Asian nations' opinions of Japan's role in the region.[23]

As noted above, to realize the desired emphasis on international cooperation, as well as open and stable seas, cooperation with the US is paramount. The argument is that in the Asia-Pacific region, where enormous shifts in the security environment are taking place, it is the Japan-US alliance above all that must be placed at the core of Japan's national security strategy. In the next section, I will consider how the Japan-US alliance and the direction in which it should be developed are discussed in the 2013 Guidelines.

The National Security Strategy and the Japan-US Alliance

Prime Minister Abe has made strengthening the Japan-US alliance central to his vision of foreign policy. This may have arisen from the destabilization of the Japan-US relationship by the issue of the Futenma base relocation under the DPJ administration of Prime Minister Yukio Hatoyama from 2009 to 2010, and the lessons learned from that crisis.

At the same time, the foreign policy ideology put forth by Prime Minister Abe also emphasizes that Japan is a "major player in the international community" and a "maritime state." It may be necessary to strengthen the Japan-US alliance in order to ensure the openness and stability of the seas and advocate for international cooperation. Amid major shifts in the global balance of power, it is important that Japan maintain the rules-based international order by cooperating with the US via the Japan-US alliance, as well as by strengthening partnerships with Australia, India, and other democratic nations whose values it shares.

Based on this foreign policy vision, the National Security Strategy lists six strategic approaches that Japan should adopt for its national security. The first is "strengthening and expanding Japan's capabilities and roles." Prime Minister Abe has often emphasized the importance of "the spirit of defending one's own country by oneself." Consequently, it is important first for Japan to not neglect its own defense efforts. The second strategic approach is "strengthening the Japan-US Alliance." The third is "strengthening diplomacy and security cooperation with Japan's partners for peace and stability in the international community." Here the priority is to strengthen "cooperative relations with countries with which Japan shares universal values and strategic interests, such as the Republic of Korea, Australia, the countries of ASEAN, and India." The fourth strategic approach, "proactive contribution to international efforts for peace and stability of the international community," truly falls under the rubric of "proactive contribution to peace based on the principle of international cooperation." Specific items mentioned include "strengthening diplomacy at the United Nations," "strengthening the rule of law," and "leading international efforts on disarmament and nonproliferation." The fifth strategic approach is "strengthening cooperation based on universal values to resolve global issues." Here, the National Security Strategy states, "Through a partnership with countries with which Japan shares universal values, such as freedom, democracy, respect for fundamental human rights including women's rights, and the rule of law, Japan will conduct diplomacy that contributes to addressing global issues." The "human security" which the Japanese government has addressed to date also falls under this approach. Finally, the sixth strategic approach is "strengthening the domestic foundation that supports national security and promoting domestic and global understanding." This includes, for example, "maintaining and enhancing defense production and technological bases" and "boosting communication capabilities."

Japan's National Security Strategy should be developed with these six pillars in mind. The Japan-US alliance is particularly important. As stated in the National Security Strategy, "The Japan-US Alliance is the cornerstone of Japan's security. Likewise, for the US, the alliance has served as the core of its alliance network with countries in the region, including the Republic of Korea, Australia, Thailand and the Philippines. In this context, the Japan-US Alliance has been serving as a foundation for the US strategy in the Asia-Pacific region."

The National Security Strategy expresses the importance of the Japan-US alliance to both countries, as well as the need to position the alliance as the "cornerstone of national security." It places special importance on the Japan-US alliance above all because that partnership is seen as contributing to the peace and stability of the region. It is definitely not a vestige of the Cold War that generates antagonism in the region. Rather, as stated in the National Security Strategy, "For more than sixty years, the Japan-US Alliance, with the Japan-US security arrangements at its core, has played an indispensable role for peace and security in Japan as well as peace and stability in the Asia-Pacific region. In recent years, the Alliance has also played a more critical role for peace, stability, and prosperity in the international community."

Conclusion

The idea of positioning the Japan-US security alliance at the core of Japan's National Security Strategy is widely shared in the Japanese security community. For example, former Japanese ambassador to Thailand Hisahiko Okazaki, who was said to have had great influence on Prime Minister Abe in the field of foreign affairs, wrote as follows. "I firmly believe we can maintain the freedom, security, and prosperity of Japan in the twenty-first century as well if we can achieve two tasks. First, the Japan-US relationship must be positioned as the cornerstone; second, we must always interpret information from the US accurately. This is the conclusion I have reached from trial and error over my forty years working at the Ministry of Foreign Affairs and twenty-two years since retirement from public service."[24]

Shōtarō Yachi, who is known as the "brains" behind Prime Minister Abe's foreign policy and who has played an important role as the secretary general of the National Security Secretariat since it was established in January 2014, makes the following argument: "Japan should continue to base its diplomacy and security on the Japan-US alliance for the foreseeable future. This would maintain the diplomatic moral principles followed since the Meiji era (1868–1912). At the same time, it is also critical for Japan to be aware of and actively fulfill its global roles and responsibilities in anticipation of newly emerging shifts in the balance of power. It is important for Japan to choose the Japan-US alliance from its own subjective position, and not simply maintain the status quo since the Allied occupation of Japan."[25]

In this way, the National Security Strategy was drafted placing the importance of the Japan-US alliance, which is widely recognized by Japan's national security community, at its core. Essentially, the National Security Strategy was formulated to maintain "Open and Stable Seas" and to establish peace and stability in this region in response to changes in the balance of power. If that is the case, then Japan's National Security Strategy and the Japan-US alliance should be supported by the nations of this region. In other words, the real value of the Japan-US alliance may depend on how much Japan can actually contribute to the peace and stability of the region and establish international cooperation and stability in the international community. For the Japan-US alliance, which is an alliance between maritime states, to become a "commons" in the true sense, it must be welcomed more widely by all the countries concerned, and they must trust that it is linked to regional stability.

1   Shinichi Kitaoka, "Sekkyokuteki 'heiwa-shugi' ni tenkansuru Nihon no anzen hoshō seisaku" [Japanese security policy shifting to "proactive pacifism"], *Nippon.com*, February 5, 2014, http://www.nippon.com/ja/currents/d00108/.

2   For an outline of this process, see Izuru Makihara, "Seisaku kettei ni okeru shushō kantei no yakuwari" [The role of the Prime Minister's Office in deciding policy], *Nippon.com*, June 27, 2013, http://www.nippon.com/ja/features/c00408/.

3   Toshio Sakurai, "Kantei kinō no kyōka to gyōsei zenpan no minaoshi" [Reinforcement of the functions of the Prime Minister's Office and reconsideration of overall government administration], *Rippō to Chōsa* no. 300 (January 2010), 5–7. For political science analysis of this movement toward initiative from the Prime Minister's Office, see Tomohito Shinoda, *Kantei gaikō: Seiji rīdāshippu no yukue* [Diplomacy by the Prime Minister's Office: The direction of political leadership] (Asahi Shimbunsha, 2004); Masato Shimizu, *Kantei shudō: Koizumi Junichirō no kaikaku* [Leadership by the Prime Minister's Office: Junichirō Koizumi's reform] (Nihon Keizai Shimbunsha, 2005); Harukata Takenaka, *Shushō shihai: Nihon seiji no henbō* [Control by the prime minister: Changes in Japanese politics] (Chuokoron-Shinsha, 2006); Satoshi Machidori, *Shushō seiji no seido bunseki: Gendai Nihon seiji no kenryoku kiban keisei* [Systems analysis of prime minister politics: Formation of power in contemporary Japanese politics] (Chikura Publishing, 2012).

4   Press conference by Prime Minister Shinzō Abe, December 26, 2012, https://japan.kantei.go.jp/96_abe/statement/201212/26kaiken_e.html.

5   Policy speech by Prime Minister Shinzō Abe to the 183rd Session of the Diet, January 28, 2013, https://japan.kantei.go.jp/96_abe/statement/201301/28syosin_e.html.

6   Shinzō Abe, "Asia's Democratic Security Diamond," *Project Syndicate*, December 27, 2012, http://www.project-syndicate.org/commentary/a-strategic-alliance-for-japan-and-india-by-shinzo-abe.

7   Shinzō Abe, *Atarashii kuni e: Utsukushii kuni e kanzenban* [Towards a new country, towards a beautiful country, complete edition] (Bungeishunjū, 2013), 133.

8   Shinzō Abe, *Nihon no ketsui* [Japan's determination] (Shinchōsha, 2014), 14.

9   Akihiro Sadō, *Sengo seiji to Jieitai* [Postwar politics and the Self-Defense Forces] (Yoshikawa Kōbunkan, 2006), 101.

10 Ibid, 184–87.

11 Yūichi Hosoya, "Minshutō seiken no anzen hoshō seisaku no teitai to zenshin" [Security policy stagnation and progress of the Democratic Party of Japan administration], *Nippon.com*, June 4, 2012, http://www.nippon.com/ja/currents/d00039.

12 Tomohito Shinoda, *Seiji shudō vs. kanryō shihai: Jimin seiken, minshu seiken, seikan 20-nen tōsō no uchimaku* [Political initiative vs. bureaucratic control: Inside facts of the 20-year struggle between politicians and bureaucrats under Liberal Democratic Party and Democratic Party of Japan administrations] (Asahi Shimbun Shuppan, 2013), 174.

13 Kitaoka, "Sekkyokuteki 'heiwashugi' ni tenkansuru Nihon no anzen hoshō seiskaku."

14 Ibid.

15 There is not yet much research directly addressing this 2013 National Security Strategy, but regarding its drafting process, see Akira Igata, "Kokka anzen hoshō seisaku no sakusei katei: Dai niji Abe seikenka no mittsu no kondankai" [The process of drafting national security strategy: The three advisory bodies under the second Abe administration], *Kokusai anzen hoshō* 42, no. 4 (2015).

16 Defense Posture Review Commission, "Defense Posture Review Interim Report," Ministry of Defense, July 26, 2013.

17 Advisory Panel on Security and Defense Capabilities (First Meeting), Summary of Proceedings, September 12, 2013, http://www.kantei.go.jp/jp/singi/anzen_bouei/dai1/gijiyousi.pdf.

18 Ibid.

19 Ministry of Defense, *FY 2014 Defense White Paper*, 2014, 132–33.

20 Kitaoka, "Sekkyokuteki 'heiwashugi' ni tenkansuru Nihon no anzen hoshō seikaku."

21 "National Security Strategy," Cabinet Resolution of December 17, 2013.

22 Richard L. Armitage and Joseph S. Nye, *The US-Japan Alliance: Anchoring Stability in Asia* (Washington, DC: Center for Strategic and International Studies, August 2012), 1.

23 For example, in a March 2014 public opinion poll regarding Japan conducted in the ASEAN 7 countries, Japan was chosen most often as the "country that can be trusted the most," with 33 percent of the responses. China was number five, with only 5 percent of the respondents choosing China as the "country that can be trusted the most."

24 Hisahiko Okazaki, *Kokusai jōsei handan hanseiki* [Judgment of international conditions over half a century] (Ikuhōsha, 2015), 202.

25 Shōtarō Yachi, preface to *Nihon no gaikō to sōgō anzen hoshō* [Japanese diplomacy and comprehensive security], ed. Shōtarō Yachi (Wedge, 2011), 9.

CHAPTER 3

America's Asia Strategy and China

Satoru Mori

Professor, Department of Global Politics, Faculty of Law, Hōsei University

Does the United States today have an Asia strategy? According to then Secretary of State Hillary Clinton, the "rebalance to Asia" strategy announced by the Obama administration in November 2011 was a region-wide engagement strategy designed to advance the policy goals of forging a broad-based military presence in the region, expanding economic relations, and promoting democracy and human rights. The rebalance aimed to achieve these goals by reinforcing security alliances, deepening relationships with newly emerging powers, and bolstering engagement with regional multilateral institutions.[1] As explained by President Barack Obama and then National Security Advisor Tom Donilon, the rebalance emphasized international rules, particularly the promotion of norms that were established under American initiative, and was aimed at establishing a "rules-based international system" in Asia. This way of thinking was also presented in the 2010 National Security Strategy of the United States of America,[2] and it was subsequently firmly maintained as a basic policy of the administration.

How has the Obama administration attempted to manage the power shift in Asia under this type of policy, and what are the characteristics and effects of those efforts? How have the Washington policy elites seen China in recent years, and are there differences among them in their views toward China? How have President Obama and the White House approached China? How is the United States handling its strategic competition with China? This chapter aims to answer these questions by clarifying the distinctive characteristics of the changes in the Obama administration's Asia strategy, as well as the political process concerning its approach toward China.

I. The Asia Strategy: Objectives and Approach toward Security

Asia Strategy Objectives

The policy speeches addressing the US rebalance to Asia and America's Asia policy delivered by Obama administration leaders and senior officials reveal three main objectives. The first objective is the provision of security. The rise of China brings the potential for security competition between China and neighboring states; the US seeks to reduce the competition as much as possible and to stabilize the security environment. The second objective is the promotion of rules. The idea is that having regional states share and implement international rules as much as possible will make international relations increasingly predictable, which in turn will facilitate the alignment of each county's approach in responding to transnational problems. This may even be considered a hallmark of the Obama administration. The third is region-wide economic engagement. This is an effort to bring greater dynamism to the US economy by stabilizing the regional security environment, forming a common rules-based regional order, and forging commercial and economic relations with East Asian countries under that order.

These three objectives are essential for the United States to take advantage of the economic dynamism of East Asia in a stable manner. With no bright outlook for Europe and increasing confusion in the Middle East, Asia is seen as the most promising source of economic growth. For the United States, it is vitally important that economic growth in the Asian region undergoing a rapid power shift does not run off track. This was the compelling rationale behind the Obama administration's initiatives aimed at regional stabilization.

"Dual Reassurance" toward Both China and US Allies/Partners

In East Asia, the Obama administration is working at providing security, promoting rules, and encouraging stronger region-wide economic engagement. What sort of approach is the administration pursuing for security? As China increases its military power along with its economic power, it is fueling the security competition with neighboring states. Managing this may be considered America's greatest security issue in East Asia. North Korea also poses a grave risk to regional security, but it goes without saying that the emergence of China has far greater long-term and strategic ramifications.

Although the Obama administration's security approach in East Asia can be broadly divided into two stages, its most distinguishing characteristic is that it aims to provide reassurance based on promises, rather than pursuing deterrence based on threats. While deterrence is an approach of using quid pro quo threats—if a country causes the worst consequences for another country, then that country will cause the worst consequences for the first country in return—reassurance is an approach of offering promises to cause the best results for another country, and requesting that country to also take actions to bring about the best results for the first country in return.[3]

The Obama administration's approach to security in East Asia was initially characterized by what might be called "dual reassurance." The United States is, of course, manifesting deterrence through the forward deployment of US troops in East Asia. Regardless, there are only limited cases where the Obama administration has taken the deterrence-by-threat approach of specifying problematic behavior to China beforehand and expressly stipulating in advance the retaliatory measures it would take should China adopt such behavior. (Statements by the US president and government leaders that Article 5 of the US-Japan Security Treaty applies to the Senkaku Islands are a rare exception, and even in this case, the acts that would prompt a response and the retaliatory measures that would be taken have not been specified.) The Obama administration's approach is not founded on deterrence; rather, it is centered on reassurance. This is apparently based on the idea that if the United States provided reassurance to China on the one hand, while also providing reassurance to Asian allies and partners on the other, tensions between the two sides would ease, and the security competition between them could be diminished. For example, President Obama and senior US government officials have repeatedly stated that the United States welcomes the rise of a peaceful and prosperous China, provided it observes international rules. By holding consultations on such wide-ranging policy issues as North Korea, Iran, Afghanistan, climate change, and the global economy and devoting vast amounts of time and energy to the US-China Strategic and Economic Dialogue (S&ED) and other mechanisms, the United States sought to strengthen the impression that it was sincerely encouraging China to cooperate with international rules. Meanwhile, the Obama administration also provided reassurance to its allies and partners in the region by advancing all types of defense and security cooperation, so that when skirmishes with China occurred, it urged both parties not to aggravate the situation.

This "dual reassurance" approach of providing reassurance both to allies/

partners and to China has a certain theoretical clarity, but when it was put into practice, a side effect emerged, and it became clear that there were real problems with its underlying rationale. In practice, when the United States provided reassurance to allies and partners, China's distrust of the United States intensified; likewise, when the United States provided reassurance to China, American allies and partners felt greater mistrust toward the United States. America's extension of its military presence toward the Southeast Asian region, including the rotation of a US Marine Corps unit to Australia and the stationing of a littoral combat ship in Singapore, as well as its welcoming of the development of Japan's security policy in the Japan-US foreign and defense ministers' meeting (two-plus-two) reassured America's allies and partners, but China perceived these efforts as a containment policy. On the other hand, the United States' welcoming of the emergence of China, and especially its positive reaction in 2013 to the "new type of great power relationship" proposed by China, along with the removal of any mention of military initiatives from the explanation of the rebalance by Secretary of Defense Chuck Hagel,[4] and the statement by National Security Advisor Susan E. Rice in November of that year that the United States was seeking to "operationalize" a new model of major power relations[5] led Japan and other US allies and partners to feel mistrust and anxiety toward the United States. In short, providing security to one side harmed reassurance to the other. The side effect of intensified anxiety and mistrust toward the United States from both American allies/partners and from China emerged every time.

Toward Reassurance Emphasizing Allies and Partners

In addition to this side effect, it also became clear that there were problems with the rationale on which the dual reassurance approach was based. If a country was behaving provocatively out of anxiety, reassurance could potentially moderate that behavior. However, if the country was acting not out of anxiety, but rather due to expansionist motives to alter the status quo, then reassurance could conversely wind up sacrificing the security and benefits of other countries and invite further unilateral expansionist behavior. From the time it took office, the Obama administration highlighted cooperation with China and adopted the reassurance-based approach, but as will be seen in this section, China continued to cause problems in the security arena. Even though the Obama administration repeatedly lodged diplomatic objections, China did not change its provocative behavior in the least. As a result, the ongoing approach was unsuccessful; expectations that China would eventually become a "responsible stakeholder"[6] quickly dried up, and disappoint-ment grew.

Here, I would like to step back in time and present a general summary of those developments. When the Obama administration announced the rebalance to Asia in November 2011, there was backlash in China, as it was seen as a containment policy. Perhaps because President Obama had singled out and criticized China in the context of economic problems during the 2012 presidential campaign, the reassurance approach toward China was put into play when the second Obama administration came into office in January 2013. In a speech given at the Asia Society in March of that year, National Security Advisor Donilon explained that the leaders of both China and the United States endorsed the goal of building a "new model of rela-tions" between an existing power and an emerging one.[7] President Obama held his first summit meeting with President Xi Jinping in an informal setting at Sunnylands in California in June 2013. According to the press briefing by National Security Advisor Donilon, the two leaders spoke about "a new model of great-power relations" there as well, and shared a commitment to cooperation to avert conflict between China and the US.[8] Furthermore, in November, National Security Advisor Susan Rice made remarks to the effect that the United States should now move to "operationalizing a new model of major power relations" and push it forward. Initially, the American side assumed that the "new model of relations" was a rejection of the historical imperative stating that when a new great power emerges it will collide with the leading great power, and that the United States and China would advance cooperation to avoid conflict. However, it eventually became clear that this "new model" was to include American respect of the "core interests" sought by China, and consequently, the United States backed away from it.[9] China's use of cyber-enabled economic espionage was becoming an issue of concern, but at that time there were still expectations and optimism for an improve-ment in US-China relations under the new Chinese leadership.

However, China established a new air defense identification zone (ADIZ) in the East China Sea in late November 2013. The number of vessels from China's maritime law enforcement agencies dispatched to the area around Japan's Senkaku Islands rose to a rather large number that summer, and from May through July 2014 China carried out unilateral oil drilling off the coast of Vietnam. In response to such hardline actions by China, the Obama administration quietly began to revise the "dual reassurance" approach by easing off on the provision of reassurance to China and taking more active measures to reinforce reassurance to its allies and partners. In February 2014, Assistant Secretary of State Daniel Russel began publicly criticizing the "nine-dash line," which China was using to claim sovereignty over the islands in the South China Sea, as a violation of international law. And in a media interview, National Security Council Senior Director for Asian Affairs Evan Medeiros said that the United States would have to change its military posture in this region if China were to set up another ADIZ in the South China Sea.[10] When President Obama visited Japan in April 2014, he became the first US president to declare that Article 5 of the Japan-US Security Treaty applied to the Senkaku Islands;[11] he also signed an Enhanced Defense Cooperation Agreement with the Philippines a few days later. The US embargo on arms exports to Vietnam was partially lifted that September. In addition, the Japan-US Defense Cooperation Guidelines were revised in April 2015, and the United States stepped up its capacity-building assistance to Southeast Asian countries. In May 2016, the United States announced it would supply $425 million in funding over five years to upgrade the maritime surveillance systems of the countries concerned through a Maritime Security Initiative, as well as giving $250 million over two years to the Philippines, Vietnam, Indonesia, and Malaysia and providing the Philippines with a patrol boat and a research vessel from the US Coast Guard.[12]

In its relations with China, the Obama administration stopped referring to "a new model of great power relations," and in May 2014 the US Department of Justice indicted five People's Liberation Army (PLA) officers for alleged cyber espionage. Furthermore, in November of that year, Secretary of Defense Hagel announced that the United States would pursue a "Third Offset Strategy" (TOS) to counter the modernization of weapons by China and Russia through the department-wide "Defense Innovation Initiative" (DII) (the offset strategy is discussed in section III). The DII was aimed not only at incorporating existing technologies and cutting-edge technologies into weapons systems and linking them with operational concepts, but also at securing US military dominance over the long term by reforming the organization of the Department of Defense and improving the weapons procurement process. The Department of Defense identified China and Russia by name and entered into a full-scale strategic competition with both countries.

II. Changes in Washington's Perceptions of China

It is said that there are two camps in Washington regarding strategy toward

Asia, and their differing views on China are steadily becoming more pronounced as China's behavior causes problems. On the one side there is the "China First" camp, which assumes that the entire Asian region can be well managed as long as US-China relations are on a good footing. On the other side lies the "Asia First" camp, which holds that the United States should always give priority to protecting the interests of its allies and partners and should respond to the various problems in the Asian region through active engagement in regional mechanisms.[13] When relations between China and its neighbors are proceeding well, there is no difference of opinion between these two camps regarding Asia strategy. When problems and disputes between China and its neighbors intensify, however, differences arise regarding which relationships should be prioritized, and gaps emerge in the strategy regarding Asia and the approach to China demanded of the US by each camp. The ideological bases of the China First and Asia First camps have been summarized in papers and commentary by policy experts and researchers at think tanks, and the ways of thinking presented therein are presumed to exist inside the US government. While there is also some range of opinion within each of the camps, the basic understanding of each camp can be roughly summarized as follows.

"China First"

The China First camp attributes China's external behavior to its fear and anxiety about uncertainty and to its opportunism. The argument is that while there are certainly those within China who are moved by intense patriotism to talk about hegemony, China has no long-term plan to achieve hegemony, and is not acting to expel the US from Asia based on any such long-term plan. While there is some range of opinion among China First proponents, one of the leading advocates, Michael Swaine, argues that if the US continues to base its policies on the presumption that overwhelming US superiority in the western Pacific is the only way to guarantee stability and prosperity in the Asia-Pacific region against an anxiety-ridden China, this will instead invite heightened military competition between the US and China, along with regional polarization and tension. According to Swaine, it is difficult to believe that China will give the US complete freedom of action in areas surrounding China and submit to conditions where US power can realize military victory in every crisis; if the US adopts a policy of maintaining superiority, the Chinese will view it as an effort to contain them. Consequently, if the US acts to sustain the overwhelming superiority it has maintained in the

Western Pacific region over the past several decades, the US and China will turn toward confrontation. Crises and disputes will frequently occur, and regional stability and prosperity will be lost. According to the proponents of China First, while the US is projected to maintain military superiority in the Asia-Pacific region, the defense budget is limited, and military forces must be allocated to the Middle East and Europe as well, so it is doubtful that the US can maintain the overwhelming dominance it has enjoyed in the past.

Viewing circumstances in this way, China First advocates stress that the overarching issue for both the US and China is to avert an all-out confrontation, and for that purpose, conditions should be intentionally created that prevent either country from achieving military dominance in the Western Pacific. Furthermore, negotiations should be held to remove factors causing tension in US-China relations: China should be given an appropriate voice in global and regional international bodies; and the economic interdependence between the two countries should be strengthened.[14] In other words, assuming that regional stability will be ensured by giving the highest priority to averting US-China confrontation and tensions in the bilateral relationship, China First proponents believe the US should revise its current strategy aimed at maintaining overwhelming military superiority, use diplomacy to resolve bilateral disputes, modify its own behavior when it creates tensions, give China suitable status, and cooperate on international issues where possible; furthermore, both countries should develop mutual interdependence so their economies can derive maximum benefit from one another.

"Asia First"

In the view of the Asia First camp, China is acting to reclaim its status as the leader of Asia without coming into direct conflict with the US. According to Asia First advocates, China's leaders, guided by historical memory, may think they are only taking defensive actions to secure China's own security and access to resources, the safety of its sea lanes, etc., but the reality is that China is steadily establishing regional hegemony. Asia First advocates believe that having the US manifest leadership in Asia and maintain alliances is the key to ensuring regional peace and stability. In their view, China, with regional hegemony as its goal, is behaving with the following seven objectives. First, it wishes to weaken the system of US alliances in Asia. Second, it wants the countries of Asia to come to doubt the reliability of the US and the intent of its involvement in Asia. Third, it intends to use its own economic power to lead Asian countries in the directions it desires. Fourth, it plans to build up the military power of the PLA to suppress the regional involvement of the US military. Fifth, it aims to spread doubts regarding the US economic model. Sixth, it wants to ensure that US democratic values do not exert a harmful influence on rule by the Communist Party of China. And finally, it hopes to avoid a large-scale confrontation with the US over the next ten years.

Asia First advocates also see a problem in how China fails to fulfill its obligations under international rules and even acts in violation of those rules by reducing the security of neighboring countries, even though it has been accepted by the US as a permanent member of the United Nations Security Council and as a member of the World Trade Organization to incorporate it into the existing international order. Some criticize prior US administrations, saying that they believed US interests in Asia could be protected by integrating China into the international system and by advocating for both hedging and cooperation toward China in parallel, when in fact it was becoming clear that China was not moving toward integration into the international system. Furthermore, the US nonetheless acted only to cooperate with China—which is far less costly than hedging against China—and continued to expect that China would eventually accept US leadership. These critics say this was the greatest failure of prior administrations, and harshly disparage the policies followed to date.[15]

Based on this understanding of the issues, Asia First advocates argue that the liberal international order whose benefits the US and the countries of Asia have long enjoyed is being destroyed by China's unilateral actions. They hold that it is China's problematic behavior that is impairing the peace and prosperity of the Asia Pacific, so the US and its allies and partner countries should cooperate to persuade China to change. There are a range of ideas regarding what sort of approach to take, but they typically include the following three elements. The first is to check China's behavior on each individual issue, and impose financial and other consequences.[16] The second is to suggest the potential for the US to take action on issues which are sensitive to China, and to urge China to exercise self-restraint.[17] The third is for the US to shift to a grand strategy of all-out competitive relations with China.[18]

"Asia First" Becomes Predominant

The China First and Asia First camps differ not only in their perceptions of China, but also in their positions regarding America's strategy in East Asia and its approach to China. These differences resulted in varied assessments of the Obama administration's approach to China, and drew debate regarding the approach that the US should take toward East Asia and China. In recent years, however, the expectations that the US held toward China have not been met by China's actions. Disappointment about this failure is apparently spreading among both camps in Washington, and as a result, the voices advocating Asia First have become louder than those advocating China First.

The US had, at the very least, two types of expectations toward China. The first was that as China became economically wealthy, political freedoms would advance and democratization might even be realized. But there has been a political crackdown in Chinese society since the launch of the Xi Jinping administration, and there is a sense in Washington that this expectation has been betrayed.

The second expectation was that if China gained strength as a great power, it would fulfill the role of supporting the existing international order while observing international rules; that is, it would become a "responsible stakeholder" or a status quo power. However, according to University of Virginia China specialist Harry Harding, this expectation was betrayed in two ways. First, without fulfilling such responsibilities, China asserted its rights as a great power when convenient, shirked its obligations as a minor player when they were inconvenient, and acted as a "selective stakeholder" or a "free rider." Second, China has been adopting antagonistic behavior that challenges the established international order, especially in recent years. Examples include the establishment of international financial institutions—the Asian Infrastructure Investment Bank and the New Development Bank (BRICs Bank)—and efforts to conclude the Regional Comprehensive Economic Partnership (RCEP) free trade agreement. Likewise, its military buildup, which has caused other countries in the Western Pacific to lose their security, and its unilateral construction of artificial islands in the South China Sea are a long way from the responsible behavior expected by the US.[19] The view of China as a "free rider" and a "challenger" became more prevalent in Washington, and US expectations that China will become a responsible stakeholder are now hanging by a thread.

China has continued with its troubling behavior, disregarding US diplomatic objections. As the sense of disappointment toward China has grown in Washington, since around the summer of 2015 several observers have noted that the Asia First proponents are becoming more prevalent. For example, China expert David Shambaugh of George Washington University boldly declares that the "engagement coalition," which has supported US involvement with China, is waning and the "competition coalition" is rising. He also asserts that the balance between cooperation with China and competition with China has shifted, with competition becoming the dominant factor, and that this competition is not limited to the military sphere, but now encompasses commerce, ideology, politics, diplomacy, technology, and even academia.[20] Another China specialist, David Lampton of the Johns Hopkins University School of Advanced International Studies, notes that the foremost leaders of the US policy elite have all come to view China as a threat to US dominance, support within the US for forward-looking US-China relations is becoming weaker, and US-China relations are reaching a tipping point.[21] Former National Intelligence Council analyst Robert Manning similarly states that the foundations of the nonpartisan China policy followed by the US since the Nixon administration are crumbling, and that it is becoming difficult to maintain the prior approach of balancing cooperation and competition.[22] And according to Australian international political science scholar Hugh White, the prior US consensus that China will never fundamentally challenge the US in Asia is unraveling. [23]

Furthermore, Harding points out that calls for a tougher China policy are growing stronger in the US, and that support for choosing to incorporate China in academia, the business world, and the policy community is dissipating. He says US relations with China are already competitive, and concerns are on the rise that this could transform into open conflict with China under certain circumstances. Regardless, Harding retains a strong belief that the US and China can avoid war, and remains hopeful that, since the ideal approach to China is still being decided, the US and China can develop positive cooperation, keep competition within healthy areas such as economic growth, and reach agreements on rules to limit competition in fields where it is costly and dangerous, such as trade and the military.[24] In fact, there is a debate on having China play a more constructive role and take responsibility in various international issues, while also deterring China. This type of discussion is a compromise between Asia First and China First, giving somewhat greater weight to the former, so support for it has not yet entirely disappeared.[25]

White House Perceptions of China

In this way, across the board, American China specialists and Asian policy experts are pointing out that the earlier US stance emphasizing cooperation with China is losing support. As seen in the previous section, this trend emerged in Washington when China did not respond as the US had expected.

More people are questioning the existing approach to China based on cooperation, and a security-based approach is gaining dominance.

So is the While House's approach toward China changing? As explained in section I, the Obama administration's approach emphasized reassurance more than deterrence; simply stated, however, this was based on expectations that the US could build up friendly relations both with US allies and partners and with China, and on the belief that an approach combining deterrence and reassurance could lead China to behave as the US desired. This tack would achieve a compromise between the positions of the China First and Asia First advocates. In a memoir, Jeffrey A. Bader, who served as senior director for Asia affairs at the National Security Council during the first Obama administration, says that those in the administration responsible for Asia policy shared the following strategic perspective.

> A sound China strategy should rest on three pillars: (1) a welcoming approach to China's emergence, influence, and legitimate expanded role; (2) a resolve to see that its rise is consistent with international norms and law; and (3) an endeavor to shape the Asia-Pacific environment to ensure that China's rise is stabilizing rather than disruptive.
>
> America's key alliances with Japan, South Korea, and Australia are critical to maintaining a framework of peace and stability in the region, as is developing effective political and security partnerships with other emerging and important actors, including Indonesia, India, and Vietnam.[26]

In other words, the basic thinking behind the Obama administration's China policy was that the US would strengthen its ties with allies and create cooperative relationships with new partners while welcoming China's emergence, and if China observed international rules, the US would recognize the increase of its influence and the expansion of its legitimate roles.

The US welcoming an expansion in China's legitimate roles means an increase in China's responsibilities regarding issues such as nuclear nonproliferation related to North Korea and Iran, climate change mitigation through the reduction of greenhouse gas emissions, stability in Afghanistan, the establishment of international rules regarding cyberspace, and the stable management of the global economy. These issues are easily politicized inside the US, and are considered important by President Obama. Because China is involved with all of them, there are strong expectations that the US could elicit collaboration from China and somehow maintain cooperative relations in order to advance toward their resolution.

On the other hand, if China's emergence is not stabilized, there is the possibility the Asia-Pacific region will fall into chaos. The US is also aware of the need to pressure China to observe international rules and to simultaneously strengthen US relations with allies and other countries in the region. This is the context of US efforts to reinforce defense cooperation with its allies and strengthen security cooperation with its partners. Because China's intimidating behavior in the East China Sea and its disruption of the status quo in the South China Sea violate international rules, as noted in section I, the Obama administration has gradually reinforced reassurance to allies and partners and backed off on reassurance to China. Additionally, the US is showing concern over the possibility that China may use the Asian Infrastructure Investment Bank and other Chinese-initiated financial organs to involve other countries in implementing financing outside the framework of high standards established by the World Bank and the Asian Development Bank.

Overall, for the Obama administration, China is both a partner with which the US must cooperate on global issues that have domestic political implications and a rival with which the US must compete regarding the rules underpinning the regional order in Asia. Consequently, within the US government, offices that are responsible for matters where the US cooperates with China and those responsible for matters where the US competes with China differ in their approach. There is a strong possibility that the former devise and decide policies based on the China First view and the latter do so based on the Asia First perspective.

Furthermore, the overall approach of the US government toward China is ultimately greatly influenced by whether the president wishes to give greater weight to cooperation or to competition. That is, if the president emphasizes cooperation, the response to competitive policy issues will be restrained; if the president emphasizes competition, the response will take into account the possibility that initiatives on policy issues that require cooperation could stagnate or even regress. President Obama is said to view China not through a geopolitical lens, but rather from the global perspective mentioned above; in fact, he has emphasized cooperation with China. In the words of one analyst, the Obama administration has adopted a "confrontation management" approach,[27] worked to identify issues where US and Chinese interests might be aligned, and tried to expand fields of cooperation via policy dialogue when bilateral relations come into conflict over issues such as North Korea, the South China Sea, and cybersecurity, so that US-China relations are not dominated by competition or confrontation alone.

Within this framework, the competitive policy viewpoint is considered an "obstacle" to advancing global cooperation issues, and responses are based on the idea of removing that "obstacle" via the minimum necessary containment measures. A forward-looking mindset is fostered if the US response creates the facade required to externally justify removing the "obstacle," or the US can draw the minimum necessary concessions from China. In other words, in the administration of a president who emphasizes cooperation, the idea of addressing points that conflict and compete with China from a medium- to long-term perspective and dealing with them resolutely in a costly manner loses strength. This suggests that the direction of US-China policy is being set by the perception that China has an expanded role in global policy issues, as well as by whether the US president's conceptual framework for diplomacy emphasizes (a) cooperation among great powers to address global policy issues or (b) competition and the formation of alliances to deal with geopolitical policy issues.

However, this does not imply that the Obama administration is not responsive to pending policy issues. The intensity of the response varies depending on the issue, as some involve direct harm to US interests and could have a domestic political impact, while others involve harm to the regional interests of allies and partners. As an example of the former, the problem of data theft by cyber hacking began to draw attention around February 2013. In the summer of 2015, 22.1 million records of current and former federal government employees were taken in the Chinese hacking of the United States Office of Personnel Management (OPM), worsening the discord between the US and China. The US Department of Justice indicted five PLA officers for involvement in cyber espionage in the spring of 2014, and China retaliated by suspending its participation in the US-China Cyber Working Group.

President Obama's stance toward China has hardened since the OPM hacking. In April 2015, he signed an executive order approving harsh financial sanctions against organizations and persons engaged in cyber-enabled data theft and other significant malicious cyber-enabled activities, using cyber-enabled activities to obstruct the administration of important facilities, or profiting therefrom.[28]

In the US-China Cyber Agreement concluded when General Secretary Xi Jinping visited Washington in September 2015, the US and Chinese governments agreed to a number of measures. They pledged, among other things, to provide timely responses to requests for information and assistance concerning malicious cyber activities, to refrain from conducting or knowingly supporting cyber-enabled theft of intellectual property, to pursue efforts to further identify and promote appropriate norms of state behavior in cyberspace within the international community, and to establish a high-level joint dialogue mechanism on fighting cybercrime and related issues. The agreement made a distinction between cyber espionage activities for national security purposes and cyber-enabled theft of intellectual property for commercial gain, compelling the Chinese government, which had previously refused to recognize this distinction, to accept its obligation to exercise control over the latter.[29]

President Obama's threat of financial sanctions to compel the Chinese side to respond was motivated by domestic public opinion in response to the OPM hacking case and pressure from industrial circles whose intellectual property was being stolen, as well as the likelihood that failure to respond resolutely to cyberattacks by China would become a domestic political problem. However, the US-China Cyber Agreement was ultimately about the establishment of a high-level joint dialogue mechanism to discuss cyber issues, so sanctions were not imposed. This means the Obama administration did not abandon its confrontation management approach. Rather, when driven by domestic political necessity, the administration chose the option of exerting pressure under its existing approach. It is probably not appropriate to see this as a sign of a major shift in the framework of the Obama administration's stance towards China.

Regarding the issue of the South China Sea, while the Obama administration showed subtle changes in the autumn of 2015, there are various indications that it is maintaining the confrontation management approach. China unilaterally proceeded with the construction of artificial islands in the South China Sea despite repeated protests from the US and the South China Sea claimants. In response, on the premise of navigating the high seas, on October 27, 2015, the US sent the Aegis destroyer USS *Lassen* to pass within 12 nautical miles of Subi Reef, where China was constructing a runway, to assert that China's "jurisdiction" is invalid. China's construction of artificial islands began attracting attention in Washington from around the autumn of 2014 (the construction itself started earlier). There were predictions that the artificial islands were a movement toward establishing an ADIZ in the South China Sea, and discussions began on how China might use the islands during outbreaks of military conflict and at normal times. When President Xi Jinping visited Washington in September 2015, he declared at a press conference that the islands being constructed in the South China Sea would not be militarized.

The Department of Defense and the Department of State took the position that US vessels and aircraft were free to navigate or fly anywhere at any time permitted by international law. The US Navy had been in favor of implementing freedom of navigation operations (FONOPS) for a while, but the White House had reportedly been cautious. The judgement was made to postpone FONOPS, however, prior to General Secretary Xi Jinping's September visit to Washington. There were concerns among government leaders that China might react by suspending cooperation with the Conference of the Parties to the United Nations Framework Convention on Climate Change (COP 21) to be held in Paris from the end of November. Ultimately, the option that would irritate China the least was selected, and the Department of Defense was reportedly directed not to issue any external announcements after the FONOPS took place.[30]

The implementation of FONOPS went a step beyond America's diplomatic objections to date; this can be seen as the result of China's continued activity in the South China Sea, which propelled the rise of the Asia First camp. The Department of Defense has also launched a comprehensive "Asia-Pacific Maritime Security Strategy."[31] However, if media reports on the current thinking within the administration are accurate, rather than the resolute response sought by the Department of Defense and the US military, administration leaders intend to address the construction of man-made islands in the South China Sea—which is a competitive policy issue where US interests collide with Chinese interests—within the framework of the confrontation management approach to avoid losing China's cooperation on global issues. A position paper coauthored by Jeffrey A. Bader, who served as senior director for East Asian affairs at the National Security Council during the first Obama administration, argues that while freedom of navigation in the South China Sea involves vital US interests, US credibility should not be put at stake regarding the sovereignty issue, because the US is not prepared to use force, and so the approach to the issue should be moderated.[32] It is possible that this perspective is shared within the administration.

As set forth above, President Obama and the White House are taking a confrontation management approach that balances the competitive and cooperative aspects of US-China relations. In practice, however, this framework emphasizes advancing policy issues that require cooperation with China while taking a cautious stance toward competitive issues to avoid damaging relations with China wherever possible. As for cyber issues, which have a large impact on domestic politics, while the administration is threatening sanctions and applying pressure, it has also established a high-level joint dialogue mechanism. Regarding the South China Sea issue, while implementing freedom of navigation operations and stepping up its protests, the US is also continuing military exchanges with China and devising ways to avert tensions in US-China relations. Policymakers in Washington are leaning toward an Asia First approach to China, and that trend is becoming more pronounced in competitive policy issues, especially within the offices responsible for national security at both the Department of Defense and the Department of State. In emphasizing the security of allies and partners in its approach, the Obama White House is nevertheless maintaining its confrontation management stance while stepping back somewhat from providing reassurance to China.

It should be noted that, while the Obama White House is adopting a restrained response to national security issues within this confrontation management approach, in the defense establishment there is rising opposition and wariness toward China, which is bolstering its anti-access/area denial (A2/AD) capabilities and continuing to construct artificial islands and build facilities in the South China Sea. As explained in the next section, this sense of mistrust is pushing Department of Defense leaders to pursue the "Third Offset Strategy" and leading to full-scale strategic competition between the US and China in the military arena.

III. The Defense Establishment and the Third Offset Strategy

Debate on A2/AD Countermeasures

The Asia First camp emphasizes relations with allies and partners. But the foreign policy establishment, which primarily views international relations in Asia from a diplomatic perspective, and the defense establishment, which views the military balance in East Asia from a strategic perspective, have different outlooks on China. The defense establishment—which includes personnel of the Department of Defense and the US military, defense-affiliated think tanks, and the Senate and House armed services committees—is wary of how China has rapidly enhanced its A2/AD capabilities in recent years and repeatedly acted to change the facts on the ground in the Western Pacific. A growing view is that by enhancing its A2/AD and other capabilities, China aims to have the US lose its military superiority in East Asia, to alienate US allies, and ultimately to drive the US out of East Asia. Defense strategy is being examined with a view to halting and reversing such developments. To avoid direct conflict with the US military, to date China has not directly employed the PLA, but has used maritime law enforcement agencies and other bodies to commit acts of intimidation, construct artificial islands, and carry out other acts that change the facts on the ground. Regardless, the US defense establishment is reacting strongly to China's military buildup and acts that alter the status quo.

Plainly speaking, the US defense establishment has been debating how US forces can be projected into the theater of operations and function effectively under an A2/AD environment, what must be done toward those ends during peacetime, and what issues must be addressed in pursuing long-term strategic competition with China and Russia.

Going back in time slightly to review efforts to devise operational concepts at the Department of Defense and the US Armed Forces, the Department of Defense announced the Joint Operational Access Concept (JOAC) in January 2012.[33] Under the JOAC, to counter enhanced A2/AD capabilities acquired by hostile nations, it will be essential to utilize "cross-domain synergy" which establishes superiority in some combination of the land, sea, air, space, and cyberspace domains, depending on the situation, and compensates for vulnerabilities in other domains. To implement the JOAC, thirty types of mission accomplishment capabilities must be reinforced, and there should be a greater degree of military integration than ever before.

The Air-Sea Battle (ASB) concept is subsidiary to the JOAC. ASB was announced as a US military operational concept under an A2/AD environment in the 2010 Quadrennial Defense Review. The goal of ASB is to defend allies and partners and maintain free access to the global commons while third countries are advancing their acquisition of A2/AD capabilities. Under ASB, the solution to the A2/AD issue is to implement operations across all domains (sea, air, land, space, and cyberspace) and conduct networked, integrated, in-depth attacks to disrupt, destroy, and defeat the enemy's A2/AD capabilities where necessary.[34]

A blockade at sea without attacking the Chinese mainland was also proposed as an offshore control strategy around the same time,[35] and proponents of ASB debated the merits of attacking enemy territory and the escalation risk,[36] but this soon died down. Thereafter, in January 2015, the military service chiefs from the Army, Marine Corps, Navy, and Air Force exchanged a memorandum renaming Air-Sea Battle as the Joint Concept for Access and Maneuver in the Global Commons (JAM-GC). The contents are being revised and expanded; if this proceeds smoothly the new operational concept will be established in the second half of 2016.[37]

The Launch of the Defense Innovation Initiative

During this period, developments went beyond discussions regarding operational concepts and moved toward restructuring initiatives to secure US military dominance from a more fundamental level. In a policy speech on November 15, 2014, Secretary of Defense Hagel announced the launch of the Defense Innovation Initiative (DII) and a Third Offset Strategy (TOS) to be developed by implementing the various initiatives in the DII.[38] "Offset strategy" refers to combining weapons, systems, and operational concepts in new ways to offset the military superiority of enemies, secure surplus military capabilities, and create deterrence; the DII is an organizational "innovation" initiative by the entire Department of Defense to realize the TOS. According to Deputy Secretary of Defense Robert O. Work, who is heading the effort, the TOS focuses in particular on the deterrence of other great powers by conventional forces (here, a "great power" refers to a state that can take on the United States with conventional forces and which has effective nuclear retaliation capabilities; that is, to China and Russia).[39] Work led the "Future Warfare 20XX" project when he was at the Center for Strategic and Budgetary Assessments and then the "20YY Preparing for War in the Robotic Age" project at the Center for a New American Security, conducting research on the implications of the application of artificial intelligence and robotics technology to weapons. This research presumably was the basis for the launch of the TOS at the Department of Defense.[40]

In the 1950s, the Eisenhower administration deterred the conventionally superior Warsaw Pact forces of the Eastern Bloc by using US nuclear capabilities under the so-called New Look strategy. This was characterized as the First Offset Strategy. The Second Offset Strategy refers to the series of initiatives taken in the 1970s when the USSR was achieving nuclear parity. The US integrated cutting-edge technologies of the day with its command and control network to create precision-guided munitions systems and combined these with the operational concepts of Air-Land Battle and Follow-on-Forces Attack, allowing NATO forces to regain deterrence against the USSR.[41]

Behind the Department of Defense's push to implement the DII were certain shifts in the security environment. First was the recognition that the cutting-edge weapons technology formerly monopolized by the US was now in the possession of newly emerging countries, terrorist organizations, and other non-state actors.[42] There was a growing sense of alarm that while the US was expending vast resources on stabilization operations by ground forces in Iraq and Afghanistan, both China and Russia were investing massive amounts of capital on modernizing their weapons, and as a result, the US was losing its military superiority. Second was the recognition that other countries and actors are able to access the fundamental technologies that will be used to modernize weapons in the future. Deputy Secretary of Defense Work points out that the current distribution of military technologies resembles the situation in the interwar period more than that of the Cold War.[43]

While the objective of the DII is to create the TOS, this will require research and development initiatives to integrate technologies, systems, and operational concepts in order to secure power projection capabilities, as well as undertaking the necessary systems reforms to realize and support the TOS.

Research and development initiatives
Both short-term and long-term initiatives are being taken with respect to TOS. The short-term initiatives, centered on the Strategic Capabilities Office, use innovative methods to conduct a zero-base examination of utilizing existing military forces. They are projected to run for around five years from 2014, corresponding to the five-year range of the Department of Defense Future Years Defense Program (FYDP). The long-term initiatives take a perspective of ten years or longer, corresponding to the second FYDP cycle, and focus on "Strategic Portfolio Reviews," including planning defense investment to develop capabilities for future deployment.[44]

While there are multiple organizations that could advance and support these initiatives from a specialized technology perspective, to date only two have had their direct involvement officially confirmed.[45] The first is the Long-Range Research and Development Planning Program (LRRDPP) established by Under Secretary of Defense for Acquisition, Technology, and Logistics Frank Kendall. The AT&L (referring to this under secretary and his organization) identifies innovations that utilize state-of-the-art technologies and systems and promotes their development and deployment. The LRRDPP investigates the military application of technologies that would give the US military advantages around the year 2030, including those related to space, undersea operations, air dominance and airstrikes, air and missile defense, and all sorts of plans based on other technologies.[46] The program examines relatively mature technologies that may be applied in novel or unique ways to create fundamentally different types of system capabilities, as well as emerging technologies that can be rapidly developed to offer new military capabilities and technologies being applied to nonmilitary uses that can be used for military purposes; it seeks proposals from the private sector as well.[47] The unit that advanced the Second Offset Strategy was also called the LRRDPP, and the revival of a unit with the same name has drawn the attention of the US defense strategy community.

The second known organization is the Defense Science Board (DSB), which is also managed by the AT&L. The DSB is primarily an advisory body composed of scientists and strategists specializing in science and technology pertaining to national defense. For example, as discussed below, the DSB investigates and reports on the management of autonomous weapons systems at the request of the AT&L.[48]

In practice, the DII is supported by various units and individuals within the Department of Defense. The Advanced Capabilities and Deterrence Panel has been established as an operations liaison council under Deputy Secretary Work. This panel, which coordinates initiatives across the entire organization, includes Department of Defense's senior leadership from the areas of policy, intelligence, armed services, the Joint Chiefs of Staff, research and engineering, and acquisitions. The Department of Defense has also initiated systematic outreach efforts to acquire new technologies from outside the department. These have included the establishment of the Defense Innovation Unit Experimental (DIUx) in California's Silicon Valley in an effort to increase contact with information technology firms, which have had very little involvement with national defense in the past.[49] The Department of Defense has also invested in In-Q-Tel, a company established by the CIA to invest in promising companies engaged in technological development, and is advancing initiatives relating to the adoption of new technologies developed by private companies.[50]

System reforms

Acquisition process reform is another aspect of the DII that has been drawing attention. A given weapon generally takes thirty years to develop from the research and testing stages through to procurement and deployment, but the technology innovation cycle and the pace at which innovations are propagated are speeding up. If competitor countries are likewise able to divert those technologies to military purposes in a shorter period, the US must develop weapons that compete on this level if it is to maintain technological superiority. The global environment surrounding research and development has changed, and today many leading technologies and innovations are created not by the government but by the private sector. The Department of Defense is therefore competing with enemy countries over how fast weapons can move from development to acquisition and deployment. Under the Better Buying Power 3.0 (BBP 3.0) initiative led by Under Secretary of Defense Kendall,[51] reform efforts are being carried out to streamline the previously complex weapons acquisition process and provide both the defense industry and the government with greater incentives for acquisitions. Meanwhile, Republican senator John McCain, who was extremely dissatisfied with the existing acquisition process, incorporated additional reforms into the National Defense Authorization Act. These gave service chiefs, rather than the office of Acquisitions, Technology, and Logistics (AT&L), overall responsibility for the process from development through acquisition, and established a penalty system whereby programs with cost overruns of more than 15 percent would be transferred back to the AT&L and would have to pay a penalty of 3 percent of the overrun into a fund for development of weapon prototypes.[52] House Armed Services Committee Chair Mac Thornberry also submitted a bill in March 2016 under which major weapons developments starting after October 2018 would be designed so that the system components (modules) would be built around an open systems architecture. This would allow for continuous upgrades and further speed up the process from testing to development and on to deployment.[53] As these reforms are under discussion, the focus will be on whether they succeed in reducing costs and speeding up acquisition periods.

BBP 3.0 includes a policy to expand the production of weapons prototypes with the aim of maintaining cutting-edge research and development in the face of budgetary limitations, as well as producing a variety of prototype weapons to facilitate the switch to mass production in case of national security emergencies and preserving the technological foundations of the defense industry.

The memorandum on the DII that Secretary of Defense Hagel sent to the Department of Defense and top military officers[54] directed them to advance organizational reform and human resource development. This reflects the understanding that simply building new systems with advanced weapons and operating them based on new operational concepts will not be enough; personnel and organizations must also adapt to change if they are to be effective.

The Elements of the Third Offset Strategy

If the TOS is to succeed, it must link three elements: technologies, systems, and operational concepts. While no conclusive information on any of these has emerged, I would like to introduce the points currently being discussed.

Technologies

Technologies already in wide use are likely to be included as a matter of course. In his November 2014 speech, Secretary of Defense Hagel mentioned robotics, autonomous systems, miniaturization, and advanced manufacturing such as big data and 3D printing. There has been speculation in the US defense strategy community that these suggest small unmanned weapons equipped with artificial intelligence (AI). For example, concepts discussed by a naval research institute include arming unmanned submarines with a large number of miniature drones with AI, and using the Navy's overwhelming advantage in submarine fighting power to have the unmanned submarines penetrate all the way to the enemy's coastal areas and launch miniature drones which will form swarms that target and attack the enemy's sensors and other devices so as to disrupt the enemy's kill chain. Unlike the large drones currently in use, which are each operated by one pilot using a joystick, this strategy would involve the operation of dozens of miniature drones at once using a mouse. However, the organizational culture of the Air Force is reportedly resistant to the idea of operating multiple aircraft at once.[55]

Numerous other technologies are under development; for example, hypervelocity projectiles developed for electromagnetic railguns are being adapted for firing from howitzers, and advanced navigation systems with ultra-miniature cameras and sensors are being attached to miniature bombs to facilitate targeted attacks when off network.[56] These are just the tip of the iceberg.

Systems

Regarding systems, in his November 2015 policy speech, Deputy Secretary of Defense Work explained that a study in the summer of 2015 had offered insights into the LRRDPP and DSB autonomous systems and said several systems concepts were being devised. He noted two particularly worthy of mention:[57] human-machine collaboration and human-machine combat teaming. The details of both are still unclear, so this is an abstract explanation. The first, human-machine collaboration, rests on the understanding that weapons systems that help humans make decisions with the support of computers are superior to fully autonomous weapons systems. Deputy

Secretary Work's explanation implies that systems incorporating Americans who have been educated and lived in US society will be superior to the fully autonomous weapons systems that authoritarian states such as China and Russia[58] presumably will shift to eventually.

Human-machine combat teaming refers to manned systems combined with unmanned systems. In the Navy, for example, one idea is to link unmanned MQ-XX Stingrays, which have sophisticated data collection abilities and can take off and land from aircraft carriers, with manned aircraft such as F-35s or FA-18E/F Super Hornets.[59]

Operational concepts

As for operational concepts, the process of updating the former Air-Sea Battle into JAM-GC has begun. According to the DII directive from Secretary of Defense Hagel, however, new operational concepts will also be sought. For the time being, overcoming and breaking down A2/AD environments will certainly be one issue. The use of war games to formulate operational concepts is a growing trend in the Department of Defense, armed forces, and defense strategy community, and Deputy Secretary of Defense Work is emphasizing the importance of war gaming as well.[60]

Short-term efforts are also underway to find entirely new uses for existing weapons systems that support operational concepts. These efforts will probably not be conducted in a unified manner by a single unit of the Department of Defense or the armed forces, but will proceed in diverse formats at multiple locations. While the specific details are, of course, unknown, a variety of tactics are being actively debated. The Navy is examining the concept of "distributed lethality," which would boost the attack capabilities of fleets at sea under the present A2/AD environment.[61] This is one example of an innovation that strengthens existing weapons and applies them in novel ways.

On the other hand, the "swarm" mentioned above is an example of an innovation using new weapons equipped with new technologies and applying new methods. The report "Robotics on the Battlefield Part II: The Coming Swarm," published by the Center for a New American Security (CNAS) in October 2014, provides what I think is the most detailed explanation of the swarm, and the issues being explored inside the Department of Defense are substantially reflected in this report.[62] Written by CNAS Senior Fellow Paul Scharre, who was in charge of unmanned autonomous weapons systems policy at the Office of the Secretary of Defense from 2008 through 2013, the report assumes not a system for fighting with existing types of manned weapons while exchanging data over long distances via networks, but rather one where autonomous small unmanned vehicles with AI (the report presumes unmanned aircraft) share data with each other and synchronize and coordinate their behavior while attacking and defending. This would require a command and control model in which operators command a large number of small drones. In the swarm concept, qualitative advantages in military capabilities are not based on the performance standard of individual weapons as in the past, but rather on the activity of a group of weapons made possible by artificial intelligence and miniaturization technologies. The idea is that if 3D printing and other advances can be used to produce such autonomous, unmanned micro-drones cheaply, the US will also have the advantage in the cost-exchange ratio between the relative cost of the attack versus the cost of the countermeasures. Combining such advanced technologies and systems, devising corresponding operational concepts, and bringing them into military operations will require overcoming a number of different obstacles, beginning with organizational culture;[63] it will by no means be easy. These are just a few examples of innovations at the tactical level that support JAM-GC and new operational concepts.

Meanwhile, the strategist outside the government who probably conducted the most comprehensive examination of the A2/AD issue from the perspectives of operational concepts and regional military strategy is Andrew Krepinevich, who was the president of the Center for Strategic and Budgetary Assessments (CSBA) at the time. Krepinevich says that a "mature precision-strike regime" would arise if enemy powers possess precision-guided munitions and combine them with intelligence and command/control systems and long-range offensive weapons. He also states that opposing forces will compete over the no-go zone where their power projection zones overlap.

Especially in the maritime arena, he notes that the key areas of competition will include reconnaissance capabilities for discovering targets (code breaking, jamming communications links, cyber capabilities to corrupt an enemy's reconnaissance data, etc.); battle damage assessment to verify the results of attacks; measures to reinforce armor and control damage to surface vessel fleets so that enemies are forced to maintain more extended-range strike assets; and the transformation of the military power of submarines into mother ships that can carry unmanned underwater craft, advanced sea mines, towed payload modules, and so on. Krepinevich explains that countries and forces with the ability to dominate are those that can innovate or transform by linking existing and emerging military capabilities to skillful operational concepts in a timely manner. These operational concepts may center on winning scouting campaigns, depleting the enemy's long-range strike systems, or engaging in peripheral campaigns in regions where the enemy forces are vulnerable.[64]

Krepinevich and the CSBA have also drawn attention with their proposals for more specific military strategies for the Western Pacific region. They present ways of using the threat of punishment by the Air Force and Navy for deterrence in the CSBA report "Air-Sea Battle: A Point-of-Departure Operational Concept." This proposal is presented as an operational concept, but it is really closer to a military strategy because its contents mention specific enemy countries and war zones. In an article in *Foreign Affairs* magazine, Krepinevich and his coauthors propose the operational concept of "archipelagic defense" as a way of utilizing the army for a similar deterrence strategy.[65] These two mutually complementary concepts have apparently become one basis for discussions within the US defense establishment regarding operational concepts and military strategies in the Western Pacific region.

To summarize, there are active deliberations inside and outside the Department of Defense regarding operational concepts to counter A2/AD, and the ultimate outcome of these discussions is expected to be the fusion of weapons technologies and systems. In the medium to long term, it is entirely likely that mature new technologies will be incorporated as new systems to develop new weapons that will transform and evolve operational concepts.

Outlook for the Future

In recent years, China has expanded its military, advanced into maritime areas more actively, and asserted and pursued its own national interests more frequently. As cyber issues and the South China Sea problem have become matters of grave concern in US-China relations, the US has quietly strengthened its approach of reassuring allies and partner countries. Meanwhile, to elicit China's cooperation on global issues, the Obama administration has maintained its "confrontation management" approach to the greatest extent possible, so its responses to policy issues such as the South China Sea issue have tended to be passive and restrained. It is impossible to predict now, in March 2016, what approach the next administration will adopt to East Asia and China, but it will be greatly influenced by the diplomatic agenda the next president emphasizes, and how much the US will try to depend on China to pursue that agenda.

US-China relations will naturally change depending on whether the next president primarily emphasizes economic relations with China or instead focuses on maritime order, human rights, and cyber issues.

In light of the hardening of views on China among the Washington policy elite, the way the defense establishment has launched strategic competition with China, and the overall growing disappointment toward China, the US is very likely to adopt an Asia strategy focusing on reassuring allies and partners and pulling back on reassurance for China, without any expectations of Chinese cooperation. However, if China continues with its provocative behavior, the political cost of maintaining the confrontation management approach—which emphasizes cooperation to address points of conflict—will increase, and at some point, the US will inevitably switch to a containment approach using threats and pressure. If that happens, tensions and conflict between the US and China will become serious, significantly limiting the goal of promoting international rules. China may continue its tactic of adjusting its behavior while reading the atmosphere in Washington so that tensions are always kept under a certain level. If it is unable to assuage US distrust, and suspicion and wariness toward China continue to grow, the US may change its approach to China toward one of deterrence, and the strategic competition between the US and China will intensify. Even if the US and China do not engage in full-scale warfare, should it become clear that the long-term peacetime conditions are unraveling, then Japan will have to gather its wisdom and deeply consider what sort of national security policy it needs to pursue.

Note: Section III of this chapter was revised and amended from a report submitted to the Japan Institute of International Affairs project, titled "Major Developments in the US and China and US-China Relations amidst Turmoil in the International Order."

1 Hillary Clinton, "America's Pacific Century," *Foreign Policy*, November 2011.

2 The White House, "Remarks by President Obama to the Australian Parliament," November 17, 2011; Tom Donilon, "America is back in the Pacific and will uphold the rules," *Financial Times*, November 27, 2011; the White House, National Security Strategy of the United States of America, May 2010, 12–13.

3 Hiroshi Nakanishi, Atsushi Ishida, and Masayuki Tadokoro, *Kokusai seijigaku* [International politics] (Tokyo: Yūhikaku, 2013), 123–25, 144–61.

4 In his June 1, 2013, speech at the Shangri-La Dialogue, Secretary of Defense Chuck Hagel declared that the rebalance was "primarily a diplomatic, economic and cultural strategy." And

in a policy speech on April 8 that year, Deputy Secretary of Defense Ashton B. Carter said that "our rebalance to Asia is mostly a political and economic concept." US Department of Defense, "International Institute for Strategic Studies (Shangri-La Dialogue) as Delivered by Secretary of Defense Chuck Hagel," Singapore, June 1, 2013; US Department of Defense, "The US Defense Rebalance to Asia," April 8, 2013.

5   The White House, "Remarks as Prepared for Delivery by National Security Advisor Susan E. Rice," Georgetown University, Washington, DC, November 20, 2013.

6   The term "responsible stakeholder" drew attention when it was used in a 2005 speech by Robert Zoellick, who was then US deputy secretary of state in the George W. Bush administration. Robert Zoellick, "Whither China: From Membership to Responsibility," National Committee on US-China Relations, New York, September 21, 2005.

7   The White House, "Remarks by Tom Donilon, National Security Advisor to the President: 'The United States and the Asia-Pacific in 2013,'" Asia Society, New York, March 11, 2013.

8   The White House, "Press Briefing by National Security Advisor Tom Donilon," June 8, 2013.

9   The following article provides a detailed analysis regarding these developments: Seiichirō Takagi, "Beikoku no tai-Chū ninshiki / seisaku—dainiki Obama seiken o chūshin ni" [America's perceptions and policies on China—centered on the second Obama administration], in Japan Institute of International Affairs, *Shuyōkoku no tai-Chū ninshiki / seisaku no bunseki* [Analysis of the major powers' perceptions and policies on China], March 2015, 9–10.

10 US Department of State, "Maritime Disputes in Asia, Testimony of Daniel R. Russel, Assistant Secretary, Bureau of East Asian and Pacific Affairs" (testimony before the House Committee on Foreign Affairs Subcommittee on Asia and the Pacific, February 5, 2014); "US 'could change military posture' if China sets up second ADIZ," *Kyodo News*, February 1, 2014.

11 The White House, "Joint Press Conference with President Obama and Prime Minister Abe of Japan," Tokyo, April 24, 2014.

12 The White House, "Fact Sheet: US Building Maritime Capacity in Southeast Asia," November 17, 2015.

13 This classification is used in lectures and elsewhere by Kurt Campbell, who served as assistant secretary of state for East Asian and Pacific Affairs in the first Obama administration, and by Robert Sutter, who formerly served as a China analyst at the CIA and the Congressional Research Service and is now a China expert at George Washington University.

14 See, for example, Michael Swaine, "Beyond American Predominance in the Western Pacific: The Need for a Stable US-China Balance of Power" (Carnegie Endowment for International Peace, April 20, 2015); Lyle J. Goldstein, *Meeting China Halfway: How to Defuse the Emerging US-China Rivalry* (Georgetown University Press, 2015); David M. Lampton, "A Tipping Point in US-China Relations Is upon Us," *US-China Perception Monitor* (May 11, 2015); and Kevin Rudd, *US-China 21: The Future of US-China Relations Under Xi Jinping* (Belfer Center for Science and International Affairs, Harvard Kennedy School, April 2015). The international political scientist Charles Glaser argues that the US should end its commitment to the defense of Taiwan in exchange for China implementing peaceful resolutions to the South China Sea and East China Sea disputes and accepting a long-term security role for the US in the region. Charles L. Glaser, "A US-China Grand Bargain? The Hard Choice between Military Competition and Accommodation," *International Security* 39, no. 4 (Spring 2015): 49–90. In addition, the Australian researcher Hugh White argues that the main countries involved in Asia, including the US and China, should comprehensively negotiate all pending issues and form a "concert system." Hugh White, *The China Choice: Why We Should Share Power* (Oxford University Press, 2013).

15 Commentaries that clarify the Asia First position include the following: Patrick Cronin, "Chinese Regional Hegemony in Slow Motion," *War on the Rocks,* May 18, 2015; Robert D. Blackwill and Ashley J. Tellis, *Revising US Grand Strategy Toward China,* Council on Foreign Relations, Council Special Report No. 72 (March 2015): 19; Sean Mirski, "The False Promise of China's Integration into the Liberal International Order," *National Interest,* December 3, 2014.

16 Michael Green and Mira Hooper, then with the Center for Strategic and International Studies (CSIS), argue that because China is using intimidation to change the facts on the ground: (1) the US should cooperate with Japan to support capacity-building efforts by the Philippines and Vietnam and other Southeast Asian nations, (2) the US Navy should increase joint military exercises with its partners in the region and make clear to China that any declaration of an exclusive ADIZ over the South China Sea is unacceptable, and (3) the US should assist the Philippines and other Southeast Asian nations with their diplomatic and legal efforts to slow China's progress. Michael J. Green and Mira Rapp Hooper, "Push China toward diplomacy," *Washington Post,* March 12, 2015. Also, Center for a New American Security (CNAS) Asia-Pacific Security Program Senior Director Patrick Cronin writes that, while coordinating with allies and partners, the US should respond to China's aggression in the South China Sea not only with the use of intelligence but also by combining military, diplomatic, economic, and other instruments to pursue eight policies for halting and imposing costs on China. These include tarnishing China's reputation, imposing financial penalties, clarifying rules and setting norms, maximizing domestic political costs, diverting resources, strengthening deterrence and US credibility, exposing China's military weakness, and shifting the military balance. See Patrick Cronin, *The Challenge of Responding to Maritime Coercion* (Center for a New American Security, September 2014); Patrick M. Cronin and Alexander Sullivan, *Preserving the Rules: Countering Coercion in Maritime Asia* (Center for a New American Security, March 2015). In addition, Cronin argues that the US needs to promote the following ten existing measures more vigorously. (1) Collect information on China's military, diplomatic, legal, informational, and other relevant activities in the South China Sea, and make these facts public. (2) Use a regional maritime security information-sharing center to communicate with nations that utilize the South China Sea. (3) Widely distribute commercially available satellite imagery showing important construction and military-related activities in the South China Sea. (4) Advance a legally binding code of conduct regarding the South China Sea, starting with those parties that are willing to sign. (5) Advance initiatives to expand international legal expertise inside and outside the US. (6) Ratify the United Nations Convention on the Law of the Sea (UNCLOS). (7) Conduct more frequent freedom of navigation operations and joint military exercises with other countries. (8) Boost capacity-building assistance to regional countries. (9) Deepen regional engagement on all fronts, including promoting the Trans-Pacific Partnership (TPP) and other regional economic development initiatives, and cautiously advance military exchange with China. (10) Preserve a strong US military presence in the Asia-Pacific region. Patrick Cronin, "Pushing Back Against China's Strategy: Ten Steps for the United States," *War on the Rocks,* May 27, 2015.

17 For example, George Washington University US-China relations expert Robert Sutter argues that the US can exercise its influence on China and devise countermeasures so China will correct its expansionist behavior. Sutter asserts that, because Asia is China's top foreign priority, even without openly confronting China the US should examine its options for exploiting China's vulnerabilities. He gives several examples of possible measures to be considered. These include strengthening US defense cooperation with Japan, the Philippines, and Taiwan, forging stronger cooperation than in the past with Taiwan in particular; increasing demonstrations of US conventional missiles and attack submarines that avoid detection by China; increasing demonstrations

of surface sea and air power as part of the Department of Defense's new operational concept; countering Chinese ballistic missiles threatening US forces in Asia with prompt-strike conventional weapons systems that place targets in China at risk; responding to the nuclear threat posed by North Korea through discussions with Japan and South Korea involving possible transfers of offensive weapons to them in a way that would complicate Chinese strategic policy calculations; expressing greater support for popular sovereignty in Hong Kong and Taiwan; and pulling back from close US economic engagement with and reassurance of China. These options are all rather serious, but Sutter is not arguing that they should be implemented immediately. Rather, he explains they should be placed on the table in discussions of China policy in Washington, thereby demonstrating to China that if its provocative behavior continues, the US is prepared to take actions that will make China unhappy. Robert Sutter, "Asia's Importance, China's Expansion and US Strategy: What Should be Done?" East-West Center, *Asia Pacific Bulletin* no. 283 (October 28, 2014).

18 In a jointly authored policy proposal, Robert D. Blackwill of the Council on Foreign Relations and Ashley J. Tellis of the Carnegie Endowment for International Peace argue that China has already gained the power to threaten the security of US allies and regional countries in Asia and to slowly chip away at the foundations of the liberal international order globally. Regardless of what policies Washington takes, China will view them as containment, so without worrying about China's reaction, the US should strategically oppose China's challenge and adopt a grand strategy comprising the following four main pillars. First, the United States should work with its allies and other interested partners to revitalize the US economy, construct a new set of trading relationships in Asia that exclude China, devise policies to effectively deal with China's use of economic tools in Asia and elsewhere, and create a new technology export control mechanism versus China. Second, the United States should invest in US defense capabilities and capacity so that it can defeat China's emerging anti-access capabilities and project power successfully, even against concerted opposition from China. Third, the US should reinforce a new set of trusted strategic relationships and partnerships throughout the Indo-Pacific region that include traditional alliances but go beyond them, strengthen Asian states' ability to cope with China independently, build new forms of intra-Asian strategic cooperation, and provide them with systematic support. Fourth, the US should engage in high-level diplomacy with China to attempt to mitigate the inherently profound tensions as the two nations pursue mutually incompatible grand strategies, as well as to reassure US allies and friends in Asia and beyond that its objective is not to have a confrontation with China. The grand strategy advocated by Blackwill and Tellis is close to seeking strategic competition with and containing China, and as the authors themselves note, the costs are high, so their proposal has not become mainstream at the present time. Blackwill and Tellis, *Revising US Grand Strategy Toward China*.

19 Harry Harding, "Has US China Policy Failed?" *Washington Quarterly* 38, no. 3 (Fall 2015): 97–99.

20 David Shambaugh, "In a fundamental shift, China and the US are now engaged in all-out competition," *South China Morning Post*, June 11, 2015.

21 Lampton, "A Tipping Point in US-China Relations Is upon Us."

22 Robert A. Manning, "America's 'China Consensus' Implodes," *National Interest*, May 21, 2015.

23 Hugh White, "America's China Consensus Slowly Unravels," *Interpreter*, April 17, 2015.

24 Harding, "Has US China Policy Failed?" 119.

25 Examples include Thomas J. Christensen, "Obama and Asia: Confronting the China Challenge," *Foreign Affairs* 94, no. 5 (September/October 2015); Thomas J. Christensen, *The China Challenge: Shaping the Choices of a Rising Power* (W.W. Norton & Co., 2015); and Joseph Nye, "The Future of US-China Relations," *China-US Focus*, March 10, 2015.

26 Jeffrey Bader, *Obama and China's Rise: An Insider's Account of America's Asia Strategy* (Brookings Institution Press, 2012), 7.

27 Akio Takahata, "Bei-Chū senryaku / keizai taiwa (S&ED) to Ajia Taiheiyō kaiki senryaku" [US-China strategic and economic dialogue (S&ED) and Asia-Pacific rebalance strategy], in *Ajia kaiki suru Amerika: Gaikō anzen hoshō seisaku no kenshō* [Rebalancing to Asia: Evaluating the foreign and national security policy of the Obama Administration], ed. Fumiaki Kubo and Akio Takahata (NTT Shuppan, 2013), 30–55.

28 The White House, "Executive Order—Blocking the Property of Certain Persons Engaging in Significant Malicious Cyber-Enabled Activities," April 1, 2015.

29 Congressional Research Service, "US-China Cyber Agreement," *CRS Insight*, October 16, 2015.

30 Opinion, "South China Sea Stall," *Wall Street Journal*, December 16, 2015; Simon Denyer, Craig Whitlock, and Steven Mufson, "US Warship Sails within 12 Miles of Chinese-Built Island in South China Sea," *Washington Post*, October 26, 2015; Helene Cooper and Jane Perlez, "White House Moves to Reassure Allies with South China Sea Patrol, but Quietly," *New York Times*, October 27, 2015.

31 US Department of Defense, Asia-Pacific Maritime Security Strategy (2015).

32 Jeffrey Bader, Kenneth Lieberthal, and Michael McDevitt, "Keeping the South China Sea in Perspective," *Foreign Policy Brief* (Brookings Institution, August 2014).

33 US Department of Defense, Joint Operational Access Concept—Version 1.0 (January 17, 2012), 14–17, 34–35.

34 Air-Sea Battle Office, Air-Sea Battle: Service Collaboration to Address Anti-Access & Area Denial Challenges (May 2013). According to the US Air Force chief of staff and the chief of naval operations at that time, the fundamental reason the US emphasizes defense of allies and partners and securing access under an A2/AD environment is that, if the US appears unable or unwilling to counter an enemy's A2/AD capabilities, its partners and allies may lose faith in US security assurances, leading some to seek accommodation with resolute adversaries or to secure their own weapons of mass destruction. If an enemy were to acquire A2/AD and conditions worsened in this manner, US political influence would diminish, aggression against allies and partners become more likely, and US national power degrade as its alliances weaken. The authors also state that preparing US power projection capabilities in line with ASB allows US leaders to better manage the risks and uncertainties associated with changes in the balance of global power, especially when those changes are advantageous to states that challenge important international norms. General Norton A. Schwartz and Admiral Jonathan W. Greenert, "Air-Sea Battle: Promoting Stability in an Era of Uncertainty," *American Interest*, February 20, 2012.

35 Thomas X. Hammes, "Offshore Control: A Proposed Strategy for an Unlikely Conflict," *Strategic Forum* no. 278 (June 2012): 1–14.

36 Elbridge Colby, "Don't Sweat AirSea Battle," *National Interest*, July 31, 2013; T.X. Hammes, "Sorry, AirSea Battle is No Strategy," *National Interest*, August 7, 2013; Aaron L. Friedberg, *Beyond Air-Sea Battle: The Debate over US Military Strategy in Asia* (International Institute for

Strategic Studies, 2014); Erik Slavin, "Analysts: Air-Sea Battle concept carries risks in possible conflict with China," *Stars and Stripes*, September 28, 2014.

37 See the following for an interview with the Air-Sea Battle Office regarding the developments through November 2015: Harry J. Kazianis, "Air-Sea Battle's Next Step: JAM-GC on Deck," *National Interest,* November 25, 2015. See the following for an explanation from Department of Defense Air-Sea Battle office staff: Terry S. Morris, Martha Van Driel, Bill Dries, Jason C. Perdew, Richard H. Schulz, and Kristin E. Jacobsen, "Securing Operational Access: Evolving the Air-Sea Battle Concept," *National Interest*, February 11, 2015.

38 US Department of Defense, "Reagan National Defense Forum Keynote, as Delivered by Secretary of Defense Chuck Hagel," November 15, 2014.

39 US Department of Defense, "Reagan Defense Forum: 'The Third Offset Strategy,' as Delivered by Deputy Secretary of Defense Bob Work," November 7, 2015.

40 Robert O. Work and Shawn Brimley, *20YY: Preparing for War in the Robotic Age* (Center for a New American Security, January 2014).

41 While the First Offset Strategy is talked about as if it is the origin of the offset concept, offset as it is now framed is based on the Second Offset Strategy. The approach of intentionally combining technologies, systems, and operational concepts in response to trends in the strategic environment (i.e., the loss of military dominance in conventional forces) is viewed as the forerunner of the offset spoken about today. The idea behind the First Offset Strategy was that existing US nuclear forces would offset the superiority of the Warsaw Pact's conventional forces; that has been positioned retroactively as the First Offset Strategy. See the following paper for a discussion of the loss of the US military's technological advantage: Shawn Brimky, *While We Can: Arresting the Erosion of America's Military Edge* (Center for A New American Security, December 17, 2015).

42 This perception was by no means new. The proliferation of precision-guided technologies and other advanced technologies had been noted since the 1990s, but the actual proliferation pace was thought to be slower than initially expected. In the twenty-first century, however, it became clear that China was rapidly enhancing its anti-access/area denial (A2/AD) capabilities, and this came to be seen as a challenge to US military superiority.

43 During the interwar period, airplanes, radio, and various other technologies that were new at that time could already be broadly utilized. The question became how to skillfully combine those existing technologies to create weapons, and how they could be linked to creative operational concepts to generate military advantages. US Department of Defense, "Reagan Defense Forum: 'The Third Offset Strategy,' as Delivered by Deputy Secretary of Defense Bob Work."

44 US Department of Defense, "Reagan Defense Forum: 'The Third Offset Strategy,' as Delivered by Deputy Secretary of Defense Bob Work."

45 They have been mentioned in policy speeches by Deputy Secretary of Defense Work.

46 Under Secretary of Defense for Acquisition, Technology, and Logistics, "Memorandum for Secretaries of the Military Departments et al., Subject: Long Range Research and Development Plan (LRRDP) Direction and Tasking" October 29, 2014.

47 US Department of Defense, "Long Range Research and Development Plan (LRRDP) Request for Information" (undated).

48 Under Secretary of Defense for Acquisition, Technology and Logistics, "Memorandum for Chairman Defense Science Board, Subject: Terms of Reference—Defense Science Board 2015

Summer Study on Autonomy," November 17, 2014.

49 Sydney J. Freedberg, Jr., "'We're Allowed to Fail': Pentagon's Silicon Valley Outpost Truly Experimental," *Breaking Defense*, October 29, 2015.

50 US Department of Defense, "Reagan Defense Forum: 'The Third Offset Strategy,' as Delivered by Deputy Secretary of Defense Bob Work."

51 Under Secretary of Defense for Acquisition, Technology, and Logistics, "Memorandum for Secretaries of the Military Departments et al., Subject: Implementation Directive for Better Buying Power 3.0—Achieving Dominant Capabilities through Technical Excellence and Innovation," April 9, 2015.

52 Aaron Mehta and Joe Gould, "McCain Wins Big with Acquisition Reform," *Defense News*, October 5, 2015.

53 Katherine Blakeley, "Thornberry's 'Bold' Bill May Speed, Improve Buying Weapons," *Breaking Defense*, March 15, 2016.

54 Secretary of Defense, "Memorandum for Deputy Secretary of Defense et al., Subject: The Defense Innovation Initiative," November 15, 2014.

55 Paul Scharre, "How to Lose the Robotics Revolution," *War on the Rocks*, July 29, 2014.

56 US Department of Defense, "Remarks by Secretary Center on the Budget at the Economic Club of Washington, DC," February 2, 2016.

57 US Department of Defense, "Reagan Defense Forum: The Third Offset Strategy: As Delivered by Deputy Secretary of Defense Bob Work."

58 Deputy Secretary Work discussed the relationship between AI and military technology innovation at a CNAS speech. US Department of Defense, "Deputy Secretary of Defense Speech, CNAS Defense Forum," December 14, 2015.

59 Richard Whittle, "Navy Refueling Drone May Tie into F-35," *Breaking Defense*, March 22, 2016.

60 Deputy Secretary of Defense Work mentions the example of how, out of the three groups in the Navy prior to the Second World War—naval aviation, surface warfare, and submarine—the naval aviation community had examined creative applications of war games. When the war came, this group was able to be effective quickly, while the other two were constrained by conventional thinking and had difficulty fighting against the Japanese fleet. Robert O. Work and General Paul Selva, "Revitalizing Wargaming is Necessary to Be Prepared for Future Wars," *War on the Rocks*, December 8, 2015.

61 After the end of the Cold War, the US had overwhelming naval superiority. With no force to challenge US sea control, US anti-submarine warfare and anti-surface warfare capabilities declined. As a result, the surface fleet changed its emphasis from offense to defense and became skilled in such tasks as firing Tomahawk missiles from within its own safe sea areas. Now, the US Navy surface force perceives the challenging issue of A2/AD as a battle for control of the seas—the basis of its power—and is considering shifting to the distributed lethality concept of enhancing various attack capabilities (on cruisers, destroyers, littoral combat ships, amphibious assault ships, etc.), and forcing the enemy to invest more resources in defense. US Navy Surface Action Groups (SAGs) will not only enhance offensive operations, but are also expected to utilize "hunter-killer SAGs" which search for and destroy enemy units in dispersed formations (presumably in coordination with submarines). Furthermore, having the surface fleet maintain such capabilities will reinforce deterrence and escalation control by conventional weapons. Vice

Admiral Thomas Rowden, Rear Admiral Peter Gumataotao, and Rear Admiral Peter Fanta, "Distributed Lethality," *Proceedings* 141, no. 1 (January 2015); Scott C. Truver, "Navy's Distributed Lethality Will Reshape Fleet," *Breaking Defense*, October 9, 2015. This concept was also examined at workshops held three times at the US Naval War College in 2015. Daniel L. Kuester, "'Distributed Lethality' concept gains focus at NWC," US Naval War College, October 29, 2015. The Navy has also published a "design" for achieving superiority at sea. Chief of Naval Operations, A Design for Maintaining Maritime Superiority, Version 1.0, January 2016.

62 Paul Scharre, *Robotics on the Battlefield Part II: The Coming Swarm* (Center for a New American Security, October 2014).

63 Paul Scharre, "How to Lose the Robotics Revolution," *War on the Rocks*, July 29, 2014.

64 Andrew F. Krepinevich, *War Like No Other: Maritime Competition in a Mature Precision-Strike Regime* (Center for Strategic and Budgetary Assessments, April 13, 2015).

65 Jan van Tol with Mark Gunzinger, Andrew Krepinevich, and Jim Thomas, *AirSea Battle: A Point-of-Departure Operational Concept* (Center for Strategic and Budgetary Assessment, 2010); Andrew Krepinevich, "How to Deter China: The Case for Archipelagic Defense," *Foreign Affairs* 94, no. 2 (March/April 2015). In response to Krepinevich, Michael Swaine of the Carnegie Endowment for International Peace takes the "China First" position, arguing that a strategy that assumes US military superiority will harm stability in the Western Pacific. He holds that if China tries to claim no-fly zones and sea areas beyond the range justified by international law, the US must use force to oppose them if necessary. At the same time, however, he calls for the adoption of a "mutual denial operational concept" in which both China and the US possess sufficient A2/AD capabilities as a deterrent. Michael D. Swaine, "The Real Challenge in the Pacific," *Foreign Affairs* 94, no. 3 (May/June 2015), 145–54. From the context, it is reasonable to see this as an example of the China First proponent Swaine advocating for China and the US to have parity of conventional forces in the Western Pacific as a challenge to Asia First proponent Krepinevich, who calls for securing US military predominance.

CHAPTER 4

US Maritime Strategy and the Japan-US Alliance

Miyuki Matsuzaki

Captain, Japan Maritime Self-Defense Force, serving as Counselor to the Cabinet Secretariat

America's long-term interest has turned toward the Asia-Pacific, as clearly demonstrated by the Obama administration's strategic emphasis on this region. What is more, the heightened tensions pertaining to maritime challenges, as well as the modernization and upgrading of naval forces by countries in the region, make it clear that the sea is at the core of the challenges troubling the Asia-Pacific region.

Within this context, two important documents concerning US maritime strategy were released in 2015: A Cooperative Strategy for 21st Century Seapower[1] (the 2015 Cooperative Strategy) was released in March, and then the Asia-Pacific Maritime Security Strategy[2] was released in August.

Meanwhile, the new Guidelines for Japan-US Defense Cooperation[3] formulated in April 2015 show that the Japan-US alliance is becoming deeper. In this chapter, I will discuss the alliance from the perspective of US maritime strategy based on the issue of how the Japan-US alliance, which is expected to become even closer than it has been in the past, is positioned within US maritime strategy.

First, I will analyze US security and defense strategy documents centered on maritime strategy and clarify the US perception of the security environment, the military challenges derived therefrom, and the direction of US measures to address those challenges. Next, I will discuss Japan's perception of the security environment, defense challenges, and the Japanese measures to address those challenges in Japan's context as a US ally in the Asia-Pacific region. Finally, I will consider the expected role of the Japan-US alliance in US maritime strategy, as well as how US maritime strategy is reflected in the Japan-US alliance, using the new guidelines as a specific example.

US Maritime Strategy

In this section, I present analyses of two maritime strategies in light of the 2015 National Security Strategy, the 2012 Defense Strategic Guidance, the 2014 Quadrennial Defense Review, and the 2015 National Military Strategy.

The 2015 Cooperative Strategy and the Asia-Pacific Maritime Security Strategy are both maritime strategies, but while the former has a military focus and a global perspective, the latter goes beyond the military sphere, and is limited to the Asia-Pacific region. Although the 2015 Cooperative Strategy uses the expression "Indo-Asia-Pacific region," I will restrict the scope of this section to the "Asia-Pacific region," which does not include India and the Indian Ocean.

Strategic Background: Crisis Awareness Exhibited in Strategy

Changes in the security environment

In June 2015, US Deputy Secretary of Defense Robert Work said, "We are also leaving behind a unique unipolar moment when for more than two decades the Unites States reigned unchallenged as the world's single great power. That moment is coming to an end."[4] This statement clearly shows the US perception of the security environment. US strategies on all fronts present a similar viewpoint regarding a power shift in the international community.

The 2015 National Security Strategy notes that major changes in power among states have caused a shift in the security environment since the 2010 National Security Strategy, and predicts, "In particular, India's potential, China's rise, and Russia's aggression all significantly impact the future of major power relations."[5] In addition, the 2015 National Military Strategy states that Russia, Iran, North Korea, and China are "attempting to revise key aspects of the international order and are acting in a manner that threatens our national security interests."[6]

The 2015 Cooperative Strategy lists the characteristics of today's global security environment as follows: the rising importance of the Indo-Asia-Pacific region; the ongoing development and fielding of anti-access/area denial (A2/AD)[7] capabilities that challenge US global maritime access; continued threats from expanding and evolving terrorist and criminal networks;

the increasing frequency and intensity of maritime territorial disputes; and threats to maritime commerce. It mentions China, Russia, Iran, and North Korea by name, and identifies the following as problems attributable to those countries: naval expansion into the Indian and Pacific Oceans; military modernization, the illegal seizure of Crimea, and ongoing military aggression in Ukraine; the ability to threaten commerce transiting the Strait of Hormuz; pursuit of nuclear weapons and ballistic missile technologies; development of nuclear weapons capabilities; and deployment of long-range ballistic missiles.

When the 2007 Cooperative Strategy was being compiled, there was debate within the US Navy regarding criticizing China by name in recognition of the worsening relations between China and neighboring countries and between China and the United States regarding territorial disputes in the South China Sea and China's development of A2/AD strategy. The 2007 Cooperative Strategy did not associate China with "threats" due to the possibility of maritime and resource claims leading to disputes; it was felt that China would likely understand the criticism against it.[8] There is therefore a clear strategic difference between the 2007 Cooperative Strategy and the 2015 Cooperative Strategy with respect to mentioning China by name, indicating that in the US Navy, awareness of China as a threat increased over the intervening period.

Furthermore, the very existence of the Asia-Pacific Maritime Security Strategy was an indication of the heightened concern and sense of crisis within the US regarding the seas of the Asia-Pacific region. The US Congress ordered the Department of Defense to formulate a maritime security strategy specifically for this region, and the drafting of this strategy was legally mandated by the 2015 National Defense Authorization Act. The Asia-Pacific Maritime Security Strategy presents the viewpoint that, while the Asia-Pacific region has remained free from major conflicts for decades—which has allowed regional states to continue enjoying the benefits of the maritime domain—the security environment is changing, potentially challenging the continued stability of the region. Modernization of naval and maritime law enforcement, unsafe air and sea maneuvers, and land reclamation in the South China Sea are listed as factors causing instability. The Strategy also notes that, while many of the parties involved exhibit such behavior, China stands out in terms of both scale and aggression. For this reason, like other contemporaneous US strategies, it openly expresses concern regarding China.

Military challenges

From a military standpoint, all of the US strategies consider A2/AD capabilities and the emergence of new domains to be the main challenges to ensuring access and freedom of action.

The 2015 National Military Strategy says, "Of particular concern are the proliferation of ballistic missiles, precision strike technologies, unmanned systems, space and cyber capabilities, and weapons of mass destruction (WMD)—technologies designed to counter US military advantages and curtail access to the global commons."[9]

The 2015 Cooperative Strategy, which is a joint strategy of the US Navy, Coast Guard, and Marine Corps, focuses on maritime commons within the larger global commons. The challenges it notes include securing access to maritime commons, challenges to freedom of action, and the A2/AD capabilities of "potential adversaries."

The Asia-Pacific Maritime Security Strategy clearly identifies the challenges by stating that the US military has maintained the ability to project power and secure freedom of action in the Asia-Pacific region for decades, but other countries are now developing new technologies to counter those advantages.

The common thread among these strategies is the universal awareness that the dominance long enjoyed by the US armed forces is being eroded. This dominance has enabled "access and freedom of navigation"; that is—leaving political considerations aside and viewing this solely in military terms—it has enabled free access and freedom of action in the global commons, and even in the territories of other countries.

One important characteristic of naval power is that physical access is possible in all sea areas where naval vessels can navigate and all airspace where carrier-based aircraft can fly. Especially on the high seas and in international airspace, it is possible to act with few legal or political constraints. While this feature is not exclusively enjoyed by the US Navy, since the end of the Cold War the US Navy has taken greater advantage of it than any other force. Today, however, in certain regions, the stability of the maritime commons—which are important US sea lines of communication (SLOCs)—is being threatened. Furthermore, the US military has maintained the ability to project power not only in the maritime commons but within the territories of other nations as well. In some regions, however, that access and freedom of action "is increasingly contested by . . . actors that can hold even our most advanced forces and weapons systems at risk."[10] Ensuring access and freedom of action is no longer easy, even for the US military.

Furthermore, the emergence of new global commons, such as cyberspace and the electromagnetic spectrum,[11] has rendered US military freedom of action and access to the global commons more difficult. The Strategy for Operating in Cyberspace released by the Department of Defense in July 2011 positions cyberspace as an operational domain along with land, sea, air, and outer space. The 2015 Cooperative Strategy also points out the necessity of treating cyberspace and the electromagnetic spectrum as domains equivalent to sea, air, land, or outer space. In cyberspace, it is possible for states lacking high-level military capabilities, as well as for organizations and individuals, to harm US security. In addition, as conveyed in the 2015 Cooperative Strategy, the use of space, cyberspace, and the electromagnetic spectrum by "adversaries" poses a threat to the command and control implemented by the US military worldwide. If that command and control function is compromised, the power projection capability of the US could be neutralized or greatly diminished.

Thus, since the end of the Cold War, challenges have arisen to the "priority use" of the global commons that the US military long took for granted, and substantial effort is now required to ensure access to global commons and freedom of action.

Responses to the Challenges

In addition to the military challenges posed by the changes in the security environment, the US military is also facing significant budgetary limitations. It is nonetheless strongly committed to ensuring access and freedom of action within the global commons, regardless of the challenges. For example, the Department of Defense clearly stated its policy of "working to maintain the necessary capabilities to deter conflict and reassure allies and partners, while protecting our ability to respond decisively if required."[12] In addition, President Barack Obama and other high government officials have repeatedly stated that "the United States will continue to sail, fly and operate anywhere that international law allows."[13]

I will now analyze the two maritime strategies to clarify how the US military is responding to these military challenges and acting to ensure access and maintain freedom of action.

"The Asia-Pacific Maritime Security Strategy"

In the Asia-Pacific Maritime Security Strategy, which is based on the assumption that the Asia-Pacific region is essential to US security, the Department of Defense sets three objectives to maintain the peace and security of the seas in this region: first, to safeguard the freedom of the seas; second, to deter conflict and coercion; and third, to promote adherence to international law and standards. The document then lists four maritime security strategies to achieve these objectives: strengthening US military capabilities in the maritime domain; building the maritime capacity of US allies and partners; leveraging military diplomacy; and strengthening the development of a regional security architecture.

"Strengthening US military capabilities in the maritime domain" means reinforcing the means by which the US is able to deter conflict and coercion and respond decisively as needed. With the goal of offsetting A2/AD capabilities and ensuring access and freedom of operations even in contested environments, the US military is deploying its most advanced surface ships and air assets to the Asia-Pacific and reinforcing its forward presence in order to enhance its ability to respond from the sea, under the water, and in the air.

The US is also concerned about the disparity in military capability between China and the other nations involved, especially in the South China Sea. For that reason, the Department of Defense presents "building the maritime capacity of our allies and partners" as one of its priorities.

While the above is a direct response to the advance of China's A2/AD capabilities and its heightened activity in Asia-Pacific maritime areas, the Asia-Pacific Maritime Security Strategy also incorporates confidence-building measures, stronger risk management, and other measures to avert regional instability. To improve transparency and reduce the risk of conflict that may arise from miscalculation, the Department of Defense is pursuing bilateral and multilateral military diplomacy that includes China, and is also encouraging the development of a regional security architecture.

"A Cooperative Strategy for 21st Century Seapower"

The 2015 Cooperative Strategy is a maritime strategy published jointly by the heads of the three US Sea Services—the Navy, Marine Corps, and Coast Guard. For that reason, the 2015 Cooperative Strategy responds to challenges from a military viewpoint; this distinguishes it from the Asia-Pacific Maritime Security Strategy, which is a comprehensive strategy extending beyond the military domain. The prior Cooperative Strategy was published in 2007; this revision, eight years later, was motivated by changes in the security environment and economic circumstances, as well as the formulation of superior new strategies.

The roles of the Navy have been outlined in all the major strategic and conceptual documents released by that military branch to date, including the 2015 Cooperative Strategy. Various words are used—missions, roles, capabilities, and functions—but they all have the same meaning: the duties that the Navy must perform. Moreover, the essential functions of the Navy outlined in each document directly reflect the character of that document.

The 2015 Cooperative Strategy enumerates five "essential functions" of the Sea Services: all-domain access, deterrence, sea control, power projection, and maritime security. Of these, the last four are viewed as historically essential functions. In fact, deterrence, sea control, power projection, and forward presence have consistently been cited as primary functions in principal post–Cold War documents; maritime security was added as a new concept in 2006. Incidentally, the functions listed in the 2007 Cooperative Strategy are forward presence, deterrence, sea control, power projection, maritime security, and humanitarian assistance and disaster relief. One major characteristic of the 2007 strategy is that it places maritime security and humanitarian assistance and disaster relief (added in 1989) at a level of importance equivalent to the Navy's historical essential functions. The 2015 Cooperative Strategy also presents maintaining maritime security as a primary mission, emphasizing the importance of ensuring maritime safety in the global commons.

The 2015 Cooperative Strategy includes "all-domain access" as an essential function of maritime strategy for the first time ever in the Cold War or post–Cold War period. All-domain access ensures the ability to project power with the appropriate freedom of action in any domain—sea, air, land, outer space, and cyberspace, as well as in the electromagnetic spectrum. Considering access to the global commons to be crucial, the Navy identified maintaining all-domain access as a primary mission in response to the above-mentioned military challenges, including challenges to ensuring access and freedom of action in the maritime commons, A2/AD capabilities, and the emergence of new powers.

Forward presence, which had consistently been listed as a primary function in the past, was deleted from the 2015 Cooperative Strategy, but since this term refers to the forward deployment of naval forces, it is presumably included in all-domain access. The statement in the 2015 Cooperative Strategy that forward presence is essential to accomplishing missions also shows that the significance of forward presence has not declined.

The inclusion of all-domain access as a primary function demonstrates that the 2015 Cooperative Strategy emphasizes cyberspace and the electromagnetic spectrum as an operational domain, and power-projection capabilities as military capabilities. A similar perspective is evident in the superior strategies. The 2015 National Security Strategy mentions the importance of ensuring access to the shared cyberspace, outer-space, air, and maritime environments, and the 2015 National Military Strategy says that the US military will make investments to "counter A2/AD, space, cyber, and hybrid threats." The 2012 Defense Strategic Guidance also lists power projection in A2/AD environments as one of the "priority missions of the US Armed Forces."

Next, I would like to look at specific measures in response to the challenges. The 2015 Cooperative Strategy identifies two foundational principles: first, US forward naval presence and, second, engagement with allies and partners. These two principles are closely related.

Forward presence, which deploys maritime forces near areas of possible engagement, incurs costs in moving forces from their home ports and bases on the US mainland and other locations. The maritime strategy initiated a policy of increasing forward bases for troops overseas in order to both reduce that cost and increase that presence. Effective US military presence, beginning with reinforced overseas bases, would be difficult to achieve without the second principle of engagement with allies and partners. For that purpose, the US maritime strategy deepens security cooperation with allies and partners to advance a global naval network. The strategy states that "our most modern and technologically advanced forces are located where the combat power is needed most," and presents a policy "to increase the number of ships, aircraft, and Marine Corps forces stationed in 'the Indo-Asia-Pacific region.'" For these forward-deployed US troops to operate effectively, interoperability with allies and partners, as well as the capacities of those countries themselves, must be improved.

The 2015 Cooperative Strategy was not the first place where the idea of engagement with allies and partners was put forward. In 2005, Chief of Naval Operations Michael Mullen proposed the "1,000-ship navy" concept, which was later renamed the Global Maritime Partnership initiative. This was an effort to cooperate with the navies of US allies and like-minded countries to address piracy, narcotics smuggling, and other maritime security challenges. As the background to this, the number of warships in the US Navy had dropped by around half since the time of the Reagan administration, and with the greater complexity of the maritime security environment and the proliferation of threats, it was no longer possible for the navy of any one nation to deal with this situation alone. Moreover, the previous 2007

Cooperative Strategy was the first maritime strategy formulated by the Navy together with the Marine Corps and the Coast Guard, showing cooperation among US domestic maritime forces as well as international cooperation. So, although the idea of utilizing allies and partners is by no means new, the 2015 Cooperative Strategy is distinctive in not only applying this to nontraditional security fields, but also expecting US allies and partners to take on more military roles.

Japan's Perception of the Security Environment and Response to Issues

The Department of Defense and US Sea Services policies of forward presence and emphasizing engagement with allies and partners are clearly put forth in the Asia-Pacific Maritime Security Strategy and the 2015 Cooperative Strategy. It is also not difficult to imagine that that the US has high expectations of its allies in the Asia-Pacific region, and of Japan, as the policies presented emphasize the Asia-Pacific at each level of strategy under the US national security strategy.

In this section, I discuss Japan's perception of the security environment, defense matters, and response to problems from its position as a US ally. My conclusions are based on the National Security Strategy[14] formulated in 2013, the National Defense Program Guidelines for FY 2014 and beyond (the 2014 National Defense Program Guidelines),[15] and Defense of Japan 2015.[16]

Perception of the Security Environment

The 2014 National Defense Program Guidelines state that the security environment surrounding Japan became "increasingly serious" in the period following the formulation of the prior National Defense Program Guidelines released in 2010. The further development of China and India and the "relative change in US influence" are cited as grounds for this assessment, which aligns with US perceptions regarding shifts in the balance of power in the international community. The result of these changes is that US influence in the international community has seen a relative decline, and for Japan—which places the Japan-US security framework at the center of its security strategy and security policy, with the US as its only ally—this amounts to a worsening of the security environment.

Japan's geographical position with respect to neighboring countries is much less comfortable than that of the US. The 2013 National Security Strategy and the 2014 National Defense Program Guidelines both specify North Korea and China as contributors to global and regional instability. The US similarly views both these countries as security challenges, but Japan is in a much harsher position given its geographical proximity to these countries. Along with North Korea and China, Iran and Russia are seen as security challenges by the US; these countries are also geographically distant from the US.

Defense Challenges

Japan perceives three primary challenges related to defense: North Korea's development of nuclear power and missiles; China's buildup of its military forces and its sudden expansion of activities at sea and in the air; and the need to ensure stable access to the global commons of the seas, outer space, and cyberspace.

North Korea's development and deployment of ballistic missiles, nuclear weapons, and other weapons of mass destruction are characterized as a "serious and imminent threat." Cyberspace attacks and other asymmetrical military activities are also noted as concerns for Japan.

China is covertly strengthening its military force. There are particular concerns about its A2/AD capabilities and the broader enhancement of its operational capabilities at sea and in the air. China's expansion and intensification of its activities in these domains, including in the East China Sea and the South China Sea, are seen as direct threats to Japan, and also as serious problems from the perspective of the stable use of the seas as a global commons. Furthermore, there are growing concerns that China is threatening the stable use of space and cyberspace. For example, China is developing anti-satellite weapons, and the People's Liberation Army is suspected of involvement in cyberattacks.

As Japan's perceptions of these factors match those of the US regarding military challenges, it seems that Japan and the US share a common view on defense and military challenges.

Responses to the Challenges

To address these challenges, the National Security Strategy and the 2014 National Defense Program Guidelines recommended three broad measures: strengthening the capacity of Japan's own defense efforts, reinforcing the Japan-US alliance, and increasing cooperation with global security efforts.

Regarding the first measure, the 2014 National Defense Program Guidelines recommended prioritizing nine areas to strengthen the architecture of the Self-Defense Forces: intelligence, surveillance, and reconnaissance (ISR) capabilities; intelligence capabilities; transportation capabilities; command and control and information and communications capabilities; response to an attack on remote islands; ballistic missile attack response; outer space and cyberspace response; disaster response; and participation in international peace cooperation and similar activities. These address the need for security in nearby sea and airspace, the defense of remote islands, response to a ballistic missile attack, and stable access to space and cyberspace, all of which are defense challenges for Japan.

I will address the strengthening of the Japan-US alliance in detail in the next section.

With respect to bilateral and multilateral security cooperation with countries other than the US, Japan emphasizes capacity-building assistance and ensuring maritime security. Capacity-building assistance aims to improve the regional security environment by enhancing the capabilities of the recipient countries. The Ministry of Defense and the Self-Defense Forces are providing capacity-building assistance pertaining to maritime security to Indonesia, Vietnam, and Myanmar. In addition, the Maritime Self-Defense Force is conducting anti-piracy activities and joint training and exercises to ensure maritime security in the global commons.

US Maritime Strategy and the Japan-US Alliance

The Japan-US Alliance in US Maritime Strategy

Amid the changes in the security environment, the US is being pressed more than ever before to make use of the capabilities of its allies and partners. This is borne out by the 2014 Quadrennial Defense Review, which lists among its key steps "working with allies and partners . . . to facilitate greater contributions to their own defense," and having those capabilities reflected in US plans.[17] As stated above, Japan has itself recognized this necessity and is working to facilitate greater contributions to its own defense.

Furthermore, the nine functions and capabilities to be prioritized in strengthening the architecture of the Self-Defense Forces, as listed above, align with the key capabilities required to support national defense strategy as named in the 2014 Quadrennial Defense Review: cyberspace, missile defense, nuclear deterrence, outer space, air/sea, precision strike, and ISR, as well as counterterror and special operations. In addition, Japan's 2014 National Defense Program Guidelines state that Japan will strengthen these functions and capabilities with an eye to interoperability with US forces, and it will reinforce the Japan-US alliance through joint intelligence, surveillance and reconnaissance, and ballistic missile defense, as well as by advancing cooperation in maritime affairs, outer space, and cyberspace.

Thus, Japan and the US are emphasizing and reinforcing essentially the same functions and capabilities, and are also working to manifest those functions and capabilities more effectively via Japan-US cooperation. The 2015 Guidelines for Japan-US Defense Cooperation identify intelligence, surveillance, and reconnaissance, as well as air and missile defense, as "cooperative measures from peacetime." This demonstrates the approach of having Japan and the US strengthen their respective capabilities while reinforcing them through the Japan-US alliance.

The Asia-Pacific Maritime Security Strategy, in which the importance of the Japan-US alliance in maritime strategy is even more clear, emphasizes building up the capacity of US allies to maintain maritime peace and security in the Asia-Pacific region. While strengthening its own capabilities, Japan is providing capacity-building assistance toward improving the regional security environment, and these efforts are certainly in line with the direction of the Asia-Pacific Maritime Security Strategy. This strategy also clearly states that the cornerstone of US military forward presence in the region is, and will continue to be, the US presence in Japan.

The 2015 Cooperative Strategy emphasizes engagement with allies and partners and promotes forward presence to ensure access and freedom of action in contested environments, including cyberspace, outer space, and the electromagnetic spectrum. The 2015 National Military Strategy lists Japan and other countries as partners, and stresses "ensuring access to contested environments" through combined training exercises with partners with sophisticated capabilities. This also demonstrates that US expectations regarding cooperation with Japan are high.

Thus, the Japan-US alliance is expected to play an indispensable role in US maritime strategy, especially concerning the Asia-Pacific region, in maintaining the ability of US forces to project power and act freely.

US Maritime Strategy as Reflected in the 2015 Guidelines

The US intends for its plans to reflect the capabilities of its allies, as stated in the 2014 Quadrennial Defense Review. The revision of the Guidelines for Japan-US Defense Cooperation demonstrates how Japan's capabilities can be included in US plans. In this section, I discuss how US maritime strategy is reflected in the Japan-US alliance, using the new guidelines formulated in 2015 as one example.

The two US maritime strategies were released in March and August of 2015. The research on revisions for the new guidelines, which were released in April that same year, must have been conducted at the same time that US defense-related bodies, including the Navy, were developing those two strategies. For that reason, the policies presented in the maritime strategies are reflected in the new guidelines. The Asia-Pacific Maritime Security Strategy says the new guidelines "will enable the US Armed Forces and the Self-Defense Forces to work more closely together," and that under the new guidelines, "the DoD is working more closely than ever with our Japanese allies."

The new guidelines define in advance the basic framework of Japan-US defense cooperation for rapid response during emergencies. They present contingencies calling for Japan-US defense cooperation and state the roles of Japan and the US (the Self-Defense Forces and the US Armed Forces) in each case. However, the new guidelines do not presume specific countries or contingencies. In addition, the new guidelines were updated as necessary for the purpose of securing the effectiveness of the Japan-US alliance. When they were first formulated in 1978, the focus was on response to armed attacks against Japan, but with the end of the Cold War and other changes in the security environment, cooperation in areas surrounding Japan was added in 1997.

Japan and the US revised the guidelines in 2015 in response to the major changes in the security environment since 1997. Because the guidelines themselves do not create legal rights or obligations for either government, domestic legislation is required to secure the efficacy of the actions prescribed therein. In Japan, peace and security legislation was passed in September 2015, with efforts made to ensure that it was consistent with the new guidelines.

The two US maritime strategies are reflected in the new guidelines in the following points.

First, the guidelines state that in the event of an armed attack on Japan, the Self-Defense Forces and the US military will conduct joint operations across domains. The phrase "cross-domain operations" echoes US operational concepts in recent years. Air-Sea Battle, which was renamed the "Joint Concept for Access and Maneuver in the Global Commons" in 2015, is a concept for maintaining access to the global commons and ensuring freedom of action under an A2/AD environment. This goes beyond simply integrating operations to maximize operational advantage across the domains of sea, air, land, space, and cyberspace. Furthermore, "networked, integrated, and attack-in-depth operations," which are central to this concept, require cross-domain operations covering sea, air, land, space, and cyberspace.[18] The Joint Operational Access Concept announced in 2012 is a superordinate concept to Air-Sea Battle. Its central thesis is "cross-domain synergy"—the complementary employment of capabilities in different domains such that each enhances the effectiveness and compensates for the vulnerabilities of the others to achieve operational access while directly confronting an A2/AD strategy.[19]

Given these conditions, along with the addition of the new concept of "all-domain access" in the 2015 Cooperative Strategy, the stipulation in the new guidelines that Japan and the US will jointly implement "cross-domain operations" means that the Self-Defense Forces will bear a portion of a key US military operational concept. In developing the Joint Concept for Access and Maneuver in the Global Commons, the US Navy notes the growing importance of integration and interoperability with allies and partners to ensure access and freedom of action by allies in the global commons.[20]

Second, the new guidelines add "space and cyberspace" to the list of domains and stipulate cooperation in these domains. While all-domain access is the primary mission, the US military is placing special emphasis on these two domains. Therefore, cooperation between Japan and the US to ensure the stable use of outer space and cyberspace, which the US is focusing on as global commons, will grow even stronger. The domain of outer space is also essential for maritime domain awareness, so it is closely related to the use of SLOCs and other parts of the maritime commons.

Third, cooperation in the field of maritime security was added to the new guidelines. This is a major issue not only for Japan and the US, but also within and outside the region, as is clear from China's activities in the East China Sea and the South China Sea. While there were no statements regarding maritime security in the prior version, the new guidelines prescribe close Japan-US cooperation to maintain maritime order "from peacetime" and to strengthen maritime security in response to "emerging threats to Japan's peace and security."

Maritime security is an area in which cooperation is necessary to maintain peace and security in the Asia-Pacific region and worldwide. The new guidelines note that, like other forms of cooperation in international activities, this involves capacity-building assistance, as well as intelligence, surveillance, and reconnaissance. Considering US concerns about the capabilities gap between China and neighboring countries in the South China Sea, Japan-US cooperation in these fields will contribute to maritime security as well.

Finally, the new guidelines expand the geographical range of activities by the Self-Defense Forces and reinforce the functions of the Japan-US alliance. Regarding the former, the new guidelines state that the Japan-US alliance is to respond to "situations that will have an important influence on Japan's peace and security," which "cannot be defined geographically." Regarding the latter, the new guidelines state that even if Japan is not attacked by force, the Self-Defense Forces "will conduct appropriate operations involving the use of force" under certain conditions in "situations where an armed attack against a foreign country that is in a close relationship with Japan occurs." Asset protection was also included in peacetime cooperative measures: "The Self-Defense Forces and the United States Armed Forces will provide mutual protection of each other's assets, as appropriate, if engaged in activities that contribute to the defense of Japan in a cooperative manner." This may be deemed an expansion of the role of the Self-Defense Forces.

Conclusion

Strategy is formulated based on the perception of threats. Since the end of the Cold War, the main threats addressed by US maritime strategy have expanded from the actions of a single country—the USSR—to include regional disputes, terrorism, and nontraditional security fields. Moreover, as China's economic growth has bolstered its military, the US once again faces a powerful state as a threat.

Because the US and China share political and security interests in many fields, and they also have deep economic and trade ties, the US-China relationship is multifaceted. US perceptions of China cannot be represented in simple terms. Still, considering the documents related to US security and defense strategy presented in this chapter, as well as assessments of China's military forces released by US government bodies, it cannot be denied that the US views China as a threat from a military standpoint. China's naval power is of primary concern to the US, considering the heightened tensions between China and neighboring countries arising from maritime challenges, the existence of important US SLOCs in the Asia-Pacific region, and China's development of A2/AD capabilities. What is more, China—a potential threat capable of countering the US—is more aggressively asserting its claims in the Asia-Pacific region, which is the most important region for US economic growth.

It was against this backdrop that the Obama administration launched its Asia-Pacific rebalance. The question being posed both inside and outside the US is whether the Department of Defense can make priority investments in the Asia-Pacific while also responding to challenges in the Middle East and other regions under the restrictions of the Budget Control Act of 2011. In fact, US Navy sources have repeatedly stated in congressional testimony and other forums that if the defense budget remains restricted by the Budget Control Act, within a few years it will become impossible to fulfill all the roles and functions outlined in the 2012 strategic guidance offered by the Department of Defense. The Asia-Pacific Maritime Security Strategy and the Cooperative Strategy for 21st Century Seapower, both released in 2015, give an indication of how the US Navy will respond to China in the Asia-Pacific region while also responding appropriately to conditions in other regions under budgetary and other limitations.

These two maritime strategies show a strong awareness of the emergence of a potential threat with equivalent power, and state this openly. They also show that the US is determined to ensure access and freedom of action in the global commons, beginning with the maritime commons. These strategies propose cooperative engagement with other nations as one way to address the challenges. The 2015 Cooperative Strategy was the first to be released with official translations (in Japanese, Chinese, Korean, Spanish, French, and Arabic), demonstrating that US intentions are being presented not only domestically, but also overseas to allies and others.

The maritime security and defense policy of Japan, a US ally in the Asia-Pacific region, aligns with the policy of the US, which emphasizes its allies. Not only does Japan share the US perception of the security environment, but given its geographical proximity to China and the vital importance of East Asian SLOCs, it views China as a more pressing threat than the US does. When it comes to the reinforcement of Japan-US defenses and military power, it should be noted that the Self-Defense Forces and the US military are strengthening virtually the same the functions and capabilities to respond to China, and are working to make them even more effective through Japan-US cooperation. The national security and defense policies in the new guidelines and the peace and security legislation that Japan is aiming at match the policies of the US, which is working to strengthen engagement with its allies and partners.

The Japan-US alliance has long functioned effectively by having the Self-Defense Forces play a supplementary role to the US military. However, the most recent US maritime strategy makes it apparent that the Japan-US alliance has now become more important to the US than ever before. Because this chapter is limited to discussion of the Japan-US alliance from the perspective of US maritime strategy, it only notes the utility of the Japan-US alliance to the naval branch of the US military. In closing, however, I would like to note one important characteristic of the new guidelines from Japan's perspective. In the East China Sea, Chinese naval vessels are operating continuously, and vessels and aircraft belonging to Chinese maritime law enforcement authorities are intermittently intruding into Japanese territorial waters and violating Japanese airspace. Ensuring Japanese-US cooperation with respect to Chinese activities in these "gray zones" before they escalate into incidents is an urgent issue for Japan.

The new guidelines are designed to strengthen the functions of the Japan-US alliance, and they specify that the Japanese and US governments will devise seamless measures to ensure the peace and security of Japan across all phases, from peacetime through emergencies. Similarly, the new guidelines call for using the alliance coordination mechanism to develop appropriate responses, including flexible deterrent options, as well as actions aimed at de-escalation. By explicitly prescribing flexible deterrent options, the new guidelines strengthen Japan's deterrence in nearby sea areas during peacetime and in the gray zone. This is just one case in which the deepening of the Japan-US alliance may be viewed as an appropriate response to the challenges facing both Japan and the US.

Note: The opinions expressed in this chapter are the personal views of the author and do not reflect the views of any organizations with which she is affiliated.

1   US Navy, Marine Corps, and Coast Guard, A Cooperative Strategy for 21st Century Seapower, March 2015, https://www.navy.mil/local/maritime/150227-CS21R-Final.pdf.

2   US Department of Defense, Asia-Pacific Maritime Security Strategy, August 2015, https://dod.defense.gov/Portals/1/Documents/pubs/NDAA%20A-P_Maritime_SecuritY_Strategy-08142015-1300-FINALFORMAT.PDF

3   Japanese Ministry of Defense, The Guidelines for Japan-U.S. Cooperation, April 2015, https://www.mod.go.jp/e/d_act/anpo/shishin_20150427e.html.

4   US Deputy Secretary of Defense, "Speech for Naval Postgraduate School Commencement, as Prepared for Delivery by Deputy Secretary of Defense Bob Work," Naval Postgraduate School, Monterey, CA, June 19, 2015, http://www.defense.gov/News/Speeches/Speech-View/Article/606682/naval-postgraduate-school-commencement.

5   The White House, National Security Strategy, February 2015, 4, https://obamawhitehouse.ar-chives.gov/sites/default/files/docs/2015_national_security_strategy_2.pdf.

6   US Joint Chiefs of Staff, The National Military Strategy of the United States of America 2015, June 2015, 2, https://www.jcs.mil/Portals/36/Documents/Publications/2015_National_Mili-tary_Strategy.pdf.

7   According to the FY 2013 Defense White Paper, anti-access (A2) capabilities are a concept presented by the US. These refer to the capabilities that prevent enemies from entering a given operational domain, and are mostly long-distance measures. Area Denial (AD) refers to the shorter-range capabilities that restrict an enemy's freedom of action within an operational do-main. Ballistic missiles, cruise missiles, antisatellite weapons, air-defense systems, submarines, and mines are listed as weapons used in A2/AD.

8   Peter D. Haynes, *Toward a New Maritime Strategy: American Naval Thinking in the Post-Cold War Era* (Annapolis, 2015), 227–28.

9   US Joint Chiefs of Staff, The National Military Strategy of the United States of America 2015, 3.

10 US Navy, Marine Corps, and Coast Guard, A Cooperative Strategy for 21st-Century Seapower, 19.

11 Cyberspace was also mentioned in the 2007 Cooperative Strategy, but in the Strategy for Oper-ating in Cyberspace released by the Department of Defense in 2011, cyberspace is positioned as an operating domain equivalent to land, sea, air, and space.

12 US Department of Defense, Asia-Pacific Maritime Security Strategy, 20.

13 The White House, "Remarks by President Obama and President Xi of the People's Republic of China in Joint Press Conference," https://www.whitehouse.gov/the-press-office/2015/09/25/remarks-president-obama-and-president-xi-peoples-republic-china-joint.

14 Cabinet of Japan, National Security Strategy, December 2013, https://www.cas.go.jp/jp/siry-ou/131217anzenhoshou/nss-e.pdf.

15 Japanese Ministry of Defense, National Defense Program Guidelines for 2014 and Beyond, De-cember 2013, https://www.mod.go.jp/j/approach/agenda/guideline/2014/pdf/20131217_e2.pdf.

16 Japanese Ministry of Defense, Defense of Japan 2015, July 2015, https://www.mod.go.jp/e/publ/w_paper/pdf/2015/H27DOJ_Digest_EN_web.pdf.

17 US Department of Defense, Quadrennial Defense Review 2014, 24.

18 US Air-Sea Battle Office, "Overview of the Air-Sea Battle Concept," *Navy Live* (official blog of the US Navy), June 3, 2013, https://navylive.dodlive.mil/2013/06/03/overview-of-the-air-sea-battle-concept/.

19 US Department of Defense, Joint Operational Access Concept, January 17, 2012, https://dod.defense.gov/Portals/1/Documents/pubs/JOAC_Jan%202012_Signed.pdf.

20 Terry S. Morris et al, "Securing Operational Access."

CHAPTER 5

China's Maritime Strategy and the Japan-US Alliance

Shin Kawashima

Professor, University of Tokyo Graduate School of Arts and Sciences; Senior Researcher, Nakasone Peace Institute

Introduction

In China, there is a general sense that the nation has lost a great deal of territory over the course of its history, and that China's "proper"territory covers a larger area than that within the present boundaries of the People's Republic of China (PRC). So it is conventionally accepted that today's China is not as large as it properly should be, and there is even a propensity to wish for recovery of what was lost. The boundaries of this "proper" territory were not clear during the Qing dynasty (1644–1912), however, and cannot be determined precisely, so the details are always shifting. The areas considered to be China's inherent territory since the beginning of history are not fixed either, and have tended to expand.[1]

The nine-dash line (also called the eleven-dash line), which the PRC initially set after the Second World War, was established to assert Chinese territorial sovereignty over islands in the South China Sea where it did not have effective control. Considering the area effectively controlled by the Republic of China (ROC) in the past, this was an expansionist move. At a press conference on November 12, 2015, however, Ministry of Foreign Affairs spokesman Hong Lei clearly stated: "The Indonesian side has no territorial claim to China's Nansha Islands [Spratly Islands]. The Chinese side has no objection to Indonesia's sovereignty over the Natuna islands."[2] That statement is worth noting because it demonstrates that "China" does not expand endlessly beyond the nine-dash line, but rather does have some clear limit.

Meanwhile, in the East China Sea, the PRC began to assert territorial sovereignty over the Senkaku Islands from the early 1970s; the government subsequently held that the Senkaku Islands were attached to Taiwan and were therefore an integral part of China.[3] Recent statements by China have also called Japan's sovereignty over Okinawa into question.[4]

China's maritime advance is thus indisputably underway at present. While the future situation is highly unpredictable, some excellent papers on China's maritime advance have already been published in Japanese, including Masafumi Iida's "Chūgoku no kaiyō shinshutsu" [China's maritime advance], in *Chaina risuku* [China risk], edited by Shin Kawashima (Iwanami Shoten, 2015). While avoiding duplication of prior research results as much as possible, in this chapter I will first examine the history of China's maritime advance, and then present the points of dispute regarding China's maritime perspective and approach. Finally, I will consider how these intersect with the Japan-US alliance and raise some future issues.

China's Maritime Advance during Modern History

China has historically been a continental state, and modern China has not expanded beyond the continent. Yet this does not mean that China has been indifferent to ocean areas. There was a debate on maritime defense versus frontier defense during the 1880s, and the Qing dynasty had a powerful navy, with a northern sea fleet and a southern sea fleet. When sea routes opened across the Pacific Ocean, many Chinese laborers emigrated to the United States; Chinese migrated to Southeast Asia as well. The Qing government established consulates in such locations to protect Chinese emigrants and pursue its overseas interests. China was expanding its systems with a view to the movement of people and goods via the oceans.

In negotiations between China and Japan around the time of the First Sino-Japanese War (1894–1895), the Qing government did little to assert possession of the Senkaku Islands. During negotiations on the Treaty of Shimonoseki at the conclusion of that war, however, the Qing clearly stipulated the range of the Pescadores Islands, and made sure that Japan did not extend its realm to the coast of Fujian. This demonstrates that the Qing paid some attention to sovereignty issues regarding islands in coastal areas.

Japan and the Qing government also conducted negotiations regarding the possession of the Pratas Islands in the South China Sea in the early twentieth century. At that time, the South China Sea became surrounded by various powers in addition to China, including Japan, which took possession of Taiwan in 1895, and the US, which colonized the Philippines in 1898, as well as France (French Indochina), and the UK (northern Borneo), Thus, the islands of the South China Sea came to pose territorial issues between China and the great powers.

In the early twentieth century, the Qing government clearly demonstrated its sovereign intent over the Pratas Islands; these were also recognized as Chinese territory by the Japanese government following negotiations. The government established in Guangzhou during the late 1910s attempted at one time to obtain loans based on the resources of Hainan Island and islands in the South China Sea. The Nationalist government of the ROC also showed definite interest in the Paracel Islands starting in the 1930s. Japan occupied the South China Sea during the Second Sino-Japanese War (1937–1945), but at the conclusion of that conflict Japan clearly renounced its sovereignty over the Spratly Islands in both the Treaty of San Francisco and the Treaty of Taipei. The issues that have emerged in the South China Sea in the postwar era can be characterized as problems regarding sovereignty after it was renounced by Japan. In that respect, Japan has a complex history of involvement in these territorial affairs.

China has shown strong interest in the East China Sea and the South China Sea ever since Japan's defeat in 1945. In the East China Sea, the focus has been on the Senkaku Islands and on Okinawa,[5] and in the South China Sea, China demarcated the nine-dash line and claimed sovereignty over South China Sea islands. After the establishment of the PRC on the mainland in 1949, the Nationalist government of the ROC, which had moved to Taiwan, continued its governance over Itu Aba Island and the Pratas Islands in the South China Sea, changing the jurisdiction over these islands to Kaohsiung City in Taiwan.

The PRC was also interested in the South China Sea. When France withdrew from the Paracel Islands during the 1950s, South Vietnam and China both moved into these islands; following a battle with South Vietnam, China occupied them in 1974. In the 1980s, as the Soviet military shrank its forces in Vietnam, China strengthened its presence in the Spratly Islands. Furthermore, after US armed forces withdrew from Clark Air Base and Subic Bay Naval Base in the Philippines in 1991–1992, China occupied Mischief Reef, which is located close to the Philippines. China promulgated its "Territorial Sea Law" (Law of the People's Republic of China on the Territorial Sea and the Contiguous Zone) on February 25, 1992. Article 2 defines China's land territory as follows.

The land territory of the People's Republic of China includes the mainland of the People's Republic of China and its coastal islands; Taiwan and all islands appertaining thereto including the Diaoyu Islands [Senkaku Islands]; the Penghu Islands [Pescadores Islands]; the Dongsha Islands [Pratas Islands]; the Xisha Islands [Paracel Islands]; the Zhongsha Islands; and the Nansha Islands; as well as all the other islands belonging to the People's Republic of China.

Thus, China's maritime advance certainly did not begin with the current administration of Xi Jinping (president since 2013), but can be seen throughout the modern era. Chinese merchants were long active in the East China Sea and South China Sea, and there were considerable flows of migrants, both to the Chinese mainland and from the mainland to places like Japan, Taiwan, and Southeast Asia. These flows of people also generated flows of goods and remittances to China from overseas Chinese. This vibrant interchange was revived in modern China with the adoption of the "reform and opening up" policy in 1978. This opening up, along with the attention drawn by Hong Kong in the 1990s, led researchers to discuss viewing China not only as a continental state but from a maritime perspective as well.[6] In modern times, China's maritime perspective is oriented not only toward territory and territorial seas, but also toward routes for the movement of people and goods.

As shown above, China's maritime advance is part of a historical pattern, but there seems to be a definite trend in the timing of the formulation of related policies and the implementation of specific actions. That trend started to become particularly pronounced in the second half of the twentieth century. First, the assertion of the nine-dash line clearly emerged from the power vacuum in the South China Sea that followed Japan's defeat in August 1945. China's 1974 occupation of the Paracel Islands similarly occurred because South Vietnam, which had effective control over these islands (the western part), lost its backing with the US defeat in the Vietnam War. There were similar developments when the US withdrew from its bases in the Philippines, as demonstrated by China's occupation of Mischief Reef and enactment of the Territorial Sea Law. When the military security balance changes and even the smallest "opening" emerges, China takes advantage of that opportunity and moves in.

Decisions by international bodies are also a factor in these developments. Just as the Convention on the Continental Shelf, which entered into force in 1964, led to the claim of sovereignty over the Senkaku Islands by the

ROC (Taiwan), the potential links between various maritime regimes and China's acts cannot be overlooked. China attempted to extend its continental shelf in 2012 based on the United Nations Convention on the Law of the Sea (UNCLOS), and it is otherwise utilizing such international instruments to expand its maritime interests. China's movements with respect to international instruments parallel its de facto expansion of force in the military sphere. However, in this area, China's behavior can often be criticized or addressed directly as a problem, as it was in the case submitted by the Philippines to the International Court of Arbitration regarding Mischief Reef.

Japan needs to pay special attention to the two points above. First, from a practical security standpoint, Japan must protect its own maritime interests by not leaving any openings for China to expand its interests; it should also work alongside other countries in the South China Sea to oppose any changes to the status quo. Second, while paying attention to China's behavior in the context of history, systems, and laws, Japan must both oppose China where necessary, making its own claims clear, and encourage China so the two countries can share values and norms.

A Maritime Great Power: China's Perception of Maritime Areas

As of the summer of 2015, China had already reclaimed 2,900 acres (nearly 12 square kilometers) in the South China Sea. The scope and speed of this action puts it in an entirely different category from the reclamations carried out by the other countries disputing sovereignty in the Spratly Islands.[7] China constructed a 3,000-meter runway at Fiery Cross Reef, and may be planning to construct similar runways at Subi Reef and Mischief Reef as well, indicating that it is expanding its air and sea dominance in the South China Sea. China is recently moving to solidify the results of its maritime advance, perhaps intending to turn the East China Sea and South China Sea into so-called inland seas. China will probably not change its policies in this regard anytime soon.[8]

These developments echo statements being made inside China. The Chinese government and party are directing the media and schools to assert that the East China Sea and the South China Sea were originally Chinese seas and that their maritime interests fundamentally belong to China; this has also been codified into law. In this way, domestic perceptions of the situation are becoming fixed, leaving less room for compromise on issues regarding these maritime interests and narrowing China's policy options.

It is important to consider China's perception of space when evaluating its maritime advance. China has asserted not only its territory and its territorial seas, but also its contiguous zone and exclusive economic zone (EEZ), as well as an air defense identification zone (ADIZ). Other countries make such claims as well, so this is not necessarily a problem in and of itself, but there are issues with the way China established its ADIZ in the East China Sea, including questions regarding prior consultation and how the ADIZ is administered.

When considering China's perception of space, the "blue territory" concept, which was used in the early 1990s when the Territorial Sea Law was enacted and often cited by the Hu Jintao administration, is considered important. While President Xi Jinping does not use this phrase, it is frequently used by Premier Li Keqiang, and is still a relatively firmly established concept today.[9] "Blue territory" refers to territorial islands, of course, but also to all maritime rights pertaining to internal waters, territorial seas, the contiguous zone, the EEZ, the continental shelf, and the ADIZ. As implied by the name, this concept regards marine areas in the same way as land territory, expanding the range of China's national territory from the land area demarcated on the map into the ocean. This way of thinking was broadly adopted from the Jiang Zemin administration (1993–2003) through the Hu Jintao administration (2003–2013). Because it became established in Chinese society through education and publicity, it also supports the policies of the Xi Jinping administration.[10]

China's comprehensive maritime policy took shape during the Hu Jintao administration, especially during its latter half. One aspect was the Planning Outline for the Development of National Maritime Activities, which was proposed by the National Development and Reform Commission and the State Oceanic Administration and ratified by the State Council in February 2008. The Planning Outline began with a statement that China is a maritime power, and that maritime issues concern the fundamental interests of the state; it then summarized China's maritime strategy. Premier Wen Jiabao mentioned maritime interests in a March 2009 government report, and maritime interests were taken up as a major issue at the sessions of the National People's Congress and the Chinese People's Political Consultative Conference that same month, where there was a vibrant exchange of ideas. In a Chinese People's Political Consultative Conference subcommittee, committee member Li Guoan (from the People's Liberation Army) submitted a proposal to focus on exerting national sovereignty over China's southern sea areas and ensuring the safety of Chinese fishermen in traditional fishing grounds.[11]

In March 2010, the Law of the People's Republic of China on the Protection of Sea Islands, which had been adopted by the Standing Committee of the National People's Congress at the end of the prior year, came into force. This law made the state responsible for the protection of territorial sea bases, important sites for national defense, nature reserves, etc.; asserted that uninhabited islands are owned by the state; and declared that rights for their use could be granted to interested parties by the State Oceanic Administration. As the duties of the China Maritime Surveillance organization (under the State Oceanic Administration), the existing China Coast Guard (under the Ministry of Public Security), Fisheries Law Enforcement Command, and General Administration of Customs were judged too disparate, these bodies were integrated into the China Coast Guard established under the State Oceanic Administration in March 2013. This change kept fisheries law enforcement at the regional level while achieving organizational integration at the central level. Thus, the ideology, systems, and organizations concerned with maritime interests all underwent significant changes during the second half of the Hu Jintao administration.

Following that administration's shift toward a more active maritime policy, in May 2013 the Xi Jinping administration released a newly drafted "Twelfth Five-Year Development Plan for the National Marine Economy."[12] The plan begins with this declaration:

> Our country is located west of the Pacific Ocean. It has a coastline of 18,000 kilometers, 6,900 islands with an area of at least 500 square meters, and the area of its inland waters and territorial sea amounts to 380,000 square kilometers. Based on the related provisions of the United Nations Convention on the Law of the Sea and our country's claims, the maritime area that should be under Chinese jurisdiction amounts to 3 million square kilometers. In addition, the international seabed areas where China has exclusive exploration rights and priority exploitation rights comprise 75,000 square kilometers of manganese nodule mining areas and 10,000 square kilometers of polymetallic sulfide deposits. China has also established the Great Wall Station, Zhongshan Station, Kunlun Station, and the Yellow River Station as scientific observation bases in the Antarctic and Arctic.

The area encompassed by this description is presumably China's "blue territory." The Development Plan also outlines objectives to be achieved by 2020.

> The major overall objectives to be achieved by the development of maritime projects by the year 2020 are as follows: major advancement in the self-renewal capabilities and industrial level of marine science and technology; full-scale dominance in maritime development and continuous improvement in the intensification of utilizing sea areas; effective governance over pollution originating from land; fundamental reversal of the worsening of the littoral ecology; reversal of the declining biodiversity of marine organisms; improvement of the efficacy and accuracy of marine economy macro-adjustments; improvement of comprehensive maritime management systems; integration, adjustment, and swift response to maritime affairs; improvement of public service capabilities; greater ability to participate in and influence international maritime affairs; continuous development of scientific research activities on international sea areas and polar regions; universal increase in maritime awareness throughout society; restoration of the administration of maritime laws and regulations; and step-by-step achievement of the goals of effective protection, maintenance, and guarantee of national maritime interests and maritime security and of the maritime power strategy.

These objectives are aimed at boosting capabilities in numerous areas, ranging from governance of maritime interests to security. Individual policies in the East China Sea and South China Sea are part of the overall direction. Thus, the development of the Spratly Islands is encompassed by this comprehensive policy—specifically the part that states its purpose as "effective protection, maintenance, and guarantee of national maritime interests and maritime security." This means China is to build a port in the Spratly Islands, dispatch and deploy navy and coast guard vessels, and enhance its warning and surveillance and operational capabilities.

In the context of such wide-ranging activity involving maritime interests, certain recent comments regarding the possible military use of the islets in the South China Sea where China has conducted reclamation and built airfields demand scrutiny. At an April 9, 2015, press conference, for example, Foreign Ministry Spokesperson Hua Chunying said, "After the construction [at the Nansha Islands], the islands and reefs will be able to provide comprehensive services to meet various civilian demands besides satisfying the need for necessary military defense." He then listed some of the purposes presented in the above-mentioned "Twelfth Five-Year Development Plan for the National Marine Economy."[13] Similar language was also used at the May 31, 2015, Shangri-La Dialogue (an Asian security meeting sponsored by the UK International Institute for Strategic Studies), where People's Liberation Army (PLA) Navy Admiral Sun Jianguo said that the necessary military defense needs would be met. And at a June 30, 2015, press conference, Hua said, "The facilities, which mainly provide various civilian services, will enable China to better perform its international obligations and responsibilities in areas such as maritime search and rescue, disaster prevention and mitigation, marine scientific research, meteorological observation, ecological environment conservation, navigation safety, and fishery production service. Necessary military defense requirements will also be fulfilled."[14] Sun Jianguo used almost the same wording at the Shangri-La Dialogue. One key point of the explanation from the Chinese side was that the facilities were being constructed because "military defense needs will be met."

On September 25, 2015, however, Xi Jinping made the following comments at a joint press conference by the leaders of the US and China following their summit meeting. "We're committed to respecting and upholding the freedom of navigation and overflight that countries enjoy according to international law. Relevant construction activities that China is undertaking in the Nansha Islands do not target or impact any country, and *China does not intend to pursue militarization*" [italics added].[15]

Here, Xi Jinping stated that China does not intend to militarize the Nansha Islands; these words were repeated at international meetings in the autumn of 2015. For example, Premier Li Keqiang said that China "has no intention of militarization" at the East Asia Summit on November 22 in Malaysia.[16]

But these statements made in 2015 that "the necessary military defense needs will be met" seem to contradict subsequent assertions that "China does not intend to pursue militarization." Foreign Ministry Spokesperson Hua Chunying gave the following explanation regarding this point on October 14.

> Construction carried out by China on relevant islands and reefs of the Nansha Islands is mainly to satisfy civilian needs, to better fulfill China's international responsibilities and obligations, and to provide more public goods and services to the region and the international

community. There are certainly a limited number of necessary military facilities for defense purposes only. They fit well with the security environment around certain Chinese islands and reefs. But China is in no way "militarizing" relevant islands and reefs.[17]

China's response, then, is to admit the construction of military facilities, but to claim they are for defensive purposes and therefore do not constitute militarization. This suggests that China may continue building military facilities from now on, claiming all the while that this is not militarization. And as of the end of January 2016, statements by Chinese leaders and presentations by researchers at the National Institute for South China Sea Studies indicate there has been no change in direction since 2015.

Moreover, China characterizes other countries' concerns regarding the militarization of the Spratly Islands and the South China Sea as demands for "demilitarization of Chinese territory," even comparing it to Japan's demands for disarmament of areas around North China and Shanghai around the time of the Second Sino-Japanese War.[18] In China's view—based on the assumption that the South China Sea islands are Chinese territory—foreign opposition to Chinese militarization is equivalent to demanding the demilitarization of another country's territory—in other words, it is interference in China's internal affairs. This approach of combining the logic of violation of sovereignty and interference in internal affairs with China's history of being invaded is indisputably a discourse created by twentieth-century China, and one easily linked to nationalism. China may also apply this argument to the maritime interests it is trying to acquire these days, framing the issue not as Chinese expansionism, but rather as an act of aggression against Chinese territory by a foreign state. Thus, the extent of China's "blue territory" may become a problem involving more than just territory.

In early February 2016, Professor Liang Fang of the PLA National Defense University made several proposals regarding the situation in the South China Sea, including the following recommendations.

> First, a series of important ports, air fields, and other facilities should be completed immediately, so they can be used right away in case of emergencies. Second, military forces should be rapidly deployed to Xisha and Nansha. We do not plan to militarize, but defense measures must be prepared for all events. The scale of the defensive facilities will be determined in accordance with the threats we are facing.[19]

Naturally, the argument is that it is the United States, not China, that is militarizing the South China Sea; China is simply defending its own sovereignty from that threat. Professor Liang continues:

> Third, set air-defense identification zones when necessary. The military forces dispatched by the US already include military aircraft from warships, over an area extending from Nansha to Xisha. Their activities are constantly escalating and pushing China's boundaries. If China does not take the necessary measures, the US may next conduct military operations at Huanyan Dao in the Zhongsha Islands. And fourth, China should respond to the provocative behavior of the US and counterattack. We should prepare for such repeated provocative behavior by the US within 12 nautical miles of Chinese territory to become worse.

While the relationship between these proposals and government policy is not entirely clear, they should be noted as proposals from military personnel.

The Response by the Japan-US Alliance

As presented above, China's maritime advance is a national undertaking that has continued through history, manifest by ideology, systems, and actions. Shifts in the military balance of the US and other foreign countries are an important factor in China's activities in this regard; in systems as well, preparations have advanced from the 1990s and were pushed forward further during the second half of the Hu Jintao administration. From an ideological perspective, China's view on maritime interests has been determined by the perception of China as a nation that has been invaded from the beginning of the modern era, as well as the "blue territory" concept from the 1990s. The language used for this changed constantly and gradually morphed into a logic linked to faits accomplis and modern nationalism.

I believe that to understand China's behavior and engage in dialogue, we must take a broad perspective and pursue actions that consider the factors pertaining to ideology, systems, and deeds, while continuously confirming the other side's understanding. I also believe that the Japan-US alliance can fully participate, along with other countries, in this kind of consideration, action, and verification.

First, in the field of ideology (or discourse), a certain amount of intervention against China's internal and external propaganda is possible. Direct countermeasures against China's internal propaganda via education and the media would be difficult. There is limited room for foreign countries to engage in public diplomacy inside China. Yet that does not mean that direct dialogue with government officials and researchers inside China is meaningless. In China, there is a certain amount of relatively free discussion before the official positions of the government and the party are decided, and there are also periods of policy adjustment. Dialogue during such intervals should prove beneficial. Programs such as the Japan-China Dialogue on East China Sea Airspace Security being advanced by the Sasakawa Japan-China Friendship Fund provide important venues for such discussions.

Also, while it may be difficult to affect Chinese public opinion, that does not mean it cannot be done. Chinese intellectuals make good use of virtual private networks to view foreign websites, but most of the population does not. To reach the public, information must be packaged so it will get hits on Baidu, Alibaba, and other search engines used within China. To those ends, it is necessary to determine which foreign media have Chinese-language web pages that can be viewed inside China, and to then transmit information to Chinese society via those avenues. But it is important to note the weakness of this approach: the Chinese authorities can very easily block access to any web page. In addition, Japan and the US could exchange this kind of information and transmit it jointly, along with pursuing other collaborations.

The types of discourse taking shape inside China are also important. It is necessary to understand China's perceptions of the actions taken by the US and Japan. This merits thorough investigation, because the formation of public opinion inside China and the contents of internal propaganda sometimes subsequently become limiting factors when the Chinese government is determining policy. As for what specific information should be transmitted for domestic consumption in China, this might include accurate numbers and statistics on history, international law, and military security.

Meanwhile, China has been working actively to shape discourse overseas. Chinese publicity aimed at the West is conspicuous, as seen in ties between the *Washington Post* and the *China Daily*. Regulation of the Internet is relaxed in industrialized nations compared with China, and that is to China's advantage. On the Japanese-language Internet, the contents of the Japanese version of the *China Daily* are set to generate hits from various keywords. It is widely known that China's external publicity operations encompass the areas of public opinion, psychological warfare, and legal matters, and are being implemented with massive budgets not only by the Publicity Department of the Communist Party but also by institutions all across China. Setting aside the issue of US public relations efforts, Japan is implementing a systematic external PR policy at the Prime Minister's Office and the Ministry of Foreign Affairs, but this is by no means equivalent to China's activities in terms of either scale or experience. For example, if we look at the number of overseas diplomatic establishments and the PR duties assigned to individual diplomatic establishments, we see China places relatively high priority on external PR. It will become increasingly important for Japan to expand effective external publicity activities to a wide range of countries, including newly emerging economies, not just the advanced nations of the West. In these efforts, it will be essential not to simply counter China's external PR, but also to convey Japan's perspective and claims externally.

In the realm of discourse, China's statements regarding its activities in the South China Sea drew attention in 2015. As noted above, at a September 25, 2015, press conference, President Xi, who was visiting the US, clearly stated, "Relevant construction activities that China is undertaking in the Nansha Islands do not target or impact any country, and China does not intend to pursue militarization."[20] However, subsequent explanations by State Councilor Yang Jiechi and Vice-Minister for Foreign Affairs Liu Zhenmin diverged from Xi's statement. Liu and others gave the "defensive purposes" explanation while denying military objectives. At the East Asia Summit in November, Premier Li Keqiang explained that it is rational and legal for China to carry out development and construction on its own islands, saying that such construction is not targeted at any other country, nor does it affect any other country, that the construction will defend freedom of navigation and be helpful in times of maritime disasters, and that it does not constitute militarization. Also, according to media reports, Vice-Minister for Foreign Affairs Liu said that China is opposed to the militarization of the South China Sea. Nevertheless, he stated, "Constructing the necessary military defense facilities on distant islands far from the continent is based on the demands of national defense and island defense."[21] Other nations have difficulty accepting the view that China's acts do not constitute militarization but are simply defensive, while the activities of other countries essentially constitute militarization. Liu struggled to interpret President Xi's words so that the contrary statements would be consistent, noting that while Xi had said the facilities would not be used as military bases, he had not forbidden the construction of military facilities.

Even when, following pressure on China, we secure a pledge not to militarize, in the end China still expands its arms in the name of "defense." This 2015 example, which is by no means unusual, is presented to demonstrate how China twists words to justify its own actions. Nevertheless, Japan and the US need to form some sort of framework, possibly including Taiwan and other parties, to assist in interpreting such Chinese statements and predicting subsequent developments.

There are other areas where Japan and the US should collaborate. While these are related to the understanding of explanations from China mentioned above, they concern China's own perception of the situation. Recently, there has been an active discussion in the US regarding the imposition of costs (penalties) on China to discourage it from undesired actions. But whether the approach is cost imposition or engagement/containment, it will meaningless or will lead to unintended results unless China shares the perceptions and viewpoint of the US. In that sense, it is essential to understand how China perceives the various measures taken by the US. To prevent the frequently noted security dilemma as well, and for the future of the Japan-US alliance and shared efforts among Japan, the US, Australia, and other countries, it is essential to create a common understanding regarding China's perceptions.

Conclusion

In this chapter I have reviewed the historical development of China's advance into the South China Sea, noted certain trends, and discussed the characteristics of China's perspective on maritime areas. While "blue territory" is simply one example, by itself this demonstrates how China's perspective on the ocean can be compared with its viewpoint on its land territory. I then considered the response of the Japan-US alliance, and pointed out some possibilities and areas for improvement.

It must be noted that, even after thorough analysis of this historical development of China's maritime advance and the maritime perspective that lies behind it, there are limits to what can be grasped from inside Japan. US policy toward China includes traditional items as well as items drafted after the start of the Obama administration, but in the end, no conclusions can be drawn without incorporating the perceptions of the Chinese side. This applies to cost impositions by the US, of course, and to freedom of navigation operations as well. Japan and the US will probably have various frameworks for security cooperation from now on, but to begin with, the issue is how to perceive and analyze the voice of the other side.

1   Shin Kawashima, "Kingendai Chūgoku ni okeru kokkyō no kioku—'honrai no Chūgoku' no ryōiki o meguru" [Memory of national boundaries in modern China—Regarding the "proper" territory of China], *Kyōkai kenkyū* 1, 2010.

2   Foreign Ministry Spokesperson Hong Lei's regular press conference, November 12, 2015, https://www.fmprc.gov.cn/mfa_eng/xwfw_665399/s2510_665401/t1314306.shtml.

3   Shin Kawashima, "The Origins of the Senkaku/Diaoyu Islands Issue: The period before normalization of diplomatic relations between Japan and China in 1972," *Asia-Pacific Review* 20, no. 2, 2013.

4   Editorial, "Lun 'Maguan Tiaoyue' yu Diaoyudao wenti" ["The Treaty of Shimonoseki" and the Diaoyu Islands Issue], *Renmin ribao* [People's Daily], May 8, 2013; "*Riben weihe jupa Bocitan Gonggao dibatiao* (Wanghailou)" [Wanghailou: Why is Japan Afraid of the Eighth Article of the Potsdam Declaration?], *Renmin ribao haiwaiban* [People's daily overseas edition], July 28, 2014; Luo Huanxin, "Lun Liuqiu zai guojifa shangde diwei" [The status of Ryūkyū in international law], *Guojifa yanjiu* [Chinese review of international law] no. 1, Jan. 2014.

5   Shin Kawashima, "'Teikoku' to shite no Chūgoku" [China as an "empire"], in *Yūrashia kindai teikoku to gendai sekai* [Modern Eurasian empires and the contemporary world], ed. Tomohiko Uyama (Tokyo: Minerva Shobō, forthcoming).

6   Takeshi Hamashita, "Kaikoku Chūgoku to arata na shūen nashonarizumu—chiiki shugi to ikkoku shikan o koeru kokoromi," [Maritime state China and new peripheral nationalism—efforts to transcend regionalism and the historical view of one nation], *Shisō* no. 863, May 1996.

7   US Department of Defense, "The Asia-Pacific Maritime Security Strategy: Achieving US National Security Objectives in a Changing Environment," August 2015. https://apps.dtic.mil/dtic/tr/fulltext/u2/a627122.pdf.

8   In "Zhongguo haiyu jinnian zhoubian tiaozhan 'Zhiduo Bushao'" [There will only be more challenges around the China Seas this year], January 11, 2016, Wu Shicun of the National Institute for South China Sea Studies focuses on the consequences of island reclamation and construction projects, United Nations Convention on the Law of the Sea (UNCLOS) decisions, and the Declaration on the Conduct of the Parties in the South China Sea, http://ihl.cankaoxiaoxi.com/2016/0111/1050186.shtml.

9   Li Kequiang has been using this term since he was vice-premier, and he emphasized the importance of this term as premier in March 2014. "Zhengfu gongzuo baogao (2014 nian)" [Report on the work of the government (2014)], March 14, 2014, http://www.gov.cn/guowuyuan/2014-03/14/content_2638989.htm.

10 The first "blue territory" education discussion meeting was held in Qingdao in June 2014.

11 "Li Guoan weiyuan: Weihu woguo 'Lanse Guotu' quanyi kebu ronghuan" [(National CPPCC Member) Li Guoan: It is urgent to uphold the rights of our "Blue Territory"], March 4, 2009, http://military.people.com.cn/GB/1076/52969/8907465.html.

12 "Twelfth Five-Year Development Plan for the National Marine Economy," May 17, 2013, http://www.gov.cn/zwgk/2013-01/17/content_2314162.htm (in Chinese).

13 Foreign Ministry Spokesperson Hua Chunying's regular press conference, April 9, 2016, https://www.fmprc.gov.cn/mfa_eng/xwfw_665399/s2510_665401/t1253488.shtml.

14 Foreign Ministry Spokesperson Hua Chunying's regular press conference, June 30, 2015, https://www.fmprc.gov.cn/mfa_eng/xwfw_665399/s2510_665401/2511_665403/t1277267.shtml.

15 The White House, "Remarks by President Obama and President Xi of the People's Republic of China in Joint Press Conference," September 25, 2015, https://obamawhitehouse.archives. gov/the-press-office/2015/09/25/remarks-president-obama-and-president-xi-peoples-republic-china-joint.

16 Li Keqiang, "Zai dishijie Dongya Fenghui shangde fayan" [Speech at the Tenth East Asia Summit], November 22, 2015, http://politics.people.com.cn/n/2015/1124/c1001-27847103.html.

17 Foreign Ministry Spokesperson Hua Chunying's regular press conference, October 14, 2015, https://www.fmprc.gov.cn/mfa_eng/xwfw_665399/s2510_665401/2511_665403/t1305910.shtml.

18 "Zhongguo you quan rang Nanhai daoyu junshihua!" [China has the right to militarize South China Sea islands!], January 22, 2016, http://www.81.net/article/2016/0122/85631.html.

19 "Zhuanjia: Zhongguo ke she Nanhai fangshiqu zai Nansha Xisa bushu junli" [Expert: China can set the South China Sea Air Defense Identification Zone and deploy military in the Paracel and Spratly islands], February 2, 2016, http://mil.huanqiu.com/observation/2016-02/8488953.html?agt=15438 .

20 The White House, "Remarks by President Obama and President Xi of the People's Republic of China in Joint Press Conference," September 25, 2015, https://obamawhitehouse.archives. gov/the-press-office/2015/09/25/remarks-president-obama-and-president-xi-peoples-republic-china-joint.

21 "Waijiaobu Fubuzhang Liu Zhenmin: Jiang jixu zai Nanhai jianshe minyong he junshi sheshi" [Vice Minister for Foreign Affairs Liu Zhenmin: China will continue the construction of civilian and military facilities in the South China Sea], November 23, 2015, https://www.guancha.cn/politics/2015_11_23_342213.shtml?web.

CHAPTER 6

The Military Significance of China's A2/AD Strategy and Recommendations for the Military Response by Japan and the US

Yōji Kōda

Former Commander in Chief, Self-Defense Fleet, Japan Maritime Self-Defense Force

Introduction

Since around the year 2000, China's Anti-Access/Area Denial (A2/AD) strategy has drawn the world's attention because of China's expanded national power, increased military force, and seemingly coercive maritime activities. While there are various opinions regarding the interpretation and definition of A2/AD, in strictly military terms it is appropriate to view this as justifying the sudden large-scale buildup of the military power of the People's Liberation Army (PLA) in both quantity and quality, especially that of the PLA Navy and the PLA Rocket Force.

The PLA established its Rocket Force, Ground Force Command, and Strategic Support Force as of December 31, 2015. This can be seen as a decisive effort to make more practical reforms of military posture and preparations to boost the PLA's combat capabilities. These will, however, remain inferior to those of the US armed forces throughout the 2020s. Recognizing this, the PLA is not aiming to directly oppose the US armed forces or engage in a full-scale war. For now, it seems that China seeks to diminish the will of US leaders and ultimately the will of the US public to remain involved in the Indo-Asia region by demonstrating sufficient power in specific military fields where China can be equal to or somewhat superior to the United States and

---

Note: This chapter has been revised to reflect developments since the publication of the Japanese edition in 2016.

can strike US vulnerabilities under specific military situations. China's A2/AD can be characterized as a strategy and a rationale for military buildup that justifies this approach.

In this essay, I will apply the standard Western methods of formulating military plans I used as the officer in charge of defense force buildup planning at the Maritime Staff Office to analyze the PLA's planned expansion of its military forces with A2/AD. I will then examine the direction that Japan and the US should take in establishing policies and strategies to reinforce military and defense capabilities in order to counter A2/AD effectively.

I. The Current US Military Presence in Japan and the Indo-Pacific Region

There is no question that the stability of the Indo-Pacific region has been maintained since the end of the Second World War, and more recently the end of the Cold War, by the US military presence in Japan and the continuous deployment of other US forces in the region. US forces are also stationed in South Korea, but their purpose is to deter and repel an invasion of the South by North Korea. While these forces contribute greatly to stabilizing the regional situation by suppressing North Korea's adventurism, their flexible deployment outside the Korean Peninsula would be difficult. In short, from the perspective of the response to A2/AD and the value-added nature of the military posture that supports US regional and global strategy, which is now central to US policy and strategy in the Indo-Pacific, the US–South Korea alliance has far less added value than the Japan-US alliance and NATO.

To counter China's hardline foreign policy, which has become more overt in recent years, as well as the threat of A2/AD, the US announced that it would be placing greater emphasis on the Asia-Pacific through the "rebalancing" policy of the Obama administration,[1] followed by a series of new strategies regarding the Indo-Pacific under the current Trump administration. The strategy documents issued since the end of 2017 by the Trump administration, and the US military essentially emphasize placing greater importance on the Indo-Pacific region than other areas. These documents include the National Security Strategy (December 2017), the National Defense Strategy (January 2018), the National Military Strategy (December 2018) and the Indo-Pacific Strategy (June 2019). In these documents, China has become the focal nation in US security. And, more importantly, the Trump administration and the United States Indo-Pacific Command (USINDOPACOM), which is responsible for all US security policy and strategy in the region, seem to be determined and are ready to implement them when necessary.

The new strategy, which constitutes the basic US security concept, is supported by US armed forces stationed in Japan and units deployed to the Indo-Pacific region from the US mainland. The value and contribution of Japan—which has the will and the capacity to support these forces—is significant. Especially today, when the bases provided by Japan are the only US armed forces bases west of Hawaii and Guam with full-scale operations and rear-support functions, the US forces in Japan and these bases are essential to supporting US security strategy across the wide-ranging Indo-Pacific area encompassing the western Pacific, South China Sea, and Indian Ocean. All this depends on the Japan-US alliance and Japan's policies that strongly support it.

The countries of the region affected by China's recent hardline foreign policy all, to a greater or lesser extent, expect the US to take a resolute stance and to maintain the presence of its armed forces to address China's repeated violations of international norms. Japan, which hosts and supports the deployment of the US armed forces, and the Japan-US alliance are playing an even greater role than they have in the past. The US Indo-Pacific policy and strategy to counter A2/AD are strongly supported by the Japan-US alliance framework. In this context, the will and capabilities of Japan, which maintains that alliance and supports the US Indo-Pacific strategy, stand as the driving force that facilitates US policies and strategies in the region.

II. China's National Objectives and the Role of the PLA Navy

China's security policy and its growing naval power are means by which it can achieve its national objectives. Those objectives are presumed to be as follows:

1. Maintain the dictatorial regime of the Communist Party of China.
2. Maintain state sovereignty and dignity—that is to say, preserve China's territory and secure its interests in its exclusive economic zone (EEZ) as an independent state.
3. Build up a strategic nuclear force to match that of the US.
4. Maintain sustainable economic activities, including the security of its sea lines of communication (SLOCs), which are the foundation of domestic stability and its international prestige as a global economic giant (as is being advanced, for example, by the Belt and Road Initiative).
5. Develop the ability to exert China's influence (political, diplomatic, economic, military, and otherwise) anywhere in the world as a global power.

From a military perspective, in addition to the defense of territory and territorial seas in item 2, the maritime strategic nuclear force stipulated in item 3 is highly significant for the PLA, which currently has no strategic long-range bombers that can attack the US directly. Despite serious concerns regarding the current US-China trade war, stable maritime transport is also essential to maintaining China's economic activities, which are aimed to match or surpass those of the US in the near future. The military relevance of item 4 is the mission of the PLA Navy, which is directly in charge of protecting its networked SLOCs on a global scale. Finally, item 5 shows that China aims to gain the naval power to support its own global reach, allowing it to advance and deploy its military power anywhere in the world. Only the US, with its overwhelming naval power, has this ability at present.

Beijing takes the legitimacy of the naval power required for China to achieve these national objectives as a given. However, a proportional expansion of the range of activity is also a natural consequence of enhancing naval power; with this, friction with the navies of neighboring countries increases and confrontations regarding national interests are inevitable. While fully anticipating this situation, China has positioned its buildup of naval power and stepped-up maritime activities, which have become essential to achieving its national goals, as a major national policy that brooks no interference from foreign countries.

III. The Purposes of Enhanced Naval Force under China's Military Strategy (A2/AD)

China's greatest obstacle to achieving its national objectives is the US and its armed forces, which have a global reach and can take the initiative in constructing a security environment that is advantageous to the US anywhere in the world. As a first step in its efforts to achieve a comparable global reach, it is natural for China to try to establish a structure that facilitates "local reach" or "regional reach" to exert its influence over neighboring countries. To do so, it must weaken and expel the greatest obstacle: the US military presence in the region. The strategy for achieving this is A2/AD. So for the PLA, which recognizes it is still inferior to US armed forces in overall strength, A2/AD is not a strategy to plan and conduct head-on confrontation with the US armed forces. Rather, it is China's effort to demonstrate its ability to concentrate attacks on US military vulnerabilities and destroy US military assets in certain circumstances that are advantageous to China. The goal is to weaken or destroy the willingness of the American public to maintain the US military presence in the region during peacetime, intervene during crises, and execute military operations against China during war and other contingencies, and thus realize a regional security environment that is advantageous to China without waging outright war against the US.

1. The Ability to Attack US Reinforcements Moving into the Indo-Pacific

The specific areas where the PLA is enhancing its capabilities on this basis can be broadly divided into two fields. The first of these is the ability to attack US military reinforcement units advancing toward the Indo-Pacific region. For the PLA, which will remain inferior to the US armed forces in terms of military capabilities for some time to come, the plan is initially to develop the capacity to defeat both US military units deployed to the region and reinforcement units sent from the US mainland by sea and by air, and to do so as far from the Chinese mainland as possible. China is pursuing the following strategies to achieve this.

Development and deployment of anti-ship ballistic missiles (ASBMs)

China has been developing anti-ship ballistic missiles (ASBMs) that even the US armed forces do not possess and for which no countermeasures have been formulated, with a range that can reach the vicinity of Japan's Ogasawara Islands in the Pacific from the Chinese mainland (a 4,000- to 6,000-kilometer firing range). Development is believed to be in the final stages. It was reported that China conducted a test launch of six ASBMs in the South China Sea in June and July 2019. These ASBMs will primarily target the US Navy's aircraft carrier task forces, which constitute the core of US reinforcement units, and amphibious expeditionary units, which transport the US Marine Corps as a military force for immediate response, as well as strategic and naval logistical support units.

Upgrading and reinforcing the submarine force

Submarines have been used to effectively limit the use of the oceans by enemy forces ever since the First World War. Because torpedoes can sink large aircraft carriers of more than 100,000 tons—such as one of the US Navy's nuclear aircraft carriers (CVN), which constitute the core force of today's US military strategy—their physical and psychological effect is highly suitable for A2/AD. Even today, submarines remain the optimal service branch for A2/AD, and especially for area denial operations. China is investing significant state resources to enhance its submarine force capacity, which is a major threat to Japan and the US. Furthermore, the PLA Navy is energetically expanding both its nuclear and conventional submarine forces.

Building the capacity to neutralize the multiple-domain utilization capabilities that are essential to the US armed forces

China is working to neutralize US military command, control, communications, computer, intelligence, surveillance, and reconnaissance (C4ISR) capabilities, in which the US enjoys overwhelming superiority. This is an approach to neutralize US domain awareness and to utilize the outer space, air, sea, underwater, and cyberspace domains on which the US armed forces rely. To speak metaphorically, it aims to render the US armed forces dysfunctional by cutting off the "nerve function" (C4ISR) that connects the "brain" (command) to the powerful "muscles" (combat units), a tactic hereafter referred to as domain denial. Rather than directly attacking the core of the robust and mighty US armed forces, including US commands in Washington, DC, and Hawaii, and forward deployed units that have a powerful strike force, domain denial instead neutralizes the C4ISR capabilities that serve as the nervous system linking the two. Those capabilities are extremely important but difficult to defend. The idea is to acquire the capacity to destroy US armed forces that are incapacitated by domain denial while minimizing damage to the PLA. The specific domain denial methods are diverse; they may include the effective use of electromagnetic pulses (EMP) from nuclear explosions to disrupt wireless communications, anti-satellite (ASAT) weapons, cyberattacks, and cutting seabed fiber optic communications cables.

While these ASBM, submarine, and domain denial methods of enhancing China's offensive and destructive capabilities are all aimed at US armed forces units that are clearly at a great distance from the Chinese mainland, they are certainly also aimed at the Japanese Self-Defense Forces, particularly the Japan Maritime Self-Defense Force (JMSDF), which is engaged in combined operations with the US armed forces in the Indo-Pacific region, especially in the northwestern Pacific Ocean.

2. The Ability to Attack US Forces Stationed in Japan and the Indo-Pacific

The second area where the PLA is enhancing its capabilities is the ability to attack US armed forces stationed in Japan and US forces deployed in the Indo-Pacific. Like US reinforcement units crossing the Pacific Ocean, US armed forces units permanently stationed in the Indo-Pacific region will also be a target of A2/AD. These include US forces in Japan, which have extremely high value for US strategy, as noted above. In this case, the attack targets will not be limited to the operational military power in front, but will also include the US armed forces' fuel, ammunition, and facilities inside Japan, which support operations by US military units in the Indo-Pacific region, as well as Self-Defense Forces units and facilities and Japan's social infrastructure itself.

The fact that Japan's social infrastructure is the target of China's A2/AD may seem surprising to ordinary Japanese people. But Beijing evaluates Japan's capabilities from the viewpoint of its own national goals, regardless of Japanese policies toward China. Consequently, China views the existence of Japan—which supports democracy, fundamental human rights, and other values that are not compatible with China—and Japan's Self-Defense Forces—which, aside from the PLA, are the strongest in Asia and stand among the most powerful in the world in actual fighting power—as obstacles along with the US to China's achievement of its national objectives. Japan's position in the Japan-US security framework is the greatest reason why China views it as an A2/AD target, but further analysis also points to the distinct differences in values and political systems. From the perspective of military strategy, the present security situation and Japan's unique geopolitical characteristics have motivated the PLA to draft operational plans placing Japan as an A2/AD target.

Of course, averting military engagement activated by such operational plans is the role of politics and diplomacy. But at the same time, assuming that operational plans are being drafted within the PLA based on matter-of-fact calculations and projections like those presented here, it is also self-evident that to prepare for the worst-case scenario, as an independent country, Japan needs to examine measures for enhancing its ability to counter A2/AD by itself and jointly with the US. Considering this, I believe the PLA may adopt the following means of attack to achieve A2/AD.

Attacks with ballistic missiles and cruise missiles

The use of short- to medium-range ballistic missiles and cruise missiles to attack is a first-strike capability. The presumed targets would be US and Self-Defense Force bases and other military facilities, as well as core political and economic organizations and facilities with high strategic value throughout Japan.

Sabotage attacks on political and economic centers and other strategic targets by special units

While the likelihood of a direct invasion of any of Japan's four main islands by large-scale Chinese ground forces is low, surprise sabotage attacks by special units against key strategic points and political and economic centers throughout Japan to diminish support capabilities for the US armed forces and spread confusion and chaos within the Japanese community would be highly effective. The PLA is believed to have already developed the ability to facilitate such sabotage.

Invasion of the Nansei Islands for choke-point control

China's realization of A2/AD presumes that Chinese naval and air forces can freely advance into and return to bases from the Western Pacific. To that end, securing each choke point in the Nansei (Ryukyu) Islands (referred to in Japan as the Southwestern Islands) is essential for China. To achieve this, it is highly likely that the PLA would secure the islands that form the main channels or straits in the western Nansei Islands. It is obvious that China is developing and maintaining the capacity for a full-scale land invasion and occupation of some or all of the Sakishima Islands, which constitute the westernmost tip of the Nansei Islands, running from Miyako Island to Yonaguni Island.

IV. Japan-US A2/AD Countermeasures

To reiterate, China's A2/AD is not an operational concept or plan. Rather, its objective is to gain the ability to destroy some US military powers and functions, and then to show that directly to the US public in order to weaken the US government's will to remain actively involved in matters in the Indo-Pacific region, and thus establish Chinese dominance. The US and Japan must respond to China's moves toward strengthening its ability to attack the US and Japan as outlined above by closely coordinating and reinforcing their capacity to effectively deter China in the following two areas.

1. Countermeasures against Possible Chinese Attacks on US Reinforcements

First, we must be able to respond to Chinese attacks on US reinforcements. It is very likely that the PLA is planning to select the western Pacific as a theater for the destruction of US reinforcements, specifically the sea and air area between the line connecting the Izu Islands south of Tokyo Bay with the Ogasawara Islands and Guam on the east and the line connecting the Nansei Islands on the west. This has been an area for combined Japan-US operations ever since the Cold War era. Since then, the JMSDF has worked to expand its capacity to control threats to this sea area and airspace and ensure that the US reinforcements that provide support to US fighting forces operating in proximity to China's mainland during contingencies can implement their operations against opposing PLA forces without concern. With respect to A2/AD countermeasures in this area, the primary mission of the JMSDF is now, as it was during the Cold War, to control PLA threats to US reinforcements and other US military units. It is particularly important to be aware that China views US aircraft carriers as a primary target, and the loss of an aircraft carrier would be directly linked to diminished commitment by the US public to engage in the Indo-Pacific region. Based on this, Japan and the US need to devise the following countermeasures.

Construct a military posture for defense against anti-ship ballistic missiles (fleet ASBM defense)

We must strengthen our abilities to respond unerringly to the ASBMs being developed by China to attack US reinforcements on aircraft carriers and amphibious units near the Ogasawara Islands. ASBMs follow a normal ballistic missile trajectory until they approach the target. At the final stage, the warhead homes in on the target from midair and strikes the targeted ship at a speed of several kilometers per second (many times faster than conventional anti-ship missiles), taking a complicated, irregular flight path. ASBMs are extremely difficult to intercept. The full operationalization of ASBMs is believed to be five to ten years in the future, and constructing anti-ASBM capabilities is an urgent necessity. This is a difficult challenge, but it should be possible to apply many of the Japan-US ballistic missile defense (BMD) technologies currently in place for joint development of anti-ASBM measures. These should include not only ASBM interception, but also the ability to neutralize Chinese surveillance satellites that monitor targets and collect and transmit site data, along with all of China's C4ISR-related systems.

It is worth noting that on July 18, 2019, the USINDOPACOM announced that six "new-model ASBMs" had been fired in the missile tests reportedly conducted by China from the end of June through early July near the Spratly Islands (Nansha Islands) in the South China Sea. The announcement was made by a USINDOPACOM spokesperson at the Aspen Security Forum in

Colorado. While the type of the ASBMs and other details were not mentioned, this statement confirms that the PLA is actively developing ASBMs for its A2/AD military buildup. The joint development of anti-ASBM capabilities is a pressing need for Japan and the US.

Strengthen anti-submarine warfare capabilities and introduce ground-based BMD missiles

It is likely that the PLA Navy submarine force would deploy nuclear-powered submarines (SSNs)—which have mobility and cruise endurance capacity superior to conventional submarines (SSs)—to distant areas around the Ogasawara Islands to attack US reinforcements and JMSDF units providing fleet ASBM and anti-submarine warfare (ASW) defense. China's SSs, which have a more limited range than SSNs, would be positioned closer to the Chinese mainland in the western Pacific and in the vicinity of the Nansei Islands. Together with the SSNs, these would constitute a deep and multilayered offense system for carrying out attacks on the approaching US armed forces and JMSDF units that survived China's ASBM attack and remained operational thereafter. In this regard, ASW operations, which have been a primary mission of the JMSDF ever since the Cold War era, are central to the Japan-US countermeasures. It is imperative to rebuild and revitalize this capability, which has weakened as concrete threats by submarines have declined over the thirty years since the end of the Cold War.

Because China's submarine fleet is expected to attack the JMSDF's ASW units with anti-ship missiles and torpedoes, JMSDF Aegis-equipped destroyers will have to provide air defense for ASW units as well as fleet ASBM defense. Consequently, in responding to A2/AD, Japanese Aegis-equipped destroyers cannot be devoted solely to the ballistic missile defense of Japanese territory as they would be in response to North Korean ballistic missiles. It is now therefore crucial to introduce ground-based high-altitude BMD missile systems, which were not considered in the past, to defend the Japanese mainland from Chinese ballistic missiles. From this perspective, Japan's decision to introduce and to start funding for two sets of Aegis Ashore ballistic missile defense systems in 2017 and 2018 is quite appropriate.

Joint development and deployment of capabilities to respond to domain denial

China's domain denial may include electromagnetic pulses, anti-satellite (ASAT) weapons, cyberattacks, and disruption of seabed communications networks and other methods. Effective countermeasures against most of these do not yet exist or are not yet complete. In many areas, while practically starting from zero, the application and adaptation of state-of-the-art Japanese and US technologies is expected to facilitate the development of effective equipment for actual combat, as shown by the prior joint development of ballistic missile defense, which was previously considered impossible. Furthermore, the development and deployment of measures to counter domain denial represents a new area of Japan-US cooperation; such a project has huge potential to further strengthen the framework of the Japan-US alliance.

2. Countermeasures against Chinese Attacks on US Forces Stationed in Japan and the Indo-Pacific

The US and Japan must also take countermeasures against the PLA's ability to attack US armed forces stationed in Japan and US forces deployed in the Indo-Pacific, which are A2/AD targets, by reinforcing their defense capabilities. We need to strengthen the capacity for both Japan's own defense and for the protection of US forces in Japan against direct attacks on Japan by the PLA. The details are as follows.

Strengthen anti-missile defense: Deploy land-based high-altitude interception systems as an alternative to ship-based Aegis BMD systems

The BMD capabilities in place against China differ from Japan's conventional defense against ballistic missiles from North Korea. The PLA rocket force is believed to have more than 150 ballistic missiles that can target Japan, with a range that covers Japan's entire territory.[2] Consequently, Japan must construct a nationwide system to defend against ballistic missiles from China. This capacity building is highly significant because it is also directly linked to the protection of US forces stationed in Japan and US units operating in nearby areas.

In this process, it is necessary to introduce land-based high-altitude interception systems, which differ from ship-based Aegis ballistic missile defense systems. This will be a response to the new operational environment where fleet ASBM defense and anti-submarine warfare are key means of protecting US reinforcement units, and the JMSDF will be central to both these missions. In operations to defend the Japanese mainland, because Aegis-equipped destroyers can no longer be deployed solely for defense against ballistic missiles from China, other BMD assets, especially land-based high-altitude interception systems, must be deployed in place of Aegis-equipped destroy-ers. Japan's introduction of two sets of Aegis Ashore ballistic missile defense systems mentioned above is a wise and highly valued decision from this per-spective as well.

Strengthen anti-missile defense: Expand and reinforce defense against cruise missiles

Along with ballistic missiles, the PLA's attack arsenal includes cruise missiles. It is highly likely that cruise missiles launched from aircraft and submarines, as well as some ground-launched cruise missiles, will be used to attack Japan. Like the PLA's ballistic missiles, the cruise missiles will target key Japanese infrastructure, including political and economic centers and power plants, as well as important transportation points and other high-value targets. The serious potential damage represented by such an attack makes bolstering cruise missile defense capabilities extremely urgent.

Japan's present air-defense system has world-class capabilities, but it pri-marily targets manned aircraft, and its capacity for cruise missile defense is limited. Broader cruise missile defense capabilities, including C4ISR, must be developed. My concern here is that budgetary issues caused the Japanese government to withdraw the plan for the cruise missile defenses that were to be introduced with the Aegis Ashore ballistic missile defense systems. This decision must be promptly reconsidered and the cruise missile defense capa-bilities must be restored.

Build the capacity to respond to attacks by special forces on high-value core social nuclei such as political and economic centers

Attacks on Japan's core facilities that directly and indirectly support US mil-itary operations are also clearly part of the PLA's A2/AD strategy. In this case, it is very likely that attacks by special forces will be synchronized with ballistic missile and cruise missile attacks. Given the capabilities of the PLA, its special forces would attack targets throughout Japan, not limited to spe-cific cities and regions such as the Tokyo, Osaka, and Nagoya metropolises. Such a scenario would require preparation of a defense structure that covers all Japanese territory while emphasizing the defense of the Nansei Islands and western Japan against full-scale all-out invasion by the PLA by establish-ing a comprehensive C4ISR system that would not allow surprise attacks by special forces. It is also necessary to strengthen the Self-Defense Forces, espe-cially the Ground Self-Defense Force. The key will be a balance in the distribution of the Ground Self-Defense Force between deployment to western Japan for defense of the Nansei Islands against full-scale invasion and nationwide defense of distributed core social nuclei from the PLA's special forces.

Strengthen island defense capabilities: Prioritize island residents' safety

While this was hardly considered during the Cold War era, maintaining the safety and livelihoods of island residents is the top priority for island defense, especially for the Nansei Islands. China is capable of blockading and isolating part or all of the Nansei Islands using sea and air power. This can be countered by upgrading island defense capabilities and coastal maritime transport capacity in order to protect domestic shipping lanes. That will require additional force buildup beyond what is required for the protection of international SLOCs, which has been ongoing for many years since the establishment of the JMSDF. This is projected to differ substantially from present JMSDF missions in terms of both operations and equipment.

Strengthen island defense capabilities: Territorial defense (landing prevention and response)

Regarding direct island defense, maintaining the territorial integrity of the Senkaku Islands, which is the greatest matter of concern at present, is of the utmost importance. It is essential to ensure sufficient capacity to prevent any attempted invasion of the Senkaku Islands by the PLA so that the islands absolutely will not fall into China's hands.

It is also important to recognize that Japan's island defense must cover not just the Senkaku Islands, but also all of the Nansei Islands. To defend its national territory, Japan must construct a system that absolutely will not permit landing and invasion of the Nansei Islands by the PLA. There is a pressing need to deploy Self-Defense Force units to the main islands of Yonaguni, Ishigaki, and Miyako (the Sakishima Islands), and to establish a reinforcement system for times when the situation becomes tense. The central tenet of this will, of course, be the preparation of an integrated operating system for all the Self-Defense Forces. One positive measure taken by the Japanese government is that several Self-Defense Force units, most notably a battalion-sized composite Ground Self-Defense Force unit, have been deployed on both Yonaguni and Miyako in the Nansei Islands. Deployment of a similar unit is also planned on Ishigaki. However, additional measures should be taken to ensure that the defense posture of the Nansei Islands is more positive and certain.

Establish control of choke points

The Nansei Islands are located near Taiwan, which has been China's greatest area of concern. The westernmost of the Sakishima Islands, Yonaguni, is located only 110 kilometers east of Taiwan. The Nansei Islands also encompass the Sakishima Islands, which control the strategic choke point commonly called the Miyako-Ishigaki gap. The Nansei Islands have extremely high strategic value because they include the island of Okinawa, where key US Air Force and US Marine Corps units are deployed and Japan Self-Defense Force units are also stationed.

Furthermore, for China, as a continental superpower and a population giant that is almost completely dependent on foreign trade for its own survival and development, securing and controlling the choke points is as critical as the success or failure of A2/AD and the Belt and Road Initiative. At the same time, the choke points are vital to US-Japan strategy for the same reason.

From the perspective of both the Japan-US and the Chinese sides, control of the main channels along the arc of islands from Okinawa to Yonaguni and then on to Taiwan will be pivotal for the success or failure of A2/AD. The PLA is likely to take military action to capture the western Nansei Islands through full-scale landing, occupation, and maintenance, even if this entails political and strategic risk; it already has most of the required capabilities.

For Japan and the US, having China freely control those choke points would mean a sudden shift in the security balance of the Indo-Pacific region to the Chinese side, so that cannot be permitted. From this point of view, it is of vital importance for the Self-Defense Forces, which are tasked with protecting these islands, to secure these strategic choke points.

Assuming the PLA develops the capacity to invade these islands, probably at any cost, the mode of attack would likely begin with a preemptive strike against Japan and the Self-Defense Forces. Japan must therefore prepare by establishing a posture that can withstand a first strike and maintain the capacity to repel a full-scale armed invasion thereafter. It must also develop the operational capacity to prevent China from passing freely through channels that would allow for choke-point control.

V. A2/AD Countermeasures

China has been actively expanding its military and its ability to realize A2/AD since the beginning of the century, which may be considered an appropriate reflection of its stature and national power as one of the world's top production countries. While the PLA is gaining world-class capabilities through this policy, its actual abilities are not overwhelming; it still has many issues and deficiencies. The PLA is an ordinary large nation's army in the process of expanding, and it clearly will not be able to challenge the US armed forces in overall power for the next twenty or thirty years.

If we also consider the current US-China trade war—without jumping to conclusions—it is reasonable to suspect that China harbors intentions to become a great power equal to or surpassing the US by 2049, the centennial of the founding of the People's Republic of China.

In this context, the keys to effective Japan-US A2/AD countermeasures become evident. Specifically, the PLA has many vulnerabilities that the Self-Defense Forces and US armed forces could take advantage of in operations to facilitate the specific measures presented in section IV above. For example, the PLA cannot completely defend the long coastal area running from the South China Sea to the East China Sea and on to the Bohai Bay— which is the center of the vast production power that symbolizes China's strength—so a massive attack on this area by US cruise missiles is central to the Japan-US China strategy. This means our present capabilities, without additional military preparations, are enough to deter Chinese adventurism for the foreseeable future. Hypothetically, for China to fully defend its production facilities, which may be considered treasured state assets, in this long and large region, it would have to establish sufficient measures to counter US attack capabilities supported by Japan. That would require a massive, unprecedented investment of state resources, impede other types of military buildup, and force China to make a hard choice that would threaten and possibly sap its overall national power, which is what the Communist Party of China fears most. Thus, Japan can use its current capabilities in various ways to deter Chinese adventurism by forcing China to make policy decisions that can influence the fate of the Chinese state. Examples of such "keys" are presented below.

1. Efforts by Japan to Strengthen the Self-Defense Forces' Strategic Operational Capabilities

China now has the second-largest GDP in the world. Its increasing dependence on maritime transport and SLOCs gives the Self-Defense Forces— which operate exclusively from a posture of strategic defense—the powerful option of disrupting China's SLOCs in the Pacific Ocean and Indian Ocean.

China, which has become dependent on natural resources and markets worldwide for its economic prosperity, must allocate vast state resources to construct and maintain SLOC protection capabilities to guarantee its own existence and prosperity, and this definitely constitutes a great burden. This will include the defense of the aircraft carriers that China has staked its national prestige on building. Aircraft carriers have superior strike capabilities from the aircraft they carry, but they cannot defend themselves on their own. Especially for defense against submarine threats and air threats, multiple escort vessels (cruisers and destroyers) must be deployed around each aircraft carrier. Typically, a task force comprises one aircraft carrier with five to eight escort vessels. In addition, developing the anti-submarine and anti-aircraft capabilities against highly sophisticated threats to escort vessels requires superior equipment and long-term training.

The aircraft carrier defense capabilities of the PLA Navy are believed to be inferior to those of Japan and the US. At the same time, because the operational capabilities of JMSDF submarines and their anti-ship/aircraft carrier attack capabilities are estimated to greatly exceed China's anti-submarine warfare capabilities, China could face the worst-case scenario of losing its aircraft carriers right at the outset of hostilities. Such an outcome would deliver a greater blow to the prestige of China's Communist Party, its government, and the PLA than a similar outcome would to the US. Focusing on targeting aircraft carriers and other symbolic Chinese military targets aligns with leading strategic defense policies and with the countermeasures to A2/AD described above. It is an effective key that can fully deter Chinese adventurism.

Furthermore, the use of the JMSDF's mine warfare capabilities, in particular the use of cutting-edge high-performance mines with artificial intelligence (AI) to blockade the various choke points in the Nansei Islands and China's main ports, especially naval bases, would severely curtail the freedom of action of PLA naval units. As China's A2/AD in the western Pacific relies on this freedom of action, it needs a system to counter mine warfare by the JMSDF. However, the PLA's current anti-mine warfare capabilities are weak, and vast state resources and time would have to be allocated to upgrade those capabilities and remove the mine threats. This could serve as another key to keeping China in check.

2. Combined Japan-US Efforts to Strengthen Countermeasures

Develop capabilities to neutralize China's high-tech military systems

In addition to the combined Japan-US fleet ASBM defense capabilities noted in section IV, there are other bilateral Japan-US countermeasures that target weaknesses in China's A2/AD. It is well known that the PLA is doing all it can to catch up to the US armed forces, which are the strongest in the world, in a short period of time. One way to achieve this is by upgrading its high-tech military power. Like the US armed forces, the PLA is heavily reliant on high-tech equipment, and this reliance will certainly increase in the future. In other words, the more the PLA pursues high-level military capabilities, the greater its reliance on high technology will become. From this perspective, if the Self-Defense Forces and the US armed forces can physically destroy China's high-tech equipment, or largely annihilate China's capacities by invisible means (soft power), it will be possible to greatly weaken the operational capacity of the PLA and ultimately neutralize its capabilities across the board. This would also force China to allocate significant resources to devise measures to oppose Japan and the US.

Japan-US strategies to achieve this include destroying satellites, neutralizing digital networks, weakening C4ISR capabilities, and other means of decreasing or neutralizing China's domain awareness. Japan and the US have developed the basic technologies for most of these tactics, but they have not yet reached the stage of full operationalization. For the PLA, the negative impact of its capabilities becoming dysfunctional would be immeasurable and fatal. Neutralization of China's high-technology military systems is at the heart of our A2/AD countermeasures.

Develop capabilities to destroy and neutralize key PLA bases in coastal and island areas

Clear demonstrations of the US military's capability to strategically strike and destroy PLA bases, especially the naval and air force bases in coastal and island areas that constitute a pillar of China's A2/AD, are a particularly effective deterrent to Chinese adventurism. Conversely, if it is not possible to deter China by demonstrating the capabilities of the US armed forces and the Self-Defense Forces that support them, China will dominate in the strategic balance in the Indo-Pacific region and in the keen competition for naval and air power.

If Japan and the US do expressly demonstrate their ability to destroy PLA bases, China will be forced to make vast new investments to build up the basic defense framework required to realize its A2/AD strategy. Using only our current capabilities to force China to allocate new resources is a key Japan-US A2/AD countermeasure.

One aspect of China's construction of military bases on islands is often widely misunderstood in Japan. In Japan, island bases, especially air force bases, are frequently referred to as "unsinkable aircraft carriers," and there is a long-standing belief that these constitute strategic strong points. However, that thinking assumes that Japan (or another single country) will continue to hold on to those islands. In the Second World War, Japan ultimately failed to defend any of the islands it held in the mid-western Pacific, demonstrating the difficulty of defending islands against an invasion by superior enemy naval and air forces. Another lesson learned is that while aircraft carriers are difficult for a foe to reuse as combat ships because they ultimately sink in battle if they take heavy damage, after island air bases are invaded and occupied and rebuilt, they become bases for counterattack by the enemy; in other words, they add to the enemy's military strength. While having an aircraft carrier sink due to major battle damage is a heavy blow, that vessel cannot then be reused by the enemy. In contrast, when an island air base—i.e., an "unsinkable aircraft carrier"—is lost to enemy invasion, it can then provide great value to the enemy by functioning as an attack base against Japan or the country that held the base prior to invasion. In the later stages of the Pacific War, the US armed forces used this tactic to move rapidly from the central Pacific to the west through the continued invasion and recapture of islands, without giving the defending Japanese forces time to prepare the defense of the next islands. The PLA's reclamation of coral reefs and construction of military bases in the Spratly Islands in the South China Sea, which is drawing attention in the world today, entails similar vulnerabilities for China and strengths for Japan and the US, and the fact that these island bases are a "double-edged sword" should not be overlooked. In short, "unsinkable aircraft carriers" are not all-powerful; they have major vulnerabilities. This is a key that is worth including in considerations for enhancing A2/AD countermeasures.

Develop advantages over China in high-technology fields

It is possible to deter Chinese adventurism by advancing and maintaining our military advantages in the high-tech competition with China, which has independently developed numerous products but still must import or imitate new technology from the West and from Russia in many areas.

Japan and the US are, in general, unquestionably superior to China in many high-technology fields, especially those that can be used for military purposes or are dual use. Of course, China's capabilities in some areas already exceed those of Japan and the US, so China's capabilities should be accurately assessed and not underestimated. Reportedly, however, much of the PLA's newest equipment is imported from abroad and copied and produced in China or developed domestically by applying advanced foreign technologies that were transferred to China legally or illegally.

At the same time as it works to catch up to state-of-the-art Western military equipment as quickly as possible, China accurately recognizes that lagging behind the West in advanced technologies is holding it back. For China to gain the advantage, it would have to win the difficult high-tech competition with the West, which would require a massive investment of state resources. Thus, if Japan and the US, together with key NATO nations, adopt a strategy of maintaining technological superiority, science and technology could be utilized as yet another means of deterring China. Initiatives from this viewpoint include the "Star Wars" Strategic Defense Initiative (SDI) announced under the administration of US President Ronald Reagan. In hindsight, SDI was a major factor in the decision by the leadership of the USSR to end the Cold War, as it forced the Soviets to recognize the limits they faced in investing the state resources required to keep up high-tech competition against the US in space.

China has no security or military allies, and it tends to follow an independent path in industry as well, compared with Western nations. Isolating China technologically, maintaining superiority, and winning the high-tech competition are different from the highly visible measures listed above, but they are still considered an important aspect of planning A2/AD countermeasures. Of course, many high-tech factors are involved. The following is a simplified list of a vast number of options.

General technologies

- Space technology (use, attack, and defense technology, as well as alternatives for when space technology cannot be used)
- Cyber technology
- Network technology
- Underwater technology
- Unmanned vehicles (aerial, surface, and underwater)
- Artificial intelligence

Weapons-related technologies

- Directed energy technology (laser weapons, electromagnetic wave equipment)

- Hypersonic vehicles
- Ballistic missile defense and cruise missile defense technology
- C4ISR-related technology
- Technology to counter electromagnetic pulses that disable wireless communications
- Fleet ballistic missile defense technology
- Anti-submarine warfare technology
- New mine technology

VI. Drawbacks of the "US-Style" A2/AD Tenets

Recently, the Japan-US alliance has been presented in a negative light, mainly by some US factions. This likely arises from President Trump's doubts regarding the alliance, his dislike of US–South Korea joint military exercises, and his fundamental questioning of US alliance policy in general, including NATO. This casts a shadow on close Japan-US cooperation in formulating an aligned strategy toward China and its A2/AD.

Until just a few years ago, there was a concept that could be characterized as the US version of A2/AD (US-style A2/AD), as represented by offshore control (OSC).[3] This approach presumes that full-scale opposition or countermeasures to A2/AD would represent an excessive burden for the US, and proposes an alternative to the current forward deployment and presence of the US armed forces. This would involve pulling US forces back to the middle of the Pacific, pausing, and then concentrating US military power on military domains where China is vulnerable.

This approach may appear to overlap many of the initiatives advocated in section V above, but there is a significant difference. In this paper, section IV presents initiatives for Japan and the US to counter A2/AD directly together, and section V presents keys for realizing the approaches in section IV as measures against China's vulnerabilities. In contrast, the US-style A2/AD represented by OSC focuses solely on the types of measures presented in section V without discussing the strategies presented in section IV. It does not constitute a fundamental response to China's A2/AD buildup against Japan and the US.

This US-style A2/AD does not consider the core status of the Japan-US alliance, which has become a pillar of US global strategy. That is, it overlooks the fundamental importance of Japan as a hub for the US Indo-Pacific strategy, which relies on US military presence, and the very high support for the US military provided by Japan. Because this US-style A2/AD ultimately ignores the Japan-US alliance, which upholds US strategy in the Indo-Pacific region, it is clear that it will never be realized as a concrete policy.

There are also strong concerns that this US concept would actually further adventurism by China, as the pullback of the US armed forces could be viewed as an opportunity by China as well. Moreover, because there is a strong likelihood that Japan will be exposed to preemptive strikes by China, even a temporary withdrawal of the US armed forces that are solely responsible for strategic strikes would undermine the very foundation of the Japan-US alliance. And for the US itself, the pullback of forces proposed under this US-style A2/AD would render the positioning and significance of the Japan-US alliance unclear, and would clearly work against US policy centered on the Indo-Pacific and its new strategies.

If a stand-alone US version of A2/AD were introduced, there are strong concerns that it would not only fail to achieve the Japan-US strategic objective of solidly opposing China's A2/AD and preventing China from rampant adventurism, but would also cause new problems to emerge in the Indo-Pacific region, weakening deterrence against China and making the situation even more complicated. This US-style A2/AD simply cannot function as the main US strategy.

Conclusion

The goal of China's A2/AD is to gain enough military power to defeat the US forward-deployed forces in the Indo-Pacific region. This would diminish the US military presence in the region, as well as the will of the US to exercise its influence on countries in the region through its presence. China is vigorously building up its military forces with the goal of catching up to the US armed forces. However, it is projected to take some twenty to thirty years—assuming the US maintains its present level of military buildup—for China to gain an absolute advantage over the US armed forces. China's strategy is therefore to defeat the US without fighting. Specifically, by ensuring that the US public perceives effective PLA capabilities concentrated on specific areas where they are equal to or slightly superior to the US armed forces and can attack US vulnerabilities, China aims to significantly weaken the US government's resolve to intervene in regional issues. This will enable China to establish hegemony over the region without engaging in war with the US, which is China's worst-case scenario. The strategy China is using to achieve its national objectives and justify its military buildup is A2/AD.

It is important to note here that in actual military activities, the forces prepared based on military-buildup concepts are optimally and flexibly employed to achieve the given mission in accordance with the strategic conditions at the time. In military circles, these are referred to as "operations." Actual operational plans and military-buildup concepts typically do not match: military-buildup concepts are guidelines for the preparation of state military forces, and governments normally formulate only one type of concept. Operational plans, on the other hand, are formulated to respond to multiple strategic conditions and environments that can be foreseen at the projected time of implementation, so multiple plans (operational plans, or OPLAN) are formulated. Thus, by Western standards, A2/AD is a military-buildup concept and not an operational plan.

Although A2/AD may be a military-buildup concept, the PLA has already initiated low-intensity preparations for actual implementation, such as by examining the feasibility of A2/AD in the South China Sea and areas around the Nansei Islands. These forays include the construction of military bases in the Spratly Islands by reclamation of coral reefs, as well as frequent passage of through the gaps (choke points) in the Nansei Islands and into the western Pacific by PLA navy and air force units.

For the defense of the Nansei Islands, which involves Japan and the Self-Defense Forces directly, the basic strategy of the Self-Defense Forces is Japan-US cooperation. The traditional division of roles whereby the Self-Defense Forces are responsible for defensive operations and the US armed forces for offensive operations remains unchanged. However, now that thirty years have passed since the end of the Cold War, the Self-Defense Forces are finally casting off their Cold War posture and transitioning to a new structure. Stipulating island defense and unifying operational concepts with the US armed forces are new areas for the Self-Defense Forces, and it is only natural that they were examined in detail in the 2015 Japan-US Guidelines and in the drafting of the Roles, Missions, and Capabilities Review. It is time, however, for the two governments to initiate a new structure to fully examine and develop new aligned strategies to engage with China's A2/AD strategy.

In the future, the Japanese government must make sure that Japan and the US build up sufficient capacity to counter China's A2/AD, and it must absolutely ensure that China does not misunderstand or misjudge the effectiveness of the Japan-US alliance. We can deter Chinese adventurism by continuing to transmit to Beijing a clear and simple message that today's relatively stable regional situation, along with the extremely firm and steady

Japan-US alliance, have been products of Japan's determination to act as an enabler of US policy in the Indo-Pacific region.

The friction between Japan and China today is caused by the conflict between China's buildup of military capabilities to support its state objective of establishing hegemony over the Indo-Pacific region—which it strongly denies—on the one hand, and the US countermeasures and Japanese support efforts based on the Japan-US alliance on the other. We must never forget that if we lose this unarmed battle, the stability of the Indo-Pacific region, which has until now rested on the US-Japan alliance, will be lost, and Japan's peace and prosperity will be threatened.

The current US-China trade war is truly a battle in which both countries are using all their strengths to secure global leadership. The only difference between this and the previous world war is that the two nuclear powers, the US and China, are using economics and high technology, rather than military power, to fight an all-out war. Nevertheless, it is important to accurately recognize that, as in the previous world war, this competition will determine the future rise or fall of the two countries.

From this standpoint, the growing viewpoint that the US and China are now engaged in two types of war—a "static/cold" war to determine which country's security and military strategy is superior and a "dynamic/hot" war to determine which country can prevail in the economic sphere and eventually in overall global leadership—may be deemed accurate.

I would like to conclude by stating that Japan's security discussions, including those of the government, focus too closely on the Senkaku Islands issue, with little consideration given to maintaining the support for the US armed forces that is fundamental to the Japan-US alliance. With respect to Japan-US A2/AD countermeasures, the present focus is almost entirely on measures to respond to China's capacity to attack Japan and US armed forces in the region (section IV, subsection 2), while the ability to respond to attacks on US reinforcements (section IV, subsection 1) has not been addressed. As noted in this paper, it is essential to have balance between the former and the latter with respect to capacity building and defense buildup. However, as seen the most recent National Defense Program Guidelines announced in late 2018, as well as the Medium-Term Defense Program, I fear that the current discussions in Japan lack attention to such balance and feature an extremely dangerous type of single-pointed focus that should be avoided at all costs in levelheaded, sound security strategy debate.

1   See Robert G. Sutter, Michael E. Brown, Timothy J. Adamson, Mike M. Mochizuki, and Deepa Ollapally, *Balancing Acts: The US Rebalancing and Asia-Pacific Stability* (Elliott School of International Affairs and Sigur Center for Asian Studies, George Washington University, August 2013), 2.

2   This figure is estimated by the author based on his experience in the Self-Defense Forces. According to *The Military Balance 2014*, there are a total of 386 MRBMs and SRBMs assigned to the PLA rocket force (Second Artillery Corps). It is estimated that 30 to 40 percent of these could be targeted against Japan in an operational environment under A2/AD second-category operation to crush the US armed forces. International Institute for Strategic Studies, *The Military Balance 2014*, 231.

3   T.X. Hammes, "Offshore Control is the Answer," *Proceedings* 138, no. 12 (December 2012), https://www.usni.org/magazines/proceedings/2012/december/offshore-control-answer; Andrew S. Erickson, "Deterrence by Denial: How to Prevent China from Using Force," *The National Interest*, December 16, 2013, https://nationalinterest.org/commentary/war-china-two-can-play-the-area-denial-game-9564.

CHAPTER 7

The South China Sea Dispute and the Japan-US Alliance

Futoshi Matsumoto

Deputy Chief of Mission of the Consulate-General of Japan in New York; former Chargé d'Affaires of the Embassy of Japan in Syria

There is a sense that the South China Sea dispute has become an urgent issue for the Japan-US alliance and indeed a central issue of increasing importance. Given these circumstances, in this paper I would like to clarify the strategic difficulties that the South China Sea dispute presents for Japan-US security. I will also consider the significance of this dispute for other countries in the region, as well as for the Japan-US alliance.

The South China Sea Dispute as a Regional Strategic Issue

In fact, the South China Sea issue emerged from Japan's renunciation of all rights, titles, and claims to the Spratly Islands and other territories in the 1951 San Francisco Peace Treaty following World War II. In the wake of this treaty, multiple countries claimed territorial rights in the South China Sea.

Ever since then, the South China Sea dispute has been an ongoing issue among the countries asserting sovereignty for many years because territorial rights, exclusive economic zones, and other rights have remained undecided. In this respect, it is critical to recognize that, from the perspective of the regional order in Asia, the South China Sea dispute is essentially an issue left unresolved by Japan after the Second World War.

Since the second half of 2013, China has been engaged in land reclamation projects on seven reefs in the South China Sea, as well as the construction of multiple 3,000-meter-class runways and port facilities. The nature of the South China Sea dispute has changed dramatically with China's own admission that these facilities may be used for military purposes.

This dispute was previously limited to conflict on territorial rights involving specific claimants, but it has now become a strategic security matter directly concerning the interests of countries aside from the claimants. That is to say, the South China Sea dispute is now a strategic problem for the international community, brought about by the aggressive maritime advances China has been making since 2008.

With these actions by China, the nature of the South China Sea dispute has undergone a qualitative transformation into both a regional security issue related to the maintenance of a peaceful maritime order and an issue concerning the rule of law with respect to freedom of overflight and freedom of navigation on the high seas. In this regard, although the circumstances are different, the issues of maritime security in the East China Sea and the South China Sea bear many resemblances.

It is now clear that China's own mindset and actions in claiming almost all of the South China Sea as Chinese territory—as represented by the "nine-dash line" claim—is heightening regional tension. That is because China's claims and actions are not at all in accord with the general understanding of current international law, that is, the United Nations Convention on the Law of the Sea (UNCLOS).

In the context of international power politics, the South China Sea issue presently reflects the doubts held by China and other countries regarding the medium- to long-term US presence in the region. This itself reflects the inward-looking debate that has been taking place in the United States since the advent of the Obama administration and the increase in pressure to reduce defense expenditures. China's expansionist behavior is a reaction to these factors.

Thus, the South China Sea dispute has emerged as a strategic issue for both Japan and the US, reflecting the international political reality of China's rise, along with the collapse of the myth of US global hegemony.

China's Land Reclamation Projects on Seven Reefs

The land reclamation projects that China began in December 2013 have been conducted on seven reefs that are under China's effective control: Fiery Cross Reef, Johnson South Reef, Hughes Reef, Gaven Reef, Cuarteron Reef, Subi Reef, and Mischief Reef. Under these projects China reclaimed a total of more than 1,170 hectares[1] of land through June 2015. This is clearly on an extremely large scale compared with the land reclamations to date of 32 hectares by Vietnam, 28 hectares by Malaysia, 6 hectares by the Philippines, and 3 hectares by Taiwan.

Furthermore, the other claimants' reclamation projects were all carried out on landforms that are above water even at high tide, as stipulated by UNCLOS. The seven reefs reclaimed by China, by comparison, include landforms that are not above water at high tide. The US Digital Gazetteer of the Spratly Islands does not recognize any of those seven reefs as "islands."[2] It is also worth noting that, while the reclamations by the other claimants took place over decades, China completed its large-scale reclamations in an astoundingly short twenty months.

China is presently constructing various facilities on these reclaimed man-made islands. The most notable of these is the 3,000-meter runway on Fiery Cross Reef. According to official statements by the Chinese government, these reefs will be used for "maritime search and rescue, disaster prevention and mitigation, marine scientific research, meteorological observation, ecological environment conservation, navigation safety as well as fishery production service,"[3] and for military purposes as well.

At the end of June 2015, China made an official statement announcing that the land reclamation projects at all seven reefs had been completed. However, the construction of military facilities on these reefs is expected to continue, and the situation remains unpredictable. In fact, in January 2016 China landed civilian aircraft on the runway at Fiery Cross Reef and conducted test flights.

The Beginning of Full-Scale Restraint of China by the US

In March 2015, Admiral Harry Harris Jr., the commander of the US Pacific Fleet, criticized China's land reclamation projects in the South China Sea, saying, "China is creating a Great Wall of sand."[4] After May 2015, when these projects started to expand and speed up, the US government began taking action to restrain China. At the end of October 2015, the US demonstrated its "freedom of navigation" by having a single naval vessel, the USS *Lassen*, navigate inside 12 nautical miles of Subi Reef. Through this action, the US government finally demonstrated that it was taking a serious stance toward China's behavior, and that it was aware of world opinion. The decision to act was made following a series of extremely uncooperative responses by the Chinese government.

US Secretary of State John Kerry visited Beijing on May 16 and 17, 2015, and held meetings with Foreign Minister Wang Yi, State Councilor Yang Jiechi, and President Xi Jinping in which he conveyed US concerns and requested that China stop its land reclamation activities in the South China Sea. To promote positive US-China relations prior to President Xi's scheduled visit to the US in September, Kerry stressed US hopes that the Chinese side would not create tensions, but the Chinese did not give an encouraging response.

On the contrary, shortly after these meetings Foreign Ministry Spokesperson Hua Chunying said, "The close reconnaissance of China's maritime features conducted by US military aircraft is very likely to cause miscalculation and untoward incidents in the waters and airspace, and is utterly dangerous and irresponsible."[5] Furthermore, at a press conference announcing the defense white paper "China's Military Strategy," Ministry of National Defense Spokesperson Yang Yujun said that the Chinese military would take necessary countermeasures if US military aircraft carried out close reconnaissance. This was in effect a threat to the US.

It is not difficult to imagine that these stubborn words and actions on the part of the Chinese government have been extremely offensive to the US government. In fact, on May 21, 2015, just before the Shangri-La Dialogue (an Asian security conference), a US Navy P-8A Poseidon patrol plane took off from an air base in the Philippines to conduct reconnaissance on reefs in the South China Sea where China was carrying out land reclamation projects. The US appealed to global public opinion by carrying a CNN crew on board that filmed Chinese activities and broadcast the footage worldwide. Afterward, Department of Defense spokesperson Colonel Steven Warren said that Poseidon (P-8A) aircraft might continue to pass inside the 12-nautical-mile boundary that China claims around its man-made islands in the future, making it clear that the US intended to restrain China.

On May 27, 2015, during change-of-command ceremonies for the US Pacific Command in Hawaii, US Secretary of Defense Ashton Carter said that China's construction of man-made islands in the South China Seas should be halted immediately. Carter said, "China's actions are bringing countries in the region together. And they're increasing demand for American engagement in the Asia-Pacific, and we're going to meet it."[6] Additionally, at the Shangri-La Dialogue at the end of May, Carter repeatedly stressed that "the United States will fly, sail and operate wherever international law allows,"[7] clearly indicating that the US would go beyond words in the future and take action to address the South China Sea problem.

Furthermore, the G7 Summit Leaders' Declaration released on June 8 incorporated a statement that communicated the harsh reaction of the international community toward China: "We strongly oppose the use of intimidation, coercion or force, as well as any unilateral actions that seek to change the status quo, such as large scale land reclamation."[8]

China's Response: Conspicuous Diplomatic Rhetoric and Faits Accomplis

Every one of China's initial official and non-official responses demonstrated recalcitrance. In response to Secretary of Defense Carter's May 2015 speech, at a regular press conference on the following day (May 28), Foreign Ministry Spokesperson Hua Chunying criticized the US for making irresponsible comments regarding the construction of man-made islands within areas of Chinese sovereignty, stating, "No one else has the right to tell China how to behave."[9]

In addition, at the Shangri-La Dialogue held at the end of May, People's Liberation Army (PLA) General Staff Department Deputy Chief Sun Jianguo said that the situation in the South China Sea was stable, and that no country could stop China's actions in this sea area. He countered the US position with a statement that China would reject US requests to halt its land reclamation activities in the South China Sea.

On June 2, in an interview with a US media outlet, Chinese ambassador to the US Cui Tiankai said that the US was overreacting to the present situation in the South China Sea. He stated that the US was not only dispatching military aircraft and conducting reconnaissance, but also unfairly criticizing China. Ambassador Cui said the Chinese were surprised and concerned about this.

On June 11, Secretary of State Carter met with the head of China's uniformed forces, Vice Chairman of the Central Military Commission Fan Changlong, at the Pentagon, and requested that China cease its large-scale land reclamation projects in the South China Sea. On June 16, China's Ministry of Foreign Affairs officially announced that the land reclamation project would be completed as planned in the near future.

The South China Sea issue was then discussed again at the China-US Strategic Economic Dialogue held in Washington on June 23 and June 24. In his opening address, Vice President Joe Biden cautioned the Chinese, saying, "The notion of sea lanes being open and protected is even more crucial today than any time in human history."[10]

In response, State Councilor Yang Jiechi said, "China is firmly in favor of navigation freedom across the world." Vice Premier Wang Yang said both countries would pay a price for confrontation, and that dialogue was a better choice. As a result, China avoided a confrontation with the US.

At a regular press conference on June 30, Foreign Ministry Spokesperson Hua Chunying said that the land reclamation projects on some islands and reefs in the Spratly Islands in the South China Sea had been "completed recently as scheduled," and announced that China would now build facilities for various purposes, including military use.[11] Hua said these facilities would enable China to better perform its international obligations and responsibilities in such areas as maritime search and rescue, marine scientific research, meteorological observation, environmental conservation, and navigation safety, and stressed that "necessary military defense requirements" would also be fulfilled.

Furthermore, at the US-China summit meeting held at the end of September 2015, it was reported that President Xi Jinping did not make any concessions whatsoever to President Obama regarding the South China Sea problem. Based on this situation, the US has instituted what it calls "freedom of navigation" operations in the Spratly Islands. Specifically, at the end of October 2015, the Aegis destroyer USS *Lassen* from the US Navy's Seventh Fleet challenged China's position by navigating within 12 nautical miles of Subi Reef in the Spratly Islands, where China is conducting land reclamation.

Incidentally, Chinese diplomatic rhetoric changed, becoming friendlier, after the US began maintaining a firm stance toward China's actions. China has toned down its official position in the wake of strong objections from the US.

The Security Significance of China's Land Reclamation Projects

These assertive policies and actions on the part of the US reflect the security implications of China's land reclamation activities. The greatest concern is the 3,000-meter-class runway that China will likely have at Fiery Cross Reef. China is expected to construct runways of similar length on Subi Reef and Mischief Reef as well. The US Navy's selection of Subi Reef in particular and its navigation within 12 nautical miles seems to be sending a clear message.

To put the situation in context, the runways on South China Sea islands under effective control of other claimants are all just 550 meters to 1,368 meters in length. Vietnam's runway on Spratly Island is 550 meters; the Philippines' runway on Thitu Island is 1,000 meters; Taiwan's runway on Itu Aba Island is 1,195 meters; and Malaysia's runway on Swallow Reef is 1,368 meters.

A 3,000-meter-class runway can be used for landing J-11 fighters and other recent models of Chinese fighter aircraft, as well as H-6G strategic bombers and other military equipment with strong strategic significance. A base in the South China Sea would confer China overwhelming air superiority in the Southeast Asian region.[12] Consequently, it is becoming impossible to deny the possibility that China may soon announce an air defense identification zone (ADIZ) in the South China Sea similar to the ADIZ it announced in the East China Sea.

The runways are not the only consideration. According to an editorial in the *Wall Street Journal* by Elbridge Colby and Evan Braden Montgomery,

> China's artificial islands might host anti-ship missile batteries and air defense systems that would heighten the risk to any surface vessels and aircraft in the vicinity. If Beijing deployed these weapons to several different islands in the South China Sea, and if these weapons had sufficient range, then it might be able to create mini denial zones, where other countries' civilian and military assets could be held at risk from multiple locations. Meanwhile, a network of ground-based surveillance radars far from mainland China would provide Beijing with much better situational awareness of the region during peacetime—and targeting information on opponents in the event of war.[13]

In a recent report titled "The Asia-Pacific Maritime Security Strategy: Achieving U.S. National Security Objectives in a Changing Environment," the US Department of Defense notes, "The infrastructure China appears to be building would enable it to establish a more robust power projection presence in the South China Sea," and specifically stresses this as follows:

> Its latest land reclamation and construction will also allow it to berth deeper draft ships at outposts; expand its law enforcement and naval presence farther south into the South China Sea; and potentially operate aircraft—possibly as a divert airstrip for carrier-based aircraft—that could enable China to conduct sustained operations with aircraft carriers in the area.[14]

In other words, the land reclamation and construction of various military facilities on these seven reefs will constitute de facto military bases that may place not only the South China Sea, but a broad region of Southeast Asia, under the influence of China's military presence.

Above all, if China can slowly expand its influence while avoiding large-scale provocations that would invite retaliation, it will develop decisive influence over the medium to long term. Most of the neighboring countries, such as Vietnam and the Philippines, lack the capability to develop a significant military force. If China stations military units on these reefs, it will have a huge impact on the military balance in the region.

From this perspective, Colby and Montgomery express their concern that "forward-deployed Chinese forces could also encourage China's neighbors to stay on the sidelines during any crisis between Beijing and Washington. The US then might not enjoy much-needed access to facilities on their territory."[15] Such a scenario includes the possibility that China will not only exert air superiority, but may also deploy strategic nuclear submarines carrying JL2 and other submarine-launched ballistic missiles south from bases on Hainan Island to navigate freely throughout the entire South China Sea. Some also assume, of course, that Chinese strategic nuclear submarines will become even more active in the Pacific and in the Indian Ocean.

Yōji Kōda, the former commander in chief of the Japan's Maritime Self-Defense Fleet, notes the potential for a future security concern if China forms a "strategic triangle" in the South China Sea by conducting further land reclamation and militarizing Scarborough Shoal as follows:

> If the international community cannot stop it, the reclamation of Scarborough Shoal, which is located offshore of Manila in the eastern part of the South China Sea and has been under the effective control of China since 2012, and the establishment of a military base there will become a major concern. This would create a triangular sea and air area extending some 650 to 900 kilometers on each side in the South China Sea, linking Woody Island, Fiery Cross Reef, and Scarborough Shoal under Chinese control. This would be extremely serious for the US, which has no full-scale operational bases in the broad sea area west of Okinawa.[16]

In fact, on March 17, 2016, US Navy Chief of Naval Operations John M. Richardson pointed out that China was conducting survey activity around Scarborough Shoal, and stated that this was "a next possible area of reclamation."[17]

These observations make it difficult to deny the strategic objective that lies behind China's transformation of the seven reefs into man-made islands: to place the South China Sea, which is a global commons, under China's own sphere of influence. The military parade in Beijing on September 3, 2015, added certainty to this suspicion, as six different ballistic missiles that are the pride of the PLA Second Artillery Corps (Rocket Corps) were displayed all at once. These included the DF-5B and DF-31A long-range ballistic missiles, the DF-15B short-range ballistic missile, the DF-16 intermediate-range ballistic missile, and the DF-21D anti-ship ballistic missile known as the "aircraft-carrier killer." The highlight was the appearance of the DF-26 ballistic missile, which has roughly twice the range of the DF-21D. According to official comments from the Chinese government, the DF-26 can carry either a conventional warhead or a nuclear warhead, and in addition to land targets it can strike large and medium-sized targets at sea with precision.

The unveiling of the DF-26 at the military parade demonstrated that China had acquired an anti-ship missile with an even longer range than the DF-21D. This range, of course, includes Guam, where US military bases are located. Moreover, depending upon which bases in China they are placed at, not only the entire South China Sea, but also most countries in the Association of Southeast Asian Nations (ASEAN), as well as a substantial portion of the Indian Ocean, would lie within range of the DF-26.

The fact that the DF-26 has been fully deployed means that China has the power to implement anti-access and area denial (A2/AD) in its adjacent waters within the so-called first island chain. This decisive expansion of China's A2/AD capabilities also means the entire East Asian region is now within range of China's precision ballistic missiles.

In a simple summary, as it militarizes the South China Sea by constructing man-made islands and deploying intermediate-range precision ballistic missiles on them, China clearly intends to expand its A2/AD capabilities to cover the entire East Asian region, including Southeast Asia.

Actions by China That Erode the Basis of the Rule of Law

Other issues with China's actions in the South China Sea pertain to the rule of law. Both China's land reclamation activities and the claims asserted by its "nine-dash line" pose serious problems in light of the United Nations Convention of the Law of the Sea (UNCLOS).

To begin with, categorizing any of the seven reefs where China is conducting land reclamation as an island is highly debatable. For example, while

Fiery Cross Reef, the first of the Spratly Islands occupied by China, was originally 22 kilometers long and around 7 kilometers wide, it is a sunken reef that lies 50 centimeters to 1 meter underwater at high tide. According to UNCLOS Article 121, "An island is a naturally formed area of land, surrounded by water, which is above water at high tide." None of these seven reefs fit this definition.

Furthermore, if these seven reefs are considered low-tide elevations as defined in UNCLOS Article 13 ("A low-tide elevation is a naturally formed area of land which is surrounded by and above water at low tide but submerged at high tide"), by definition they have no 12-nautical-mile territorial waters or territorial airspace above; nor do they have a 200-nautical-mile exclusive economic zone, a continental shelf, or a 500-meter safety zone.

There is no unified opinion as to whether any of these seven reefs are land areas that are above water at high tide or low-tide elevations. It must also be noted that their legal determination under international law is still pending, as the Philippines has a case before the Permanent Court of Arbitration regarding their legal status. [Note: This is the translation of a article written prior to the judgement of the Permanent Court of Arbitration in July 2016, in which the tribunal concluded that there was "no legal basis for China to claim historic rights to resources within the sea areas falling within the 'nine-dash line.'"]

Regardless, UNCLOS specifies that man-made islands do not have the status of islands, and have no territorial waters. So, obviously, exclusive economic zones and continental shelves do not automatically come into being just because China has constructed some man-made islands.

What, then, is the legal viewpoint on the recent navigation by the US Navy destroyer *Lassen* within 12 nautical miles of Subi Reef? This should be based on the fact that Subi Reef, considered a low-tide elevation, forms part of Sandy Cay, which is effectively controlled by Vietnam and also claimed by China, the Philippines, and Taiwan. Some hold the opinion that, based on UNCLOS Article 13, if Sandy Cay is a land feature that is above water at high tide, then Subi Reef may constitute a territorial sea baseline. According to this view, whether Sandy Cay is the territory of Vietnam or of some other country, the existence of territorial seas with Subi Reef as the baseline means that navigation in those waters by the US Navy warship *Lassen* could be interpreted as innocent passage as defined in UNCLOS Article 17.[18]

To begin with, China asserted its "nine-dash line" with no rationale under international law whatsoever, and has repeatedly claimed that virtually all the South China Sea is under Chinese jurisdiction. In sea areas where it has de facto control, China has used force to expel fishing ships and official vessels of the Philippines, Vietnam, and other states when they approach. It is extremely difficult to justify those actions under international law.

Conversely, one might say that the lack of any relatively large "island" under its effective control is a weakness for China in the South China Sea, and this is the cause of China's ceaseless pursuit of islands and reefs under the effective control of others. In the Spratly Islands, the only others with de facto control over relatively large "islands" are Taiwan, Vietnam, the Philippines, and Malaysia. Specifically, these are Itu Aba Island (Taiping Island) under the control of Taiwan, Spratly Island under the control of Vietnam, Thitu Island under the control of the Philippines, and Swallow Reef under the control of Malaysia.

China's tactic over the past two years has been to bring in earth and sand and build military facilities, including runways and ports, on the reefs over which it presently has de facto control. The objective is to gain wide-area maritime domain awareness equivalent to that of other claimants. In terms of the area and the scale of the facilities, China is now working to build manmade islands that are larger than the actual islands held by other claimants.

In conducting these land reclamation projects, China has not held discussions with the Philippines or Vietnam—countries with which China is involved in disputes over territorial rights. Additionally, China's reclamation activities are causing enormous environmental destruction in the area. These facts pose serious legal questions under UNCLOS regarding China's activities.

It is clear from UNCLOS Article 123, which calls for the "cooperation of states bordering enclosed or semi-enclosed seas," that states which border the same semi-enclosed sea are to coordinate with each other in the protection and preservation of the marine environment as they exercise their rights and perform their duties. Given how systems such as exclusive economic zones and the continental shelf are recognized under UNCLOS, this renders meaningless, right from the start, the legal significance of the "historical facts" claimed by China.

Chinese government officials claim that China's construction projects in the South China Sea are similar to those of Vietnam and the Philippines, so there is no reason why only the Chinese land reclamation should be criticized.[19] However, Vietnam and the Philippines have only carried out construction on relatively large islands, while the Chinese man-made islands are on reefs that are considered low-tide elevations.

In contrast with the "nine-dash line" claim by China, which is not based on modern international law, a statement in September 2014 by Taiwanese president Ma Ying-jeou, who was originally an international law expert, asserting that Taiwan only claims sovereignty over "islands" in the South China Sea, and is not claiming sovereignty over other low-tide elevations, is in full accordance with UNCLOS.

In any case, China's mindset and the actions it has taken in land reclamation projects that completely ignore UNCLOS and the rule of law are slowly eroding the norms that underpin the international order.

ASEAN Diplomacy Facing its Limits

Yet another important aspect of the problem of man-made islands in the South China Sea is that it reveals the limits of diplomacy by the Association of Southeast Asian Nations (ASEAN). For example, for many years there has been no substantive progress on the Code of Conduct in the South China Sea (COC) that China and ASEAN are negotiating; even the provisions of the Declaration on the Conduct of Parties in the South China Sea (DOC), which the Chinese signed in 2002, are not being observed. While the DOC clearly stipulates the observance of UNCLOS, looking at China's actions in the South China Sea in recent years, China is not fulfilling that commitment in its relations with ASEAN. This situation is generating even more of a sense of powerlessness and impatience among the ASEAN countries.

Malaysia was the chair country for the 2015 ASEAN Summit. At the ASEAN Foreign Ministers' Meeting in August, Malaysian Minister of Foreign Affairs Dato' Sri Anifah bin Aman noted that the South China Sea dispute exemplified a situation where ASEAN should take the initiative in reaching a friendly resolution. He stressed that they had made a good start, but cautioned that much more remained to be done. In fact, an agreement was reached on a declaration of principles for the complete implementation of the DOC and the rapid conclusion of the COC.

Malaysia has maintained a position of neutrality and friendly relations to the greatest extent possible in its relations with China to date, but it has gradually become clear in recent years that Malaysia is greatly concerned about the security of the islands and reefs under de facto Malaysian control in the South China Sea. This is because Chinese patrol boats and warships have already visited James Shoal, which is in Malaysian territory 80 kilometers offshore of the island of Borneo, and have confronted Malaysian naval authorities each time. In March 2013, four PLA Navy warships fired warning shots in waters near James Shoal. Then, in January 2014, three PLA Navy warships approached once again and even held a ceremony declaring Chinese sovereignty.

In response to these developments, in October 2014, the government of Malaysia decided to build a naval base on the island of Borneo at Bintulu, which is also an LNG export base. For Malaysia, it is essential to ensure the maritime security in the coastal waters of Borneo, as the island is a shipping base for Malaysia's natural resources.

Furthermore, in August 2015, Malaysian officials in charge of local government instructed local government bodies to name all uninhabited islands, coral reefs, and reefs under their respective jurisdictions and give notice. In response, the defense authorities in Indonesia, which had maintained neutrality in its diplomacy, indicated greater concern.

Statements made by the leaders of Indonesia's defense authorities merit special attention. In an April 24, 2014, *Wall Street Journal* article, Indonesia's commander of the national armed forces, TNI Moeldoko, wrote, "Indonesia is dismayed . . . that China has included parts of the Natuna Islands within the Nine-Dash Line, thus apparently claiming a segment of Indonesia's Riau Islands province as its territory."[20] For that reason, he explained, "The Indonesian military has decided to strengthen its forces on Natuna," adding that Indonesia had deployed offensive Apache helicopters and Sukhoi fighter jets on the Natuna Islands.

There is clearly growing recognition, especially in the Philippines and Vietnam, that a response by ASEAN alone is not sufficient. At the August 2015 ASEAN Foreign Ministers' Meeting, Philippines Secretary of Foreign Affairs Albert Del Rosario revealed that the Philippines had requested that China suspend its land reclamation and facilities construction, and refrain from extreme actions that might intensify tensions. At the same time, Del Rosario reminded China that these requests by no means justify land reclamation by China.

The Philippines asked the Court of Arbitration to rule on the legal interpretation under UNCLOS of the land features involved with China's land reclamation in the South China Sea. In October 2015, the Court of Arbitration ruled that it does have the jurisdiction to address this issue. There is great interest in the court's future ruling on the case.

Moreover, in the Philippines, the fact that China's land reclamation is taking place without any consultation with the Philippines' government, and is also causing huge environmental damage, is viewed as a serious problem. China's land reclamation activities across wide-ranging areas are clearly having a severe impact on the ecosystems of the South China Sea, and there are concerns that they may have irreversible effects on the ecosystems of sea turtles and birds.

Given this context, what should ASEAN do? At the 2015 ASEAN Foreign Ministers' Meeting, China's Minister of Foreign Affairs Wang Yi reiterated China's position that ASEAN is not an appropriate platform for discussing the South China Sea issue. However, this view is not accepted by the ASEAN countries, as articulated by Institute of Strategic and International Studies Malaysia senior fellow Tan Siew Mun, who raises the following three points.[21]

First, the South China Sea issue is an important security issue between four of the main ASEAN members and China, and it will continue to feature prominently in ASEAN discussions. Second, the South China Sea issue also concerns the interests of ASEAN states that are non-claimants (states that do not claim territorial rights in the South China Seas while denying the claims of other states), as the security of claimant states is not separate from that of non-claimant states. Third, the establishment of a legally binding code of conduct is important for ASEAN, which holds international law as a norm.

It would clearly be particularly grave for ASEAN if the norm of international law were obstructed. Mun emphasizes, "The Code of Conduct is more than a means to stabilize the stormy South China Sea disputes. More importantly, it serves to ingrain international law as a framework for ASEAN members to manage their relations among themselves and with external parties, especially the major powers." Mun further notes, "Beijing's pressure on ASEAN to remove the South China Sea issue from the regional discourse undermines the value of ASEAN and the ASEAN-led processes as avenues to manage differences through diplomatic channels."

US Relations with Southeast Asian Countries

Amid these developments, the US is reinforcing its relations with countries in the region and providing maritime capacity-building assistance. During the Shangri-La Dialogue at the end of May 2015, Secretary of Defense Carter presented the $425 million Southeast Asia Maritime Security Initiative to improve the maritime domain awareness of Southeast Asian countries. Under this initiative, joint training and equipment will be provided to the

Philippines, Vietnam, Thailand, Malaysia, and other Southeast Asian countries over several years starting from 2016, in order to boost maritime domain awareness.

In implementing such programs, the US views Japan as an important partner, and close cooperation between Japan and the US in the field of maritime security is expected.

The strengthening of relations between the US and Southeast Asian countries, especially the Philippines and Vietnam, is accelerating. An Enhanced Defense Cooperation Agreement (EDCA) was concluded between the US and the Philippines when President Obama visited Manila in April 2014, and an agreement was also reached on regular port calls by US warships in the Philippines. In March 2016, based on this EDCA, an agreement was concluded to allow the use of five Philippine air force bases on Palawan, Luzon, and other islands as bases for the US military. Meanwhile, the US plans to provide the Philippines with coastal radar equipment and training facilities. This assistance is expected to boost maritime domain awareness.

There have also been dramatic changes in US-Vietnam relations in recent years. Vietnam's supreme leader, General Secretary of the Communist Party of Vietnam Nguyen Phu Trong, met with President Obama at the White House on July 7, 2015. This was the first visit by a general secretary of the Communist Party of Vietnam since the end of the Vietnam War in 1975, and it indicated that the bilateral relations had entered a qualitatively different epoch.

Regarding the South China Sea dispute and China's activities, the United States–Vietnam Joint Vision Statement issued following the summit meeting declared, "Both countries are concerned about recent developments in the South China Sea that have increased tensions, eroded trust . . ."[22] The statement shows support, once again, for the peaceful resolution of disputes in accordance with international law, including UNCLOS.

Unlike the Philippines, which has a military alliance with the US, Vietnam has no military support in countering China. This is certainly the reason Vietnam is now turning toward defense cooperation with the US. In response, the US has already decided to provide Vietnam with $18 million to purchase a patrol boat, and in October 2014 the US announced that it would partially lift the prohibition on arms exports to Vietnam.

The above-mentioned Asia-Pacific Maritime Security Strategy report issued by the US Department of Defense explicitly stipulated four measures to be taken: strengthening US military capabilities in the maritime domain;

building the maritime capacity of allies and partners; using military diplomacy to reduce risk and boost transparency; and strengthening the development of a regional security architecture. This makes clear the reinforcement of US engagement in the Asia-Pacific region.

Japan's Increased Security Cooperation with the Philippines and Vietnam

Japan has fostered the maritime law-enforcement institutions of Southeast Asian nations and assisted their training for many years. Due to the tensions surrounding the South China Sea issue, efforts have been made to further strengthen such cooperation.

The deepening of maritime security cooperation based on the strategic partnership between Japan and the Philippines is a noteworthy example. President Benigno Aquino Jr. visited Japan in June 2015 as a guest of state. This was Aquino's sixth visit to Japan, and the close relations between President Aquino and Prime Minister Shinzō Abe are worth noting. During the visit, the two countries stressed their "strengthened strategic partnership" anew.

In the security field, the two countries agreed on four measures: the enhancement of security dialogues as contained in the Action Plan for Strengthening of the Strategic Partnership; the initiation of negotiations to conclude an agreement on the transfer of defense equipment and technology; the strengthening of cooperation between the relevant authorities of both countries on the participation of Japan Self-Defense Forces in disaster relief activities in the Philippines; and the expansion of bilateral and multilateral training and exercises for capacity building in areas including those covered by the "Memorandum on Defense Cooperation and Exchanges between the Department of National Defense and the Ministry of Defense."[23] The Action Plan also stressed that the provision of patrol vessels from Japan to reinforce the Philippines Coast Guard was progressing smoothly.

Defense exchange between Japan and the Philippines is becoming noticeably stronger and broader. In 2015 alone, Maritime Staff Office Chief of Staff Tomohisa Takei visited the Philippines in February, and Joint Staff Office Chief of Staff Katsutoshi Kawano visited in August to inspect the Pacific Partnership 2015 activities. At the end of June, the Japan Self-Defense Forces and the Philippine Army conducted their first joint search-and-rescue training exercise, using a Self-Defense Forces P-3C patrol aircraft and a Philippines air force base for maritime surveillance. Maritime Self-Defense Force ships and the Philippine Navy also conducted joint training in sea areas to the west of Manila. It should be noted, too, that the initial working-level discussions regarding defense equipment and technology cooperation between the Philippines and Japan are moving forward.

High-level exchanges between Japan and Vietnam based on the Japan-Vietnam strategic partnership are ongoing, including the March 2014 visit to Japan by President Truong Tan Sang as a guest of state. At that time, an agreement was reached to upgrade relations to an "Extensive Strategic Partnership for Peace and Prosperity in Asia."

Also, following the maritime dispute between China and Vietnam regarding China's installation of large-scale oil drilling equipment, an agreement was reached in August 2014 for Japan to grant patrol vessels to Vietnam in response to a request from the Vietnamese government. Six 500-ton-class Japanese vessels were provided: the Fisheries Agency vessel *Shōkaku* was provided to the Vietnam Coast Guard and the former Fisheries Agency fisheries patrol boat *Hayato* was provided to Vietnam Fisheries Resources Surveillance.

At the Japan-Vietnam summit held in Tokyo in July 2015, Prime Minister Nguyen Tan Dung made an additional request for new patrol boats. Furthermore, when Communist Party General Secretary Nguyen Phu Trong visited Japan in September, an agreement was reached on the provision of additional used vessels. Relations between Japan and Vietnam are expected to continue growing stronger.

Meanwhile, Vietnam has also emphasized its relations with China, which like Vietnam has a communist government. Trong visited China in April 2015 and discussed the oil drilling around the Paracel Islands in the South China Sea, which China implemented by force in May 2014. Regardless, China conducted exercises in that same sea area from July 22, which Vietnam protested as a serious violation of Vietnamese sovereignty. The fact is that the relations between Vietnam and China remain tense.

The South China Sea Issue as a Challenge to the Japan-US Alliance

Thus, the South China Sea dispute remains a grave issue for regional security, and also poses questions regarding the observance of UNCLOS and other international norms. In that sense, in the South China Sea we are directly facing a serious challenge to the international order itself. That being the case, the South China Sea dispute is certainly testing the true value of the

Japan-US alliance, which embodies such values as freedom and democracy in the international community.

For that very reason, the April 2015 joint statement of the Japan-US Security Consultative Committee reads, "The Ministers affirmed that the Japan-U.S. Alliance, strengthened by the new Guidelines and the two countries' respective security and defense policies, continues to serve as the cornerstone of peace and security in the Asia-Pacific region as well as a platform for promoting a more peaceful and stable international security environment."[24]

Accordingly, the joint statement emphasizes the following measures regarding the South China Sea problem: "continued close coordination on partner capacity building, particularly in Southeast Asia, including through the provision of coastal patrol vessels and other maritime security capacity building endeavors," and "expanded trilateral and multilateral cooperation, particularly with key partners such as the Republic of Korea (ROK) and Australia, as well as the Association of Southeast Asian Nations."

The South China Sea issue tests the true value of appropriate burden-sharing by both sides of the Japan-US alliance. At the same time, it calls into question whether Japan's solid position in the Japan-US alliance can be firmly maintained while upholding a balance between the importance of universal values in the international arena and Japan's national security interests.

Considering that the South China Sea issue encompasses both cooperation in nonmilitary fields—such as diplomatic engagement with Southeast Asian countries and assistance in strengthening maritime law-enforcement capabilities—and cooperation in military fields, including arms provision as well as information sharing and surveillance activities, Japan's role will become considerably broader. In this regard, it is especially necessary to note that—as represented by the "Three Warfares" (public opinion warfare, psychological warfare, and legal warfare)—China's expansion of power over the South China Sea is not limited to military force, but is also being carried out via such nonmilitary means as the use of China's Coast Guard and maritime militia.[25]

Consequently, Japan and the US should keep the need for such comprehensive policies in mind as they fulfill their respective duties. In particular, Japan's relations with Southeast Asian countries are deeper and broader than those the US has with them. Japan must understand these countries' needs and subtleties and take them into consideration as it carries out its duties.

From a political and security standpoint—especially that of recent years—there is a need for highly refined diplomatic and defense cooperation that considers the centrality of ASEAN, which is reinforcing regional integration, while still respecting the autonomy of each ASEAN member state. It is also important for Japan to remain aware that its involvement in the South China Sea issue will have a decisive impact on the future order of the region.

Note: This chapter presents the personal opinions of the author. It is a revised version (rewritten in April 2016), based on the latest information available at the time, of a paper originally published in Kaigai jijō *(Journal of world affairs), October 2015.*

1   US Department of Defense, The Asia-Pacific Maritime Security Strategy, August 2016, https://dod.defense.gov/Portals/1/Documents/pubs/NDAA%20A-P_Maritime_SecuritY_Strategy-08142015-1300-FINALFORMAT.PDF.

2   For example, in a verbal note from the Philippines Department of Foreign Affairs to the Chinese Embassy in the Philippines dated January 22, 2013, the Philippine government stated that it regards Subi Reef, Mischief Reef, and Gaven Reef as "low-tide elevations" and the rest of the seven reefs as "rocks." The Digital Gazetteer of the Spratly Islands does not consider any of the seven reefs to be "islands." Meanwhile, the Japanese government, in Diet deliberations to date, has stated that it may not have accurate knowledge regarding each of the landforms in the South China Sea and that it is difficult for Japan to make a definitive judgment.

3   Chinese Foreign Ministry Spokesperson Hua Chunying's regular press conference on June 30, 2015, https://www.fmprc.gov.cn/mfa_eng/xwfw_665399/s2510_665401/2511_665403/t1277267.shtml.

4   Admiral Harry B. Harris Jr., speech delivered at the Australian Strategic Policy Institute, March 31, 2015, https://www.cpf.navy.mil/leaders/harry-harris/speeches/2015/03/ASPI-Australia.pdf.

5   Chinese Foreign Ministry Spokesperson Hua Chunying's regular press conference on May 25, 2015, https://www.fmprc.gov.cn/mfa_eng/xwfw_665399/s2510_665401/t1266733.shtml.

6   Remarks by US Secretary of Defense Ash Carter, *PACOM News*, "U.S. Pacific Command Change of Command," May 28, 2015, https://www.pacom.mil/Media/News/Article/589963/us-pacific-command-change-of-command/.

7   US Department of Defense, "Remarks by Secretary Carter and Q&A at the Shangri-La Dialogue," Singapore, June 5, 2016, https://www.defense.gov/Newsroom/Transcripts/Transcript/Article/791472/remarks-by-secretary-carter-and-qa-at-the-shangri-la-dialogue-singapore/.

8   Leaders' Declaration, G7 Summit, June 7–8, 2015, https://www.mofa.go.jp/files/000084020.pdf.

9   Chinese Foreign Ministry Spokesperson Hua Chunying's regular press conference on May 28, 2015, https://www.fmprc.gov.cn/mfa_eng/xwfw_665399/s2510_665401/t1267839.shtml.

10 US Department of State, "The US-China Strategic & Economic Dialogue: Consultation on People-to-People Exchange," June 23, 2015, https://2009-2017.state.gov/secretary/remarks/2015/06/244120.htm

11 Chinese Foreign Ministry Spokesperson Hua Chunying's regular press conference on June 30, 2015, https://www.fmprc.gov.cn/mfa_eng/xwfw_665399/s2510_665401/2511_665403/t1277267.shtml.

12 See Center for Strategic and International Studies, Asia Maritime Transparency Initiative, "Airpower in the South China Sea," http://amti.csis.org/airstrips-scs/.

13 Elbridge Colby and Evan Braden Montgomery, "Changing tides in the South China Sea: Analysts who think China's artificial islands will not affect the US are too sanguine," *Wall Street Journal*, August 25, 2015, https://www.wsj.com/articles/changing-tides-in-south-china-sea-1440523898.

14 US Department of Defense, The Asia-Pacific Maritime Security Strategy, August 14, 2015, https://dod.defense.gov/Portals/1/Documents/pubs/NDAA%20A-P_Maritime_SecuritY_Strategy-08142015-1300-FINALFORMAT.PDF.

15 Colby and Montgomery, "Changing tides in the South China Sea."

16 See Yōji Kōda, *Chūgoku no Minami Shinakai kanshō umetate to Nihon no anzen hoshō* [China's land reclamation on South China Sea atolls and Japan's security], *Nippon.com*, July 28, 2015, http://www.nippon.com/ja/currents/d00190/.

17 David Brunnstorm and Andrea Shalal, "Exclusive: US sees new activity around South China Sea Shoal," Reuters, https://www.reuters.com/article/us-southchinasea-china-scarborough-exclu-idUSKCN0WK01B.

18 Bonnie S. Glaser and Peter A. Dutton, "The U.S. Navy's Freedom of Navigation Operation around Subi Reef: Deciphering U.S. Signaling," *The National Interest*, November 6, 2015.

19 See, for example, the June 30, 2015, *Sankei Shimbun* article at https://www.sankei.com/smp/world/news/150630/wor1506300039-s.html. According to this article, Chairman of the Chinese People's Political Consultative Conference Yu Shengsheng, who is ranked fourth in the Communist Party of China, met with former Japanese minister of home affairs Takeshi Noda of the Liberal Democratic Party on June 29 and expressed strong displeasure with intervention by the US and others, saying, "They make no mention of the various efforts to date by the parties involved with the dispute. Why do they speak only about China? Is this fair?"

20 TNI Moeldoko, "China's Dismaying New Claims in the South China Sea," *Wall Street Journal*, April 24, 2014, https://www.wsj.com/articles/moeldoko-chinas-dismaying-new-claims-in-the-south-china-sea-1398382003

21 Tang Siew Mun, "ASEAN Must Speak Up More on South China Sea Matters," *Straits Times*, August 13, 2015, http://www.straitstimes.com/opinion/asean-must-speak-up-more-on-south-china-sea-matters.

22 The White House, "United States–Vietnam Joint Vision Statement," July 7, 2015, https://obamawhitehouse.archives.gov/the-press-office/2015/07/07/united-states-%E2%80%93-vietnam-joint-vision-statement.

23 Ministry of Foreign Affairs of Japan, "Japan-Philippines Joint Declaration: A Strengthened Strategic Partnership for Advancing the Shared Principles and Goals of Peace, Security, and Growth in the Region and Beyond," June 4, 2015, https://www.mofa.go.jp/s_sa/sea2/ph/page4e_000280.html.

24 The Security Consultative Committee, "A Stronger Alliance for a Dynamic Security Environment: The New Guidelines for Japan-US Defense Cooperation," https://www.mofa.go.jp/mofaj/files/000078186.pdf.

25 Regarding China's "Three Warfares," see the paper by the author in *Sekaishi no gyakushū* [The revenge of world history] part I, chapter 7, (Kōdansha, 2016).

CHAPTER 8

The Defense Policies of ASEAN Countries: ASEAN-5 and Vietnam

Kōichi Satō

Professor, J. F. Oberlin University; Lecturer, Japan Maritime Self-Defense Force Staff College

Overview of the Issues

What are the diplomatic and military strategies and policies for the security and defense of the members of the Association of Southeast Asian Nations (ASEAN), and what is their future direction? The ASEAN-5 countries (Indonesia, Malaysia, the Philippines, Singapore, and Thailand), which originally comprised ASEAN when it was established in 1967, and Vietnam, which joined ASEAN in 1995, are all small nations that lack the military, economic, and strategic power to independently affect Japan, the United States, China, or other major powers outside of the region. Any such strategies or policies they do have are geared toward survival, and characterized by total defense and a certain ambiguity as seen by countries outside the region. From a military standpoint, the ASEAN nations have adopted such policies for several reasons. First, they have a history of being continually interfered with by the great powers. Second, almost all the ASEAN countries perceive diverse and multilayered threats. Third, most ASEAN countries face budgetary limitations on their military, as well as military and diplomatic weakness as they make the transition from public security forces to defense forces. Fourth, because ASEAN must remain open to most major countries outside the region and reflect the greatest common denominator among its member states, it pursues conference diplomacy as an organization.

In the following sections, I will analyze the defense policies of these ASEAN countries, which are affected by the first three factors,[1] and then separately address the fourth factor, which is ASEAN conference diplomacy. I will conclude with a few observations regarding the future direction of ASEAN countries' defense and diplomacy.

Factors Affecting ASEAN Countries' Defense Policies

History of Interference by Major Powers from outside the Region

In premodern times, the countries of Southeast Asia had a "mandala" or "circles of states" structure whereby countries encompassed small regional kingdoms with poorly defined borders. Their residents included overseas Chinese and were divided into multiple groups by religion and language. These became the respective ethnic groups as these countries modernized and formed pluralistic societies. Their residents were not homogenous, as these individual ethnic groups were socially distant from one another in terms of language, religion, cultural values, historical background, genetics, and other characteristics, and this became an obstacle in the process of nation building. At times, groups of residents formed movements to break away from their rulers, and at times they changed affiliations as the relative power of the small bordering kingdoms shifted.

Southeast Asia has long been known for its spices. Following colonization, it became a production region for goods and resources essential for trade and the conduct of war, such as rubber, rice, sugar, coffee, bananas, palm oil, and other agricultural products, along with iron, zinc, copper, gold, nickel, bauxite, limestone, and other minerals, and petroleum, coal, natural gas, and other fossil-fuel resources. Southeast Asia is also strategically important as a transit point connecting East and West through the Strait of Malacca, the Sunda Strait, and the Lombok Strait, which are sea-lane choke points. Control of this region has been extremely important for major powers outside the region aiming at global hegemony ever since the seventeenth century, when the competition over colonization began.

As a result, by the time of the Second World War all the countries of Southeast Asia except Thailand had been made into Western colonies. In exchange for the abolition of extraterritorial rights, Thailand ceded its southern states of Kelantan, Terengganu, Kedah, and Perlis to British Malaya in the Anglo-Siamese Treaty of 1909. Starting in the nineteenth century, many migrant workers from China and India came to British Malaya and Singapore. During the Second World War, all of Southeast Asia was occupied by the Japanese army and placed under its military administration, except for

Thailand, which became a Japanese ally, and French Indochina, which was under the Vichy regime collaborating with Nazi Germany.

The countries of Southeast Asia all followed a path to independence after the end of the war. During the Cold War, however, Vietnam was split: North Vietnam aligned with the East (China and the USSR) and South Vietnam with the West (France and subsequently the US). Fighting continued until the end of the Vietnam War in 1975. During those years, the ASEAN-5 nations, which all had domestic Chinese-affiliated communist guerrilla groups, depended on the West for their security. In 1968, however, the British government declared the withdrawal of all British forces east of Suez, and in the 1969 Guam Doctrine, the US indicated its intention to withdraw from the Vietnam War. North Vietnam, which had enjoyed the support of China and the USSR, had to grapple with the US-China reconciliation in 1972, prior to the end of the Vietnam War. The unified Vietnam that formed in 1975 at the end of the Vietnam War was dependent on the USSR. Vietnam fought against the government of Democratic Kampuchea (Cambodia), which was backed by China, from 1979 through 1991, and also fought against China in the 1979 Sino-Vietnamese War, in which China launched a punitive attack on Vietnam at the Vietnamese-Chinese border.

In this way, the present ASEAN countries were manipulated by the major powers from the colonial era through the Second World War, and then from the Cold War era to the post–Cold War era. This has resulted in a deep-seated distrust of the major powers outside the region. Furthermore, the vague national boundaries among the kingdoms of the premodern era do not match the national boundaries set from the nineteenth century by the colonial powers, which were great powers from outside the region; in some cases the same ethnic groups live across national boundaries. Consequently, the ASEAN counties have national boundary disputes among themselves based on irredentism (policies advocating the restoration of former territory).

Diverse and Multilayered Threats

As a result of the historical circumstances described above, the threats perceived by each country that influence defense policy are diverse and multilayered, comprising threats from outside the region, threats from neighboring countries within the region, and domestic threats. For example, Singapore, the smallest ASEAN country, which has a majority population of ethnic Chinese and a minority population of Malay people, has been threatened by China, Japan, Russia (the USSR), India, and other countries outside the region. Domestically, it has experienced military confrontation and separation and independence from the neighboring countries of Indonesia and Malaysia, which have large numbers of Malay people. Moreover, because Singapore must rely on those very countries for its drinking water and fresh foods, it works toward coexistence despite feeling threatened.

Such factors affect other ASEAN countries as well. Indonesia, the largest country in ASEAN, has had border and boundary line disputes on land and at sea with both Malaysia and the Philippines, and has felt strongly threatened by China—a major power outside the region—ever since the 30 September Movement, an attempted coup in 1965. China's recent delineation of a U-shaped line on the map of the South China Sea in connection with the exclusive economic zone (EEZ) of the Natuna Islands has added to Indonesia's insecurity. Indonesia has also faced domestic challenges from separatist movements in Aceh, Papua, and East Timor and from its ethnic Chinese residents.

Malaysia is involved in disputes in the South China Sea with non-ASEAN parties—namely, China and Taiwan—and with other ASEAN countries, including the Philippines, Vietnam, and Brunei. Moreover, within the ASEAN region, it has issues regarding national borders and maritime boundary lines (territorial seas, EEZs, the continental shelf) with Brunei, Indonesia, the Philippines, Singapore, Thailand, and Vietnam. On the domestic front, there was a conflict between ethnic Malays and ethnic Chinese in May 1969 that led to the establishment of the Bumiputra policy favoring ethnic Malays; this strife is still ongoing.

The Philippines has a territorial issue with Malaysia regarding the state of Sabah (formerly North Borneo), and feels strongly threatened by China regarding possession of the Spratly Islands (called the Nansha Islands by China) and the Macclesfield Bank. The Philippines also has a dispute with Taiwan regarding the boundary between their EEZs. Domestically, it has substantial problems with Muslims in the south, and it still faces the problem of the communist New People's Army as well.

Thailand felt strongly threatened by communist Vietnam during the Vietnam War and during the Cambodian Civil War, and was also wary of the Heng Samrin regime installed in Cambodia with Vietnamese backing. Domestically, Thailand faces a longstanding Malay separatist movement in the south. During the Vietnam War, North Vietnam naturally viewed Thailand, where US armed forces were stationed, as an enemy; however, in January 1974 the South Vietnamese navy lost a battle over the Paracel Islands with China's People's Liberation Army (PLA) Navy. After its reunification,

Vietnam was in conflict with China over territorial boundaries from the start of the Sino-Vietnamese War in 1979 until a settlement was reached in November 1991 (the boundary was demarcated in 1999). Vietnam and China exchanged fire in the seas near the Spratly Islands in March 1988, and minor clashes continued in the Gulf of Tonkin as well until that boundary was demarcated in 2000. Vietnam is still in confrontation with China regarding both the Spratly Islands and the Paracel Islands in the South China Sea.

Military Readiness in the Transition Period

Most ASEAN countries have pluralistic societies comprising multiple ethnic groups, which include overseas Chinese. They also have disputes with neighboring countries regarding the affiliations of ethnic groups and land boundaries. Moreover, from the 1950s through the 1980s, almost all the ASEAN countries had problems with Chinese-affiliated communist guerilla groups inside their countries. The ASEAN states, which are mostly developing nations that gained independence after the Second World War, have limited defense budgets. With the exception of Singapore's armed forces since the 1980s, the military forces in each country do not comprise fully equipped armies for national defense in the event of war with a foreign state. Rather, they are lightly armed public security forces intended to protect the country's government and systems from internal security problems.

The economic development of ASEAN countries progressed with an influx of foreign capital investment starting in the late 1980s. Since 1988, when China's PLA Navy began making active forays into the South China Sea, there have been calls for ASEAN countries to upgrade their naval and air forces. These efforts were delayed somewhat by the 1997–1998 Asian financial crisis, but are now continuing. While the change is slow, the ASEAN nations are in a transitional state of upgrading their military from public-security forces to defense forces.

The status of naval personnel and equipment in each country is presented in table 1. Compared with Japan, these are all small-scale forces with annual spending ranging from 4.3 percent to 16.3 percent of Japan's total defense budget. While some of these countries have many vessels, these are almost all coastal patrol boats with a displacement under 1,000 tons; even their main surface combat craft are mostly frigate-class vessels of less than 4,000 tons. The navies of most ASEAN countries have yet to become blue-water navies that can operate on the open sea; they are in various stages of transition from green-water navies focused on coastal security.

Table 1: Naval Personnel and Equipment of ASEAN Countries (2014)

Country	Defense budget (US $ millions)	Naval personnel (thousands)	Ships	Submarines	Major surface combat vessels	Aircraft
Brunei	405	0.74	13			20
Cambodia	346	2.8	4			
Indonesia	7,740	45	203	2	6 (frigates)	65
Malaysia	4,830	17.9	49	2	2 (frigates)	16
Myanmar	1,880	12.2	117		4 (frigates)	
Philippines	2,590	22	78		3 (frigates)	13
Singapore	9,680	4.5	72	5	6 (frigates)	41
Thailand	5,500	63	168		10 (1 light aircraft carrier)	76
Vietnam	3,330	16	139	4	7 (frigates)	2
East Timor	64	0.25	7			
Japan	59,400	45.8	141	16	47 (41 escort vessels)	289
China	102,000	217	891	63	78 (1 aircraft carrier)	624
USA	676,700	312.6	485	72	118 (10 aircraft carriers)	2,807
Taiwan	10,300	46.5	287	4	26 (4 destroyers)	66

Source: *Sekai no kaigun 2014–2015* [Navies of the world 2014–2015] (Kaijinsha, 2014).

The Defense Policies of the ASEAN-5 Countries and Vietnam

This section presents the main elements of the national defense policies and military equipment upgrades of the ASEAN-5 and Vietnam, the countries discussed in this paper. Many of these countries have developed their national defense policies around a total defense concept similar to the Japanese concept of comprehensive security.[2] Because their brief is to maintain the government or regime in addition to dealing with external threats (which are not explicit in some cases), these defense policies also address internal threats. Generally speaking, priorities change with the advance of democratization, which represents a key turning point in the approach to national defense policy.

Indonesia

The core concept of Indonesia's national defense policy is "national resilience" (*ketahanan nasional*). This concept was presented as an alternative by President Suharto when the Zone of Peace, Freedom, and Neutrality was proposed by Malaysia as ASEAN's common goal in 1971. The objectives of national resilience are, domestically, to be capable of securing necessary social change while maintaining the national identity with all its fragilities and, externally, to be able to deal with all threats from outside the region, both declared and undeclared. National resilience therefore includes reinforcing all the constituent factors for the complete development of the people. It encompasses ideological, political, economic, social, cultural, and military factors, and is essentially the same as the concept of total defense.

A national defense policy report published in 1995 puts forth two other central concepts in Indonesia's defense policy: the "archipelagic principle" (*wawasan nusantara*) of national unity, and the "dual functions" (*dwifungsi*) of the Indonesian national armed forces: the defense/security function and the sociopolitical function.[3] The significance of the archipelagic principle is obvious, considering the regional rebellions in Aceh and East Timor (the insurgency in Aceh ended, and East Timor became independent in 2002), and it will probably continue to be emphasized. The sociopolitical role of the armed forces' dual functions was abolished along with the military's bloc of seats in the parliament with the passage of the National Defense Law in 2002, when democratization began following the resignation of President Suharto in 1998.

The national defense issues identified by Indonesia are maritime security, including the South China Sea dispute; terrorism; denuclearization, including the Southeast Asian Nuclear-Weapon-Free Zone Treaty; transnational crime (narcotics, human trafficking, armed robbery at sea); and humanitarian assistance and disaster relief. As for the South China Sea dispute, China—which has its eyes on the Natuna Islands EEZ—is positioned as the greatest threat in the ASEAN Regional Forum (ARF) Annual Security Outlook 2013,[4] even though it is not explicitly mentioned by name. Islamic extremists engaged in terrorism are apparently the greatest domestic threat. The Indonesian government has support from Nahdlatul Ulama, Indonesia's largest Islamic organization, in promoting the moderation of Islam. Additionally, while the issue is not mentioned at all in the Annual Security Outlook, Indonesia has a dispute with Malaysia regarding the Ambalat block (the sea area around Sipadan and the Ligitan Islands offshore Borneo, where there is a natural gas field) that has been heating up in recent years; there are also issues with the treatment of migrant workers. At the East Asian summit on November 13, 2014, President Joko Widodo, who took office in October 2014, announced the pillars of a new five-item maritime policy, "Indonesia's Global Maritime Fulcrum"; these include stronger prosecution of illegal fishing and maritime defense. Attention will be focused on the future development of this policy.

The upgrading of defense equipment is limited because the government of Indonesia follows the "Minimum Essential Force" concept. As of 2014, the Indonesian navy plans to deploy twelve submarines; it has already signed a contract to purchase two from the Daewoo Shipbuilding & Engineering Company of South Korea. There is also a plan for the domestic production by 2018 of a Korean Chang Bogo–class submarine (1,306 tons, Germany's 209/1200 model produced under license by South Korea). The Indonesian navy deployed two Bung Tomo–class corvettes (2,300 tons) manufactured in the UK to the Belawan Naval Base in northern Sumatra on September 20, 2014. Meanwhile, the Indonesian air force is scheduled to receive twenty-four F-16 fighters with improved functions (F-16C/D) from the US. The Indonesian marine police also received three 27-meter patrol boats from Japan in 2007 (similar patrol boats in Japan are around 68 tons). In addition, before former president Susilo Bambang Yudhoyono retired, he increased the FY 2015 defense budget by 14 percent from the previous year to around $8.1 billion. The main focus of Indonesia's military cooperation with major powers outside the region is with the US, including ongoing joint exercises and the provision of arms (see tables 2 and 3).

Malaysia

The longstanding core concepts of Malaysia's national defense policy are the "counterinsurgency" used in the battle against Communist Party of Malaya guerrillas and "security and development" (*kesban*, a combination of the two Malay words *keselamatan* [security] and *pembangunan* [development]). The term "total defense" (*hanruh*) is presented in the ASEAN Regional Forum's Annual Security Outlook 2013 as follows.

> Total and integrated defence involves many government agencies, the private sector, NGOs and the citizenry in all circumstances. National defence is not the sole responsibility of the MAF [Malaysian Armed Forces] but the responsibility of all levels of society. All should know the role and contribution that they could play in times of disaster and conflict. National defense has to be based on self-confidence and not depending on external parties. Within this context patriotism and nationalism among Malaysians always need to be nurtured and with the realization that national prosperity and peace override individual needs and political ideology.[5]

The national defense issues identified by Malaysia are terrorism, border security, denuclearization (nonproliferation, Southeast Asian Nuclear-Weapon-Free Zone), transnational crime (narcotics, human trafficking, cybercrime), humanitarian aid and disaster relief, and maritime security (piracy). On the domestic front, former deputy prime minister Anwar Ibrahim, from the opposition party, has been charged and found guilty of sodomy; this may lead to domestic political instability.

Among these issues, Malaysia is prioritizing terrorism countermeasures and maritime security. Regarding the former, according to the ASEAN Regional Forum's Annual Security Outlook 2013, Malaysia established the Southeast Asia Regional Centre for Counter-Terrorism in July 2003 to contain Islamic extremist activities. It is also implementing comprehensive measures against money laundering and promoting dialogue among different religions. Regarding piracy, the Annual Security Outlook 2013 states that Malaysia is emphasizing the security of the Strait of Malacca and areas offshore Sabah; it introduces the trilateral Malacca Strait coordinated patrol MALSINDO and the "Eyes in the Sky" surveillance program, and also mentions the Malaysian Maritime Enforcement Agency, which was established in 2004. China's advance into the South China Sea, however, is not addressed. The advance of the PLA Navy into the sea area around James Shoal at the southern edge of the Spratly Islands in recent years could split Malaysia's national territory into east and west on either side of the South China Sea. This is a troublesome issue for the administration of Najib Razak, which is taking care not to irritate China.

As for the upgrading of military equipment, training has begun using two Scorpène-class submarines (1,755 tons) purchased from France. In light of the South China Sea dispute and the border defense of Sabah, Malaysia has also decided to create a marine corps. There are plans to build six 3,000-ton-class littoral combat ships domestically, with the first ship scheduled to be commissioned by 2019. Malaysia's military cooperation with major powers outside the region mostly comprises armaments provision arrangements and military exercises with the UK, its former colonial power, as well as engagement in the UK-centered Five Power Defense Arrangements since 1971. Malaysia has participated in few joint military exercises with the US, aside from taking part in the US-Thai Cobra Gold joint multilateral military exercise since 2011. It has also received cooperation from India in submarine detection exercises using sonar.

The Philippines

The Philippines' national defense policy uses a "total defense" approach. The 1996 defense white paper explains this as follows. Defense policy does not only envisage the application of armed force to meet a threat; it also requires the organization and mobilization of all elements of national infrastructure, population and all resources should circumstances demand.[6] The term "total defense" does not appear in the ASEAN Regional Forum's 2013 Annual Security Outlook, but the Philippines' section on countering terrorism and transnational crime uses similar expressions: "whole-of-government and whole-of-nation approach" and "comprehensive approach."

The national defense issues identified by the Philippines are the South China Sea dispute; the framework agreement with the Moro Islamic Liberation Front (MILF) in Mindanao; denuclearization (nonproliferation and the Southeast Asian Nuclear-Weapon-Free Zone), and in relation to that, the Korean Peninsula problem; terrorism and transnational crime (measures against terrorism, chemical, biological, and nuclear weapons, money-laundering, and human trafficking); humanitarian aid and disaster relief (notably in the wake of typhoons); and maritime security (freedom and safety of navigation, piracy countermeasures, conservation of the marine environment). Among these, the Philippines prioritizes the issues of the South China Sea dispute, the framework agreement with the MILF, and anti-terrorism, along with the Korean Peninsula problem related to denuclearization. With respect to the South China Sea, the Philippines is protesting the frequent intrusion of Chinese naval, coast guard, and fishing vessels into waters around the Spratly Islands (called Kapuluan ng Kalayaan by the Philippines and the Nansha Islands by the Chinese) and the Scarborough Shoal (called Huangyan Dao by the Chinese) in the Macclesfield Bank (the Zhongsha Islands in Chinese). To this end, it has submitted a query to the International Court of Arbitration requesting judgment regarding the propriety of a claim by a party to the dispute in this sea area (while not mentioned by name, this refers to territory within the "nine-dash line" that China has drawn in the South China Sea). Domestically, the Philippines has entered a reconciliation process with the MILF, and Islamic extremist terrorism has subsided, but these problems require continued attention. Meanwhile, while not explicitly stated, the reason for the Philippines' emphasis on the Korean Peninsula problem in connection with denuclearization is North Korea's provocative stance toward South Korea, which is one of the main countries where migrant laborers from the Philippines work overseas.

To upgrade its military equipment, the Philippines is reportedly considering the purchase of a third Hamilton-class cutter (3,353 tons) from the US, and is scheduled to receive ten 40-meter-class patrol vessels (around 200 tons) in aid from Japan. There is a rumor in other ASEAN countries about the purchase of submarines by the Philippines, but there is no information about that at present. As for military cooperation with major powers outside the region, the Philippines has maintained close ties with the US, its former colonial power, ever since the Mutual Defense Treaty between the Republic of the Philippines and the United States of America was concluded in August 1951 (see table 3). While US military forces withdrew from the Philippines in 1991, they have been received under a Visiting Forces Agreement since 1999. Also, the Philippine navy held its first joint exercises with Japan Maritime Self-Defense Force vessels and antisubmarine patrol aircraft in May and June 2015.

Singapore

The core concept of Singapore's national defense policy is "Total Defence." This concept was formulated in 1984 under former Prime Minister Goh Chok Tong, who was first deputy prime minister and minister for defense at that time. Singapore was the first ASEAN country to use the term "total defense," and its approach is the most refined among the six countries addressed in this chapter.

> The concept of Total Defence aims to achieve a seamless and integrated all-round capability to defend our national interests. Consisting of six elements—Military Defence, Civil Defence, Economic Defence, Social Defence, Digital Defence and Psychological Defence—it unites and commits all sectors of society to the defence of Singapore. Military Defence: It is about building a strong and formidable defence force that makes potential aggressors think twice before attacking us. That is deterrence at its best. And if that fails, we must be able to defend ourselves when attacked. Civil Defence: Singaporeans—whether at the individual, organization or community level—must pitch in to help and be able to take care of themselves. We can be alert to signs of threats and, when a crisis occurs, we can be effective first responders, helping one another regardless of race, religion, or self-interest. . . . All this helps us bounce back quickly as one people, confident and strong. This is what a strong Civil Defence means. Economic Defence: It is

about strengthening the competitiveness and attractiveness of Singapore's economy so that we are special and relevant to the world. Economic Defence is also about keeping our economy strong and resilient, enabling it to carry on and recover quickly should we be confronted by any challenge or crisis in the future, such as a global downturn or economic strangulation that could shake investor confidence in Singapore. Social Defence: In a multiracial, multi-religious and multi-cultural society like Singapore, peace and progress is possible only if Singaporeans of all races and religious live together in harmony and look out for one another. It requires constant effort to build understanding and trust among different communities and to ensure that potential sources of misunderstanding and insensitivity are nipped in the bud quickly. This is Social Defence. Digital Defence: While the digital revolution presents opportunities for Singapore, it also makes us vulnerable to threats from the digital domain. We need to be able to respond to cyberattacks that target our networks and infrastructure, as well as threats that can be perpetrated through the digital domain such as fake news and deliberate online falsehoods. . . . We must build robust defences and have effective recovery plans to remain resilient even when things go wrong. This is what a strong Digital Defence means. Psychological Defence: Singapore's ability to overcome threats and challenges that come our way depends on the collective will of our people to defend our way of life, the resolve to stand up for Singapore when pressured by forces that undermine our national interests, and the fighting spirit to press on and overcome crisis together. This is Psychological Defence.[7]

The national defense issues identified by Singapore include the following: the direction of US-China relations; the Korean Peninsula problem; the South China Sea dispute; the Middle East problem, which has political, economic, and personal (Muslim) links to Southeast Asia; denuclearization; nonproliferation, arms control, and arms reduction of weapons of mass destruction; terrorism; transnational crime (piracy, cybercrime, human trafficking); humanitarian aid and disaster relief; and maritime security in general (including piracy). Because Singapore is a fragile city-state without a hinterland, all of these issues are important. Still, in recent years Singapore has given special emphasis to the South China Sea dispute and maritime security in general, and to counterterrorism, which also involves the Middle East problem. Many of these issues are maritime issues, because Singapore is a trading nation that emphasizes the security of sea lanes and defines itself as a maritime state. However, the inclusion of the South China Sea dispute and the concern about the direction of US-China relations indicate that the focus of the problems is China, although that is not explicitly stated. Singapore also exercises extreme caution in addressing the piracy problem, because it requires the cooperation of Indonesia and Malaysia, with which Singapore has had disputes in the past in the Strait of Malacca and the Singapore Strait. Underlying the priority of counterterrorism, which involves the Middle East problem, is the concern that Islamic extremism in the Middle East could influence the Muslims who make up around 40 percent of the population of the ASEAN countries. In fact, members of Jemaah Islamiyah, which collaborated with the Taliban of Afghanistan, were arrested in 2003. Singapore is addressing this issue in collaboration with the US, of course, and with Indonesia and Malaysia.

With respect to military upgrades, Singapore has five used submarines: two Swedish Västergötland-class vessels (1,626 tons, with air-independent propulsion systems) and three Sjöormen-class vessels (1,229 tons). It has also signed a contract to purchase two new submarines with air-independent propulsion systems from the German company ThyssenKrupp AG. The three branches of the Singapore armed forces are all well equipped, and also conduct thoroughgoing research on state-of-the-art weaponry. As for military cooperation with major powers outside the region, in addition to engaging in the Five Power Defense Arrangements centered on the UK, its former colonial power, Singapore has granted access to US armed forces aircraft and vessels. It actively participates in joint military exercises with the US and carries out joint exercises with India and China, and is engaged in military technology cooperation with France.

Thailand

The core concept of Thailand's national defense policy is "total defense strategy." This concept was made clear in the national defense policy reports, The Defence of Thailand, published in 1994 and 1996, as follows.

> Total Defence Strategy is a defence system aimed at deterrence, protection and responding to enemy operations by the planned integration of all available forces, including main forces, local forces and citizens, with continuous political, economic, socio-psychological and military support, to deal with conflicts at every level. The Total Defence Strat-

egy combines the systems of military Strategic Defence, Area Defence and Internal Defence against both domestic and external threats into a complete single system which can assist in coordinating socio-economic development with national security. Development in the border area is especially useful for border defence.[8]

Thailand also emphasizes the importance of protecting the monarchy, because of the devotion shown by the royal family to the welfare of the people when various political ideologies threatened the political system. At that time the king and queen took the initiative to deal with regional poverty and brought about economic improvements and popular solidarity, which led to victory over the Communist Party of Thailand.

The national defense issues identified by Thailand in the above-mentioned defense policy reports, which are still emphasized in recent years, include disputes with Cambodia and Myanmar regarding national boundaries and minority peoples, the South China Sea dispute, illegal migrants and human trafficking, smuggling, and drug dealing. The problem of Malay separatism is a long-standing problem for Thailand that has grown greater in recent years. Among these issues, Thailand is apparently prioritizing the territorial rights issue regarding the Temple of Preah Vihear and surrounding land at the border with Cambodia, where there are occasional skirmishes between border security forces, and the Malay separatist issue in the three southern provinces of Yala, Patani, and Narathiwat. The Malay separatists in the three southern provinces are reportedly receiving support from the Malaysian state of Kelantan, whose residents speak the same Malay dialect (Jawi) as the Malays in southern Thailand. Regarding the South China Sea dispute, Thailand exercises caution because it is not a party to the dispute. It is also wary of the opposition between China, which is Thailand's largest trading partner, and the US, with which Thailand maintains strong military ties. An issue related to the South China Sea, however, is Thailand's dispute with Indonesia regarding fishing in the seas around the Natuna Islands.

Thailand's nontraditional security issues include the aftermath of the December 26, 2004, tsunami that struck southern Thailand and caused 8,000 deaths, as well as the 2011 floods, which caused massive damage. The other problem presently stressed in Thailand, though it is not discussed openly, is the conflict between the "Red Shirts"—supporters of the administrations of former prime minister Thaksin Shinawatra (Thai Rak Thai Party), who was democratically elected and removed in a coup d'état, and of his younger sister, former prime minster Yingluck Shinawatra (Pheu Thai Party)—and the "Yellow Shirts," who are supporters of former prime minister Abhisit Vejiajiva (Democrat Party), the army and conservatives who launched the coup, and the royalists.

With respect to the upgrading of military equipment, Thailand is considering the purchase of submarines (there was a report in July 2015 that a decision had been made to purchase a Chinese submarine). As for military cooperation with major powers outside the region, Thailand has maintained its closest ties with the US since the Vietnam War era, but is also conducting recurring navy and army drills with China.

Vietnam

The core concept of Vietnam's national defense policy, "all-people national defense," was introduced in the 1998 national defense white paper "Vietnam: Consolidating National Defence Safeguarding the Homeland." The contents include the following.

> In the all-people's national Defence, the people have a decisive role. . . . "Nothing is more precious than independence and freedom." . . . A posture of "all-people's national Defence" means that all the people preserve the country; and that of people's security implies safeguarding security by the whole people. All the activities of the country aim at achieving the objective of a prosperous people, a strong country and an equitable and civilized society, including the objective of creating an all-round strength of the all-people's national Defence of which the most important task is to create potential strength in the politico-spiritual, economic, scientific, technological and military aspects. The state also advocates building provinces (cities) into strong Defence zones as required. Each Defence zone should be capable of being independent, self-reliant, and self-resilient, of regularly building the whole people's aggregate strength, of firmly defending the locality in the common posture of the whole country. Should wars occur, such a zone can be capable of taking initiative in fighting the enemies at the very beginning of attacking.[9]

This approach suggests a kind of scorched-earth strategy of drawing the enemy into Vietnam's own territory. The lessons from past wars against the US and against China can be seen in this strategy, and the spread of defense zones across maritime areas, islands, and territorial airspace, while not explicitly stated, hint at China as a hypothetical enemy disputing land and sea borders. Vietnam's armed forces are unique in that they comprise regular forces—which include the Vietnam People's Ground Force, the Vietnam People's Navy, and the Vietnam People's Air Force—as well as local forces, the Vietnam Border Defense Force, the Vietnam Civil Defense Force, and the militia.

The national defense issues identified by Vietnam in the above-mentioned white paper, which are still considered important in recent years, include the South China Sea (in Vietnam, this is called the "East Sea") dispute, human rights and democratization movements and political instability (i.e., the existence of antigovernment movements) inside Vietnam, illegal immigrants, illegal fishing, human trafficking, and the smuggling of weapons and drugs. In the South China Sea dispute, Vietnam is disputing the sovereignty of the Spratly Islands (Truong Sa in Vietnamese) and the Paracel Islands (Hoang Sa in Vietnamese; the Xisha Islands in Chinese) with China. From May through July 2014, China conducted resource exploration in sea areas near the Paracel Islands, and the dispute continued at sea. From July through August 2019, China conducted resource exploration in sea areas of the Spratly Islands, as well as Vanguard Bank. Vietnam also has many problems with illegal fishing by China in the seas around the Paracel Islands. Vietnam shares borders with China in three locations: on land, in the Gulf of Tonkin, and in the South China Sea. (The land border was demarcated in December 1999 and the Gulf of Tonkin border in December 2000.) Dealing with conflicts individually so they will not ignite disputes in other border areas and stabilizing relations with China are the highest priorities for Vietnam.

Regarding military equipment upgrades, Vietnam has signed a contract to purchase six Kilo-class submarines (3,125 tons) from Russia, all to be delivered by 2017. Vietnam is also scheduled to receive six used patrol vessels (500 tons or more) in aid from the Japanese government. As for military cooperation with major powers outside the region, Vietnam's "Three Nos" policy—no military alliances with foreign countries, no foreign military bases on Vietnamese territory, and no reliance on any country to fight against another—preclude it from forming military alliances. Recently, however, Vietnam has purchased arms from Russia, its former ally, and begun naval vessel repairs and medical cooperation with the US. Also, in addition to receiving used vessels from Japan, Vietnam has received a $100 million export credit from India; there is speculation that this will be used to purchase Brahmos anti-ship cruise missiles manufactured in India.

Table 2: Joint Military Exercises and Training Conducted by China and ASEAN Countries in Recent Years

Year/month/day(s)	Exercise (code name)	Implementation area
2005/12	China-Thailand joint naval exercise (China-Thailand Friendship 2005)	Siam Bay, Thailand
2007	China-Thailand joint special troops exercise (Strike-2007)	Guangdong Province, China
2008	China-Thailand special troops exercise (Strike-2008)	Chiangmai, Thailand
2009	China-Singapore joint special troops training (Cooperation 2009)	Guilin, Guangxi Province, China
2009	China-Singapore joint naval exercise (no code name)	Location unknown
2010/10	China-Thailand special troops training (Strike-2010)	Guilin, Guangxi Province, China
2010/10	China-Thailand joint marine corps training (Blue Strike 2010)	Sattahip, Thailand
2010/11	China-Singapore joint special troops training (Cooperation 2010)	Singapore
2010	China-Vietnam joint naval search and rescue training (no code name)	Location unknown
2011/6/17	China-Indonesia joint special troops airborne exercise (Sharp Knife 2011)	Bandung, Indonesia
2011/6/21	China-Vietnam joint naval patrol (no code name); 11th since 2005	Gulf of Tonkin
2012/5	China-Thailand joint marine training (Blue Strike 2012)	Zhanjiang, Guangdong Province, China
2012/6	China-Indonesia joint special troops airborne exercise (Sharp Knife 2012)	Shandong Province, China
2013/6/23	China-Vietnam joint naval patrol (no code name); 15th since 2005	Gulf of Tonkin
2013/11	China-Indonesia joint special troops airborne exercise (Sharp Knife 2013)	Bandung, Indonesia
2013/12	China-Thailand joint special troops training (Strike 2013)	Lopburi, Thailand
2014/11/1–9	China-Singapore joint army exercise (Cooperation 2014)	Nanjing, China
2015/5/25	China-Singapore joint naval exercise (Maritime Cooperation); first time	South China Sea off the east coast of the Malay Peninsula

Sources: China Department of Defense website; the *China Daily* website; Xinhua News Agency; *Dangdai haijun* [Modern navy]; the Singapore National Defense Force journal *Pioneer*; the *Straits Times*; the *Bangkok Post* website; VietNamNet website; Annual Report to Congress by the Office of the Secretary of Defense; Military and Security Developments Involving the People's Republic of China 2014; US Department of Defense website.

Table 3: Joint Military Exercises and Trainings Conducted by the US, Japan, Australia, and ASEAN Countries in Recent Years

Year/month/ day(s)	Exercise (code name) Participating countries	Implementation area
2011/7	US-Vietnam naval medical/dental exchange	Da Nang, Vietnam
2011/5–10	US-Bangladesh/ASEAN bilateral joint naval exercise (Carat); Bangladesh, Brunei, Cambodia, Indonesia, Malaysia, Philippines, Singapore, and Thailand	
2011/7	US-Australia joint naval training	Off Brunei, South China Sea
2011/8/23	US Navy cargo ammunition supply ship repaired at a Vietnamese shipyard for the first time since the Vietnam War	Cam Ranh Bay, Vietnam
2011/10/26	US Air Force transport aircraft C-17 landed at Noi Bai International Airport	Hanoi, Vietnam
2012/2/8–17	US-Thailand tri-service joint exercise (Cobra Gold); multinational joint exercise by Thailand, Singapore, Indonesia, Malaysia, Japan, South Korea and other countries, focused on humanitarian aid, peace cooperation, interoperability improvement, etc.; held annually since 1982	Chonburi, Thailand, and other locations
2012/3/12–23	US-Singapore-Thailand joint air force exercise (COPE Tiger); held annually since 1994, first part in December 2011 in Singapore	Korat, Thailand
2012/4/17–27	US-Philippines combined army and navy military exercise (Balikatan); annual project since 1991 that includes humanitarian aid, disaster management, and school construction along with port and base recovery exercises, etc.	Palawan, the Philippines
2012/4/23–27	US-Vietnam joint naval exchange; dredging and disaster training	Da Nang, Vietnam
2012/5–7	US-ASEAN bilateral joint naval exercise (Carat), held annually, joined by the coast guard forces; Thailand, Indonesia, the Philippines, Malaysia, Singapore, Brunei, and East Timor (participated for the first time)	
2012/6/27–8/7	Rim of the Pacific Exercise (RIMPAC 2012), held since 1971; US, Australia, Canada, Chile, France, Japan, Mexico, New Zealand, South Korea, Russia, and Singapore sent vessels; Colombia, India, Indonesia, Malaysia, the Netherlands, Norway, Peru, the Philippines, Thailand, Tonga, and the United Kingdom also participated.	Off Hawai
2012/8/27–9/3	US-ASEAN joint counterterrorism annual exercise (Seacat), since 2001; US, Brunei, Indonesia, the Philippines, Singapore and Thailand	

Year/month/ day(s)	Exercise (code name) Participating countries	Implementation area
2012/9/16–23	Japan-US-Australia joint naval exercise, antisubmarine patrol, etc.	Darwin, Australia
2013/2/11–21	US-Thailand multinational tri-service joint exercise (Cobra Gold); included training for rescue of Japanese nationals	Chiang Mai, Thailand, and other locations
	Thailand, Singapore, Indonesia, Malaysia, Japan and South Korea; Myanmar participated for the first time as an observer.	
2013/3/12	US Navy dispatch of a state-of-the-art battleship to Singapore as part of its Asia-Pacific regional strategy against China	
2013/4/15	US-Philippines joint military exercise focused on disaster relief (Balikatan); US military attaché in China participated for the first time	
2014/2/11	US-Thailand multinational tri-service joint exercise (Cobra Gold)	Phitsanulok, Thailand, and other locations
	Thailand, Singapore, Indonesia, Malaysia, Japan, and South Korea; 17 military personnel from China's PLA participated for the first time, although the PLA had been sending observers since 2002.	
2014/6/21–8/1	Rim of the Pacific Exercise (RIMPAC 2014)	
	US, Japan, and 20 other countries; first-time participation by the PLA Navy (1,100 military personnel, 4 ships, and 2 helicopters) and the Royal Brunei Navy	
2014/8/25–9/12	Multinational naval exercises sponsored by the Australian navy (Kakadu 14)	
	Joined by 14 countries including the US, Japan, the Philippines, Singapore and Thailand; 1,200 personnel, 8 ships, and 26 aircraft	
2014/10/2	US-Philippines joint naval exercise (Phiblex 2015); exercise to recapture islands from sea and air	Off Palawan
	2 US fighters, 19 rubber boats, 119 US and Filipino marines and Japan Self-Defense Force observers	
2015/5/13	Japan Maritime Self-Defense Force and Filipino Navy joint training Code for Unplanned Encounters at Sea (CUES)	Off Subic Bay
2015.6.23-24	Japan-Philippines joint naval exercise with P3C anti-submarine patrol aircraft in the South China Sea	

Sources: *Pioneer*; *Philippine Daily Inquirer*; US Pacific Fleet website; US Navy website; *Asagumo Shimbun*; UPI; *Wall Street Journal* (Japanese edition); *Sankei Shimbun*; *China.org.cn* (Japanese edition).

ASEAN's Conference Diplomacy

The main body of ASEAN, which was established on August 8, 1967, is the ASEAN Foreign Ministers' Meeting (AMM), a conference diplomacy venue with few restraints that operates as a consensus-based forum for policy decisions. Initially, ASEAN's main activities were mitigating and regulating the disputes among the small non-communist countries of Southeast Asia, rather than its stated purposes of economic and cultural cooperation. The 1968 announcement that UK forces would withdraw from east of Suez and the 1969 US Guam Doctrine led to the 1971 ASEAN Zone of Peace, Freedom, and Neutrality (ZOPFAN) declaration calling for non-interference of major powers outside the region, with the neutrality of Southeast Asia as a condition.[10] Subsequently, with the conclusion of the Vietnam War in 1975, Vietnam's invasion of Cambodia from the end of 1978, and the exodus of large numbers of Indochinese refugees, the ASEAN Post Ministerial Conferences were established in 1979 as expanded foreign ministers' meetings with ASEAN and major powers outside the region, making ASEAN conference diplomacy multilayered. Through group negotiations, diplomatic appeals were made to outside powers (mostly in the West) for support of ASEAN and regional stability.

After the end of the Cold War, the ASEAN countries established separate international forums for discussion of important international issues pertaining to the region at the AMM and the ASEAN Post Ministerial Conferences. Items concerning the economy of the entire region are addressed at meetings of the Asia-Pacific Economic Cooperation (APEC) forum, while those concerning the security (and defense) of the entire region are addressed at the ASEAN Regional Forum. ASEAN countries have been involved in the administration of these forums as the chair or host, and they began to seek cooperation and concessions from major powers outside the region through group negotiations. Thus, ASEAN conference diplomacy became multi-dimensional. In this process, the ASEAN nations concluded the Southeast Asian Nuclear-Weapon-Free Zone treaty in 1995 and agreed on the Declaration on the Conduct of the Parties in the South China Sea with China in 2002. ASEAN also successfully conducted dialogue with partners from outside the region, including the signing of the Treaty of Amity and Cooperation in Southeast Asia (concluded in 1976) by Japan, the US, China, and India. This agreement calls for non-interference in internal affairs and renunciation of the use of force.

However, because all of these security achievements by ASEAN are based on consensus within the ASEAN region at the AMM, a forum which follows the format of unanimous agreement, they do not strongly reflect the interests of any one country. The content of agreements may become even less substantial in group negotiations at conference diplomacy venues with countries from outside the region. There is also a tendency to prevent any single major power outside the region from exerting disproportionate influence. In other words, to achieve this sense of balance in its policy decisions, the format of international conferences sponsored by the group of small ASEAN countries that adopt policy by consensus is characterized by ambiguity. For this reason, major countries outside the region are not hesitant to deal with ASEAN. The ASEAN members and those major powers came to see the value of diversifying and expanding their own diplomacy through ASEAN's conference diplomacy, leading to their current prosperity. This gives even outside major powers like China—which has disputes in the South China Sea with multiple ASEAN nations—reason to participate in ASEAN conference diplomacy.

In 2006, ASEAN established the ASEAN Defense Ministers' Meeting, which is held annually; it then established the ASEAN Defense Ministers' Meeting Plus (ADMM-Plus) in 2010. In June 2013, ADMM-Plus implemented disaster relief exercises in Brunei with all ten ASEAN countries, along with Japan, the US, Australia, China, India, South Korea, New Zealand and Russia. It should be credited for developing a new form of nontraditional security cooperation that includes countries that are in conflict over matters in the South China Sea and East China Sea.

Conclusion: Future Direction

In closing, I would like to make a few observations regarding the future direction of the national defense policies of the six countries described above and of ASEAN's security and national defense policies. As of 2014, the economic cooperation between ASEAN countries and China is outstanding, but in military cooperation, their ties with the US are even stronger. As shown in table 2, while the number of joint military exercises with China is increasing, it is still small. In contrast, as shown in table 3, the joint military exercises with the US almost always take place annually. The national military forces of ASEAN members are in transition from public security forces to defense forces and cannot do much, regardless of whether they hold exercises with the US or with China. For the time being, they are expected to monitor the situation while conducting military exercises with both major powers.

However, because China has many submarines, and because the incursions of the PLA navy, the Chinese coast guard, and Chinese fishing vessels into the South China Sea are becoming conspicuous, the ASEAN countries are all increasing purchases of submarines as noted above, and they have an increasing desire to operate them. Of course, some are also calling for the US and other major powers outside the region, such as Japan, to maintain a military presence, especially in sea areas. Meanwhile, many of the countries have border disputes with their neighbors; there are still many troubles in ASEAN, as there were during the Cold War.

Furthermore, the domestic public security problem of "internal enemies" is growing more serious in ASEAN countries where the progress of democratization is lagging, where there are many government opponents, and where there are many Muslims. These countries will carefully monitor the connection between democratization movements, domestic government opponents, and the South China Sea dispute, and the relations between Islamic extremists and the Islamic State. Also, as made clear by the 2003 Severe Acute Respiratory Syndrome (SARS) epidemic, continued caution is required to address the spread of infectious diseases, such as Ebola hemorrhagic fever and avian influenza, which result from globalization, and to address major earthquakes, tsunamis, typhoons, and other natural disasters. While dealing with such problems individually, ASEAN countries will use ASEAN conference diplomacy venues to ask countries outside the region to help mitigate problems concerning the entire region, such as the intensification of the South China Sea dispute, issues with major powers outside the region that are beyond ASEAN's capabilities, and non-traditional security matters.

Acknowledgement: I would like to thank Professor Takayuki Ogasawara of Yamanashi Gakuin University for providing the Vietnamese defense policy papers.

1   The summaries that follow are based on the national defense policy papers of each country published as part of the ASEAN Regional Forum (ARF) confidence-building measures during the late 1990s. See Kōichi Satō, "ASEAN shokoku to hōkatsuteki anzen hoshō gainen" [Comprehensive security concepts of the ASEAN countries], *Journal of Pacific Asia*, vol. 8, 2002, 21–34, which analyzes those papers, and descriptions in the ARF Annual Security Outlook 2013.

2   Regarding comprehensive security, see Shinkichi Etō and Yoshinobu Yamamoto, *Sōgō anpo to mirai no sentaku* [Comprehensive security and future choices] (Kōdansha, 1991). This comprehensive ("total defense") security concept being advocated by each ASEAN nation may be

referred to as a military doctrine; however, a true military doctrine presents a concrete framework or principles for implementing wars; it covers operations, logistics, C4ISR (command, control, communications, computers, intelligence, surveillance, and reconnaissance), etc. These countries' total defense policies are not so detailed or specific. They simply present the action guidelines and preparations for defense of the nation. Regarding military doctrines, see Ryō Asano, "Gunji dokutorin no hen'yō to tenkai" ["Military doctrine changes and developments"], in Tomohide Murai et al., *Chūgoku o meguru anzen hoshō* [Security pertaining to China] (Minerva Shobō, 2007), 243.

3   Indonesian Ministry of Defence, The Policy of the State Defence and Security of the Republic of Indonesia, nos. 12–13, 1995, 46–54. The sociopolitical aspects of the dual functions include everything from peacekeeping and search and rescue to family planning, reforestation, increased rice production, poverty countermeasures, and social and cultural development (countermeasures regarding religion).

4   ASEAN Regional Forum, Annual Security Outlook, 2013, http://aseanregionalforum.asean.org/wp-content/uploads/2019/01/ARF-Annual-Security-Outlook-2013.pdf

5   Zakaria Haji Ahmad, "The Military and Development in Malaysia and Brunei, with a Short Survey on Singapore," J. Soedjati Diwandono & Yong Mun Cheong, eds., *Soldiers and Stability in Southeast Asia, Institute of Southeast Asian Studies*, 1988, 231–54; Abdul Ghani Yunus, "The Malaysian Armed Forces and Vision 2020," Abdul Razak Abdullah Baginda and Rohana Mahmood, eds., *Malaysia's Defense & Foreign Policies*, Pelanduk Publications, 1995, 1–9; "Malaysia," in ARF Annual Security Outlook 2013, 89.

6   Department of National Defense, *In Defense of the Philippines*, 1996, 33.

7   Ministry of Defence, Singapore, "What is Total Defence?" https://www.mindef.gov.sg/web/portal/mindef/Defence-matters/Defence-topic/Defence-topic-detail/total-Defence. Digital defense became the sixth pillar in Singapore's national defense framework in February 2019. See "Digital Defence to be sixth pillar of Total Defence," *Straits Times*, February 15, 2019, https://www.straitstimes.com/singapore/digital-Defence-to-be-sixth-pillar-of-total-Defence; and Ministry of Defense, Singapore, *Defending Singapore in the 21st Century* (Grace Communications Pte. Ltd, 2000), 12.

8   Ministry of Defence, Thailand, The Defence of Thailand 1996, 27; Ministry of Defence, Thailand, The Defence of Thailand 1994, 40–41.

9   Ministry of Defence, the Socialist Republic of Vietnam, Consolidating National Defense Safeguarding the Homeland, 1998, 21–31.

10 Regarding ASEAN, see Tatsumi Okabe, ed., *ASEAN o meguru kokusai kankei* [International relations pertaining to ASEAN] (Japan Institute of International Affairs, 1977); Tatsumi Okabe, ed., *ASEAN no 20 nen* [Twenty Years of ASEAN] (Japan Institute of International Affairs, 1987); Yoneji Kuroyanagi, *ASEAN 35 nen no kiseki "ASEAN Way" no kōyō to genkai* [Thirty-five years of ASEAN: The usefulness and limits of the "ASEAN Way"] (Yūshindō Kōbunsha, 2003); Kōichi Satō, *ASEAN rejīmu* [The ASEAN regime] (Keisō Shobō, 2003); and Kōichi Satō, *Chūgoku kyōiron to ASEAN shokoku* [The China threat theory and the ASEAN nations] (Keisō Shobō, 2012).

CHAPTER 9

India's Diplomatic and Security Policies

Takako Hirose
Emeritus Professor, Daitō Bunka University

Eyes on India

While the rise of China is often perceived as a threat, not only by its neighbors but also by countries outside the region, the developments in India, another major nation that is quickly gaining power in Asia, are drawing attention. India was actively pursuing nonaligned diplomacy in the early stages of the Cold War era, but it built up close relations with the USSR starting in the 1970s, and then suddenly moved close to the United States once the Cold War ended. India declared itself a nuclear-weapons state after conducting nuclear tests in 1998, but despite that, its relationship with the US has continued to progress. In the meantime, India's relations with China have undergone major changes, and today India maintains stable relations with the colossus to its north amid a certain tension.

How does India perceive the present international situation? What actions is it taking externally, and what are the objectives behind them? What are the goals of the diplomatic policies of the Bharatiya Janata Party (BJP) administration led by Prime Minister Narendra Modi, who took office in May 2014? In particular, what sorts of policies has India developed toward Japan and the US? The purpose of this chapter is to consider these questions.

There are a few points I would like to call attention to when examining India's diplomacy. The first is the present significance of India's nonalignment policy in its diplomacy. To be certain, the rationale behind this policy ended with the Cold War, and many analysts believe that India abandoned the practice of nonaligned diplomacy when it concluded the 1971 Indo-Soviet Treaty of Peace, Friendship, and Cooperation. Nonetheless, the basic stance of nonaligned diplomacy continues to have great force in India's foreign policy today. Even though common threats are recognized, forming alliances to counter those threats is not an option in Indian diplomacy.

India's resolute commitment to nonaligned diplomacy is the product of its strong determination to decide its own foreign policy on every point of dispute. India, whose former defense minister, George Fernandes, called China "enemy number one," has strongly resisted participating in efforts by the US, Japan, and other countries to rein in China. For Japan, which wants to go beyond the Japan-US alliance and reinforce positive ties with India, accommodating India's commitment to nonalignment is a major challenge.

Another point is India's undeniable dominance in South Asia, which typically refers to the seven countries of India, Pakistan, Bangladesh, Sri Lanka, Nepal, Bhutan, and the Maldives. (In some cases, Afghanistan, which recently became a member of the South Asian Association for Regional Cooperation, is included, and when discussing security problems, China is sometimes included and the area referred to as "Southern Asia.") In the context of these seven countries, the national power of India—whether measured by population, area, GDP, or other figures—is around three times that of the other six countries combined. Geographically, India shares land or sea borders with all the other countries, whereas the other countries—aside from Sri Lanka and the Maldives, which are separated by sea channels—do not share boundaries with each other.

Although India's pride in its overwhelming power is understandable, neighboring countries have traditionally strongly opposed India's hegemonistic attitude. To a certain degree, India considers its relations with neighboring countries to be an extension of domestic policy. Only recently has it developed cautious diplomatic relations with them. For India, which is on its way to becoming not only a regional but also a global major power, however, relations with neighboring countries have become a major hurdle, leaving room for China to interfere. To oppose India's overwhelming force, Pakistan has often moved closer to China, as have Nepal and Sri Lanka, creating the very situation India most wants to avoid. This is why Prime Minister Modi visited neighboring countries immediately after his administration came into power.

The third point, which is related to the second, is that when international relations in South Asia are discussed, the first thing that comes up is the conflict between India and Pakistan. The origins of this confrontation go back to the bloody partition of the two countries when they gained their independence from Britain in 1947. This led to the current situation in which the "brother countries" of India and Pakistan are squaring off against each other with nuclear weapons. Moreover, Pakistan has significant connections with terrorism. As it is unlikely that there will be any major changes in India-Pakistan relations in the near future, herein I have taken the India-Pakistan confrontation as a given condition, and focus on India's relations with China, the United States, and Japan.

Diplomacy by the Modi Administration

The BJP won an overwhelming victory in the Lok Sabah (lower house) elections held in April and May of 2014, taking an outright majority, and formed a coalition government at the end of May with parties that were allies before the election was held. Prime Minister Modi had served as chief minister of the western Indian state of Gujarat for more than a decade, greatly improving the state's infrastructure during that time, and his leadership was highly acclaimed nationwide. There were high expectations for his talents, especially regarding economic development, but they proved difficult to meet. The road building, electrification, and other infrastructural improvements that had succeeded in Gujarat presented difficult problems when attempted on a national scale.

India has a federal system in which electricity, agriculture, education, and other areas are under the jurisdiction of the states. Regardless of what the central government declares, results cannot be expected unless the state governments comply. The fact is that the circumstances of individual states make it difficult for them to take action. Although India's economic growth rate has improved since the Modi administration took office, there have been no breakthroughs in infrastructure upgrades or other domestic areas. On the other hand, the field of diplomacy, in which the central government faces comparatively few restrictions from the states, offers the BJP ample room to demonstrate its originality. Prime Minister Modi initiated diplomacy with neighboring countries right from the start of his administration, and has energetically made repeated trips abroad thereafter as well.

The Modi administration's stated objective in pursuing these actions is a "Strong India." The BJP is a right-wing party that forcefully advocates Hindu nationalism, and it is known to take a hard-line external stance. The

"Strong India" of BJP aspirations is not only strong militarily, but strong in the economic, political, and cultural spheres as well. Culturally, the BJP paints a unified image of Indian citizens based on adherence to Hinduism, which is a concern for minorities, especially Muslims. Even within the BJP, Prime Minister Modi stands out for his support of hard-line Hindu nationalism. His handling of the 2002 Gujarat riots, in which a large number of Muslims were killed, has been questioned, and both the US and the UK have denied him an entry visa in the past.

The Rashtriya Swayamsevak Sangh (RSS) national volunteer association is generally considered to be the parent of the BPJ. As the largest non governmental organization in the world, the RSS has tens of thousands of branches nationwide, and provides its own education and training in various formats to a vast number of people ranging from children to the elderly. It advocates a unified, strong India based on Hindu nationalism. It has a vast number of related groups, including labor unions, student organizations, women's organizations, and religious organizations, as well as the BJP. These groups collectively form the Sangh Parivar ("the family of the RSS"). While their mutual relations are informal, persons trained by the RSS have been appointed to key government positions, and the will of the RSS is reflected in policies through their personal relations. Even within the BPJ, Prime Minister Modi is seen to have a strong connection with the RSS, and its influence can be seen in the staffing of his administration and in its domestic and foreign policies.

Prime Minister Modi might be characterized as a "pragmatic nationalist." The pragmatism is clearly evident in his economic policies, and the nationalism emerges in policies dominated by Hindu nationalism. His foreign policy is a skillful combination of both, as shown by India's relations with Japan under his administration.

The principal architects of the Modi administration's foreign policy are National Security Advisor Ajit Doval and Foreign Secretary Subrahmanyam Jaishankar. As former director of the Intelligence Bureau, Doval's achievements included the operations and public security measures in disputes in Mizoram, Punjab, and Kashmir and negotiations with hijackers within India. He also worked at the Indian embassy in Pakistan. Foreign Secretary Jaishankar is a top-level diplomat who served as ambassador in Beijing and Washington and who also spent time at the Indian embassy in Tokyo. He supports India's development of nuclear weapons and missiles, and he follows a hard-line diplomatic approach close to that of the BJP.

India, being a democratic country, must adjust its foreign policy to accommodate Parliament, the mass media, and different interest groups, all of them outspoken. In spite of the competing interests, the Modi administration is the first in twenty years to have a majority in Parliament, and has achieved stability in its relations with the ruling coalition and the RSS. It could be said that the Modi administration's diplomacy has a relatively high level of freedom to realize its political vision of a "Strong India."

India's Relations with China

Over the decades since India gained independence, its relationship with China has been through major ups and downs. The two countries experienced a honeymoon phase in the early 1950s, but their relations as "brother countries" in Asia suddenly deteriorated over a border dispute in the late 1950s, leading to the 1962 Sino-Indian Border Conflict. India's humiliating defeat in this war influenced its subsequent national defense policies greatly. Sino-Indian relations became steadily worse, reaching their nadir with China's first nuclear test two years later. Diplomatic relations were finally normalized with an exchange of ambassadors in 1976, and improved with regular bilateral consultations regarding border issues from the 1980s. This rapprochement gained momentum with Prime Minister Rajiv Gandhi's visit to China in 1988. In 1993, the two countries signed an agreement to maintain peace in the India-China border areas, and in the economic sphere the bilateral trade that was resumed in the 1980s has increased dramatically through to the present day. While there is still a strong wariness of China in India, the strengthening of economic relations is overshadowing the political tensions.

In this context, the Modi administration's handling of India-China relations plainly demonstrates Prime Minister Modi's pragmatism. Although its willingness to pursue military action in border areas remains unchanged, in a sense India has grown accustomed to the border disputes and its measured response is notable. The border problem is the greatest area of conflict with China, and sporadic firefights occur across the line of actual control. When President Xi Jinping visited India in September 2014, there was a firefight in the Ladakh region of Kashmir just as the two leaders were holding friendly discussions in Prime Minister Modi's home state of Gujarat, and India expressed strong concerns regarding the incursions by the Chinese side. Furthermore, China does not recognize the existence of the state of Arunachal Pradesh in northeast India, claiming that this area is Chinese territory, and it refuses to issue regular visas to people born in this state. When Prime Minister Modi visited Arunachal Pradesh on February 20, 2015, China reacted strongly, and the two sides were unable to agree on a further schedule for border negotiations.

India is also concerned about the ties between China and Pakistan, and is observing China's aid to Pakistan closely. China and Pakistan have maintained amicable relations through thick and thin, and they have grown even closer in recent years with the huge flow of Chinese aid for upgrading domestic infrastructure in Pakistan. In April 2015, when President Xi made the first visit by a Chinese head of state to Pakistan in nine years, he signed an agreement for massive Chinese financing of $46 billion over fifteen years to construct roads, railroads, pipelines, power plants, and other infrastructure in an "economic corridor" stretching from Gwadar Port on the Arabian Sea to the Xinjian Uygur Autonomous Region. The $7.5 billion in development assistance to Pakistan which the US pledged over five years from 2009 pales in comparison with China's recent investment. Furthermore, because the US aid was spread thinly across the entire country, it ended in a "dramatic failure"[1] without achieving concrete results. By comparison, the construction of Gwadar Port began in 2002 with Chinese aid, and in 2013 the operating rights were transferred to China, making the port one major base of China's "string of pearls" strategy to build ports along the coast of the Indian Ocean in countries including Pakistan, Sri Lanka, Bangladesh, and Myanmar. China is working to develop this economic corridor as a route for transporting goods to and from Europe and the Middle East without passing through the Strait of Malacca; it constitutes an important part of China's Belt and Road Initiative, which aims to form a "New Silk Road" over land and sea. In fact, the first project financed by China's newly established Silk Road Fund was the construction of a hydroelectric power plant in Pakistan, with a total investment of $1.65 billion. Pakistan and China are also strengthening their military relations: the Parliament of Pakistan approved the purchase of eight Chinese-made submarines at a cost of $6 billion prior to President Xi's visit.

India takes a dim view of China's support for Pakistan. When Prime Minister Modi visited China in May 2015, he was positive toward cooperative economic relations, but the resulting joint declaration made no mention of the Belt and Road Initiative or the New Silk Road, and the Indian side clearly expressed its concerns regarding China's intentions. Regardless, India has announced its commitment to the Bangladesh-China-India-Myanmar Economic Corridor initiative, and Minister of External Affairs Sushma Swaraj visited Kunming, which is the base for this corridor on the Chinese side.

India also joined the Asian Infrastructure Investment Bank, which is head-quartered in China, as a founding member, and sent an Indian official to serve as one of the vice presidents. In addition, India is actively engaged in the three-nation dialogue among India, Russia, and China. To summarize, India is increasingly wary of the ties between China and Pakistan, but does not hesitate to collaborate with China in other regions and fields.

Chinese cooperation in the economic field has become essential for India, with trade growing from $2.92 billion in 2000 to $41.85 billion in 2008, when China surpassed the US as India's largest trading partner. Bilateral trade between the two countries increased to $71.59 billion in 2014, according to a Ministry of External Affairs announcement. While India's large trade deficit in this trade is an issue, China is certainly an important economic partner for it. Chinese investment in India is likewise increasing steadily. When Prime Minister Modi visited China in 2015, he said that India now welcomes Chinese investment in Indian infrastructure, which had previously been restricted.

Being a pragmatist, Prime Minister Modi recognizes the importance of maintaining a relationship with China. However, India's cautious stance regarding other political and security issues, especially the border problem and China's relations with Pakistan, has not changed.

India's Relations with the United States

Relations between India and the United States grew closer after the end of the Cold War, especially from the late 1990s, but bilateral relations had grown cool by the time Prime Minister Modi took office. The arrest by US authorities of a female diplomat from the consulate general of India in New York at the end of 2013 heightened anti-US sentiment within India, and mutual distrust intensified thereafter. On the US side, there was concern regarding the Civil Liability for Nuclear Damage Act (an Indian law under which not only operators but also manufacturers can be considered liable in the case of a nuclear accident), and criticism and dissatisfaction about how Indian opposition prevented the adoption of measures to facilitate trade at the World Trade Organization (WTO) Doha Round negotiations. On the Indian side, there was enormous anger over reports that the US had spied on the Indian embassy in Washington and the BJP. Furthermore, in 2005 the US had refused to issue a visa to Modi because of questions about his responsibility in the above-mentioned 2002 Gujarat riots. From the start of his administration, Modi faced the major issue of how to restore India-US relations.

In September 2014, Prime Minister Modi attended the UN General Assembly and then had his first summit meeting with President Barack Obama in Washington. A Vision Statement for the US-India Strategic Partnership[2] was issued the night before the meeting, and a US-India Joint Statement[3] was released afterward. This summit enabled the leaders to share their recognition of the terrorism issue and the need to strengthen economic ties, and also to discuss international relations in general, particularly security issues. While the joint statement did not mention China by name, it reaffirmed the shared interests that India and the US have in the Asia Pacific and expressed concern about ongoing tensions in the South China Sea. The summit also confirmed the importance of the trilateral dialogue incorporating Japan; a decision was made to explore holding this dialogue among foreign ministers rather than bureau heads. Overall, Prime Minister Modi was successful in restoring some trust to the relationship.

The foundations for relations were further reinforced with President Obama's visit to India in January 2015 as the guest of honor for India's Republic Day (Prime Minister Shinzō Abe had been the guest of honor the year before). In addition, nuclear power cooperation was improved by a solution to the issue of the Civil Liability for Nuclear Damage Act. The US agreed to a proposal to establish an insurance system using a pool of funds to be arranged by the Indian side, which basically resolved the issue by having the Indian government effectively bear the burden for compensation without making any changes to India's domestic legislation under foreign pressure.

In the security field, the two countries signed the Framework for the US-India Defense Relationship covering the next ten years, confirming progress in defense cooperation, including joint development and production of weapons. The US-India Joint Strategic Vision for the Asia-Pacific and Indian Ocean Region[4] was issued following the summit. Like the joint statement of September 2014, the Joint Strategic Vision mentions the South China Sea, restraining China by affirming freedom of navigation and overflight and by stressing the importance of resolving territorial disputes through peaceful means in accordance with international law. The two countries also agreed to hold summits on a regular basis. Up to that time, India had been holding regular summits only with Japan and Russia.

Even as the framework for cooperation between India and the US has grown stronger, India's multilateral diplomacy remains alive and well. At the trilateral Russia-India-China Foreign Ministerial Meeting held in China just after Obama's visit to India, Minister of External Affairs Swaraj expressed sympathy with Russia and China as the confrontation between the West and Russia intensified over the situation in Ukraine. A joint communiqué issued after the meeting expressed opposition to unilateral sanctions and stressed the importance of multilateralism and the United Nations system. In fact, India is not participating in the Western-led sanctions against Russia, but this is because India has a long-standing policy of not participating in multinational sanctions.

A significant reason for the state of India-US relations remaining amicable, despite the ups and downs, is the large number of ethnic Indian residents of the US. As of January 2015, the total population of the ethnic Indian diaspora exceeded 25 million; of these, 4 million reside in the US. The living conditions and social status of ethnic Indians abroad varies by country of residence. The descendants of those who relocated to Southeast Asia and other regions as plantation workers during the British colonial era still have relatively low social status. Since the Second World War, aside from professionals, the short-term migrant laborers working in the Middle East for a few years at a time have been forced to toil under very harsh conditions. In contrast, many of the Indian migrants to the US are doctors, lawyers, IT engineers, and other professionals. The US had policies banning nonwhite immigrants in the first half of the twentieth century, but the Immigration Act was revised in 1965 and the racially discriminatory clauses deleted. After that time, there was a sharp increase in the immigration of highly educated Indians into the US. The 1975 census categorized 93 percent of Indian immigrants as professionals. According to a 2000 survey by the government of India, ethnic Indians residing in the US have the highest average income of any ethnic group in the US.

The negative aspects of this migration were criticized in India as a "brain drain," but the migrants came to be seen in a new light with the economic liberalization and rapid growth that started in India in the 1990s. The networks of US-based entrepreneurs have a global reach, and they provide advice and introduce partners to entrepreneurs in India. The members of the Indian diaspora have expanded economic ties between India and the US, and as their economic strength increases, they are also expanding their political power. Many ethnic Indians are active in US government organizations; their lobbying activities are now as influential as those of the Jewish community, and exert a major impact on the governments of both the US and India. For example, lobbying by Indian-Americans reportedly had a strong influence on the US-India nuclear power agreement.

The Indian government has taken up the BJP's enthusiasm for maintaining direct connections with Indian expatriates with an eye to using their wealth and power for the economic development of the homeland. It has introduced policies that make it easier for ethnic Indians abroad to return to India, to invest in India, and to transfer funds, and has revised laws to recognize dual nationality for Indian immigrants residing in industrialized nations. The BJP can use the activities of its international support body, the "Overseas Friends of BJP," to spread party policies and policy lines overseas. Prime Minister Modi is exceptionally enthusiastic about building ties with Indians abroad, and always arranges a venue for large-scale exchange with the local Indian community whenever he travels overseas. Ethnic Indians abroad provide the material benefits of investments and remittances, and constitute a powerful weapon for spreading Hindu nationalism overseas, thus satisfying both the pragmatic and nationalistic leanings of Prime Minister Modi.

India and the US also maintain active intergovernmental communication, which supports the India-US Global Strategic Partnership. In addition to summit meetings, the two countries have some forty bilateral dialogue mechanisms across a wide range of fields. At India's Ministry of External Affairs, these are grouped into five main categories: strategic cooperation; energy and climate change; education and development; economy, trade, and agriculture; science and technology; and health and hygiene. There are ministerial-level meetings covering such fields as domestic affairs, finance, commerce, human resources development, science and technology, and energy. The Ministry of External Affairs has organized a ministerial-level strategic dialogue on foreign affairs every year since 2009; there are also consultations covering a wide range of fields at the vice-ministerial level. Defense exchange has been stepped up since 2005, when the New Framework for the US-India Defense Relationship was created, involving cooperation in defense-related trade, joint exercises, personnel exchanges, and maritime security and anti-piracy measures, along with exchanges by all three services of the armed forces. These relations have deepened further since the 2013 US-India Joint Declaration on Defense Cooperation, and the two countries now conduct more joint exercises than any other countries. There is no doubt that the close dialogue and exchange is boosting the mutual trust between India and the US.

Japan-India Relations

Japan-India relations, which cooled precipitously in the wake of India's 1998 nuclear tests, reached a breakthrough with Prime Minister Yoshirō Mori's visit to India in August 2000. Since that time, bilateral relations have steadily grown stronger, particularly in the political and security fields. Annual summit meetings have been held since 2005, except for 2012, when there was a change of administration in Japan. Since coming into power, the Modi administration has brought Japan and India closer at a faster pace. Some say that Abe and Modi are both nationalists and are on the same wavelength; in any event, they are both running stable administrations, having won majorities in their elections.

Modi chose Japan for his first overseas visit after being appointed prime minister. Prior to this, he did visit Bhutan and other neighboring countries, but Japan was the first country he visited outside the region. He arrived a day earlier than initially planned and headed for Kyoto. He reportedly chose Kyoto because he wanted the Hindu sacred city of Varanasi, which is his electoral district, to find ways to modernize while retaining tradition, as Kyoto has done. Abe provided hospitality at the state guesthouse in Kyoto, guided Modi around Tōji temple, a World Heritage site, and arranged a partner-city agreement between Kyoto and Varanasi. This showy Modi-style performance came as a surprise to other countries, and the US embassy in Delhi reportedly began scrambling to prepare for a visit to India by President Obama.

Abe and Modi moved to Tokyo for their full-scale discussions. After their summit, they released a joint declaration on September 1, 2014, under which Japan pledged ¥3.5 trillion in investment and financing over five years, including official development assistance. To achieve this, a goal was set to double the number of Japanese firms with operations in India. Incidentally, the joint declaration with President Xi Jinping, who visited India just after this, called for investment of $20 billion (more than ¥2 trillion).

From a political and security standpoint, Japan-India relations were positioned as a "Special Strategic and Global Partnership." The term "special" was also used in the joint declaration following Abe's summit with Australian Prime Minister Tony Abbott in July 2014. The fact that India agreed with the use of the same term for both Australia and India is quite significant. This term is associated with the Asian "Democratic Security Diamond" concept advocated by Prime Minister Abe. Abe presented this concept of linking the four democracies of Japan, the US, Australia, and India in 2007, during his previous term as prime minister, thereby drawing a strong negative reaction from China. India had subsequently been extremely cautious in dealing with this concept, which would have the effect of encircling China. While the use of the term "special" is only a matter of expression, it may be interpreted as a sign that India is modifying its stance.

India's joint exercises also show a clear trend toward closer relations with Japan. On October 14–19, 2015, a trilateral Japan-US-India naval exercise, Exercise Malabar, was conducted in the Bay of Bengal. Exercise Malabar, which has been held annually since 2002, originally began in 1992 as an India-US joint exercise. In 2007, Japan, Australia, and Singapore were invited to participate, and the five countries conducted the exercise in the Bay of Bengal, but this met with fierce opposition from China. Subsequently, Japan's Maritime Self-Defense Force participated in Exercise Malabar at other locations, but Japan was not invited to participate in exercises in the Indian Ocean. For the Maritime Self-Defense Force, the 2015 exercises were their first in the Indian Ocean in eight years. Yet India was also participating in joint exercises with China—the fifth between the two countries—at Kunming right around the same time. This demonstrates India's shrewdness.

Things are also moving in the diplomatic sphere. A Japan-US-India trilateral foreign ministers' meeting was held in New York in September 2015. This was the seventh trilateral meeting since 2011, but the prior meetings had been at the bureau chief level. As mentioned above, Japan and the US wanted to upgrade these meetings to the ministerial level, and had lobbied Prime Minister Modi to do so, but India simply would not agree. The 2015 meeting was the first time this was achieved. In a media note[5] released following the meeting, the three countries confirmed their shared interests in the Indo-Pacific region and stressed the importance of international law and peaceful settlement of disputes and of freedom of navigation and overflight. The expression "Indo-Pacific" was used as a strategic regional concept. The "confluence of the two seas" is a concept that has long been emphasized by Prime Minister Abe.

Abe visited India in December 2015 for the annual Japan-India summit meeting. General interest was focused on developing a nuclear power agreement, but there was little substantive progress in that area. There was, however, progress in the security field. In the Japan-India Joint Vision 2025 issued after the meeting,[6] the two countries declared their determination to transform the Japan-India Special Strategic and Global Partnership into a deep, broad-based and action-oriented partnership that would work for the peace, security, and development of the Indo-Pacific region through the peaceful

settlement of disputes, as well as for freedom of navigation and other principles. India also agreed to make the Japan Maritime Self-Defense Force a
permanent partner in Exercise Malabar. Furthermore, the two governments
concluded an agreement concerning the transfer of defense equipment and
technology, as well as another agreement concerning security measures for
the protection of classified military information. These two agreements are
reportedly laying the groundwork for the export, technology transfer, and
domestic production of the Japanese US-2 rescue aircraft in India. In addition, the Joint Vision called for further promoting the Japan-India-US trilateral dialogue and the Japan-India-Australia trilateral dialogue.

This visit to India also brought results in the economic sphere. A memorandum was exchanged on adopting the Japanese Shinkansen system for
a high-speed railway planned to cover the roughly 500 kilometers between
Mumbai and Ahmedabad. The leaders called for cooperation in subway
projects, the energy sector, and other fields, and announced that an agreement had been reached in principle on a nuclear power agreement. After the
summit, as a gesture of thanks for his visit to Kyoto, Modi invited Abe to the
sacred city of Varanasi in his own electoral district; Abe was the first foreign
VIP that Modi had ever brought there. The two leaders participated together
in a Hindu ceremony on the banks of the Ganges. In relations with Japan, the
Hindu nationalist Modi is quite eager to stress not only science and technology and security but also the shared heritage of Buddhism and Asian values.

As seen in all these actions, Japan and India have been steadily reinforcing bilateral relations in various areas. With government backing, trade and
investment are expected to increase greatly in the future. India has a very high
opinion of Japanese technology, and there are hopes to create a "Strong India"
by using imported Japanese technologies to advance rapidly in this field. That
trend has accelerated since the launch of the Modi administration. The personal relations between Modi and Abe are also having a positive effect.

Conclusion

Indian diplomacy in the post–Cold War era can be characterized as being
multifaceted. Even as it moves closer to the US, India is still upholding its
traditionally amicable relations with Russia and maintaining a cautious relationship with China. During this period, it has worked to steadily strengthen
relations with Southeast Asian countries, Australia, and members of the European Union. Although India has some problems in relations with its neigh-

bors, Prime Minister Modi invited the top leaders of neighboring countries to attend his own inauguration ceremony, personally visited those countries, and also sent his minister and deputy minister for external affairs and other diplomats to work toward improving relations. As a result, India has succeeded to some extent in improving its relations with its neighbors except Pakistan, and by so doing, demonstrating anew its presence in South Asia. Considering how these countries have repeatedly moved closer to China to maintain balance, this may also be interpreted as a means of restraining China. Meanwhile, India's relations with Pakistan remain difficult, and China's massive infrastructural aid to that country is a development that India cannot ignore.

Given these circumstances, it seems that India has adjusted its traditional nonaligned diplomacy, if only a little bit. Having been harshly criticized by China for its arrangement of the five-nation 2007 Exercise Malabar, India subsequently made friendly overtures to Japan and the US, which counter China, while still maintaining a certain distance from them. It limited trilateral Japan-US-India meetings to the bureau chief level, and has maintained dialogue with China and Russia via BRICS (Brazil, Russia, India, China, South Africa), RIC (Russia, India, China), the SCO (Shanghai Cooperation Organization) and other associations. India's refusal to participate in a permanent encirclement of China may have irritated Japan somewhat, as the latter values the ties of alliance.

The adjustments in Indian diplomacy are evident in the Japan-US-India trilateral dialogue. These dialogues have taken place regularly since 2011, but were limited to the bureau head level. In September 2015, India, which had been reluctant to escalate the dialogues to the ministerial level, finally agreed, sending Minister of External Affairs Swaraj to the meeting. India also invited the Japan Maritime Self Defense Force to participate in trilateral joint exercises in the Indian Ocean and accepted the Maritime Self Defense Force as a permanent partner in Exercise Malabar. These were major changes considering India's stance up until that time. The Japan-India-Australia dialogue was launched as well, and the relationships between Japan and India and between Japan and Australia were both recognized as "special," marking a change of direction from India's prior foreign policies. It seems that, faced with the sudden expansion of Chinese power, Indian diplomacy can no longer function on principle alone.

Nevertheless, the pragmatist Modi views relations with China as extremely important from an economic standpoint, and his position and the reality of the situation are unlikely to change in the near future. Consequently, Japan needs to implement cautious but proactive measures so that India continues to move in this new direction with its foreign policy.

1 Jane Perlez, "Xi Jinping Heads to Pakistan, Bearing Billions in Infrastructure Aid," *New York Times*, April 19, 2015, https://www.nytimes.com/2015/04/20/world/asia/chinas-president-heads-to-pakistan-with-billions-in-infrastructure-aid.html.

2 The White House, Office of the Press Secretary, "Vision Statement for the U.S.-India Strategic Partnership—'Chalein Saath: Forward Together We Go,'" September 29, 2014, https://obamawhitehouse.archives.gov/the-press-office/2014/09/29/vision-statement-us-india-strategic-partnership-chalein-saath-saath-forw.

3 The White House, Office of the Press Secretary, "US-India Joint Statement," September 30, 2014, https://obamawhitehouse.archives.gov/the-press-office/2014/09/30/us-india-joint-statement.

4 The White House, Office of the Press Secretary, "U.S.-India Joint Strategic Vision for the Asia-Pacific and Indian Ocean Region," January 25, 2015, https://obamawhitehouse.archives.gov/the-press-office/2015/01/25/us-india-joint-strategic-vision-asia-pacific-and-indian-ocean-region.

5 Ministry of Foreign Affairs of Japan, "Inaugural U.S.-India-Japan Trilateral Ministerial" (media note), September 29, 2015, https://www.mofa.go.jp/files/000102078.pdf.

6 Ministry of Foreign Affairs of Japan, "Japan and India Vision 2025 Special Strategic and Global Partnership" (report on Prime Minister Abe's visit to India), December 12, 2015, https://www.mofa.go.jp/s_sa/sw/in/page3e_000432.html.

CHAPTER 10

Australia and the Japan-US Alliance

Teruhiko Fukushima

Professor, Department of International Relations, National Defense Academy of Japan

Japan-Australia security cooperation has developed rapidly in recent years to the point that Australia can now be viewed as a quasi ally of Japan linked by common alliance relations with the United States. To understand why and how such close ties have been established, it is necessary to review the progress of Japan-Australia diplomatic and security relations to date, as well as the historical development of the Australia-US alliance. In this paper, I will discuss the relationship between Japan-Australia security cooperation and the Japan-US alliance by focusing on Australia's approach to security cooperation with Japan. This relationship can be divided into five periods: post–World War II, post–Cold War, post-9/11, after the 2007 Japan-Australia Joint Declaration on Security Cooperation, and since the start of the second (current) Shinzō Abe administration in December 2012.

Japan-Australia Security Relations: Postwar through the Cold War

Visible security cooperation between Japan and Australia did not begin until after the Cold War ended. In the years after the Second World War, there was extremely strong anti-Japanese sentiment among the Australian people, as Japan was the only former enemy that had threatened Australian territory. In fact, Australia pursued building an alliance with the Unite States in order to prepare for the possible resurgence of Japan as a military power. However, the US showed no interest whatsoever in making a military commitment in the Pacific.

Washington maintained that stationing US troops in Japan would be enough to prevent a resurgence. Canberra, however, insisted on concluding a full-scale security cooperation agreement with the US. The prospect of a Japan-US alliance was a cause of concern for Australia, because if Japan were to undertake to invade Australia again with such an alliance in place, Australia would be relying on the US—a Japanese ally—for help. Consequently, there were strong demands for an Australia-US alliance as a reliable hedge. After the outbreak of the Korean War in 1950, the military significance of Australia, which voluntarily sent large numbers of army, navy, and air force troops to the front lines from the outset, was raised considerably when the Chinese People's Liberation Army (PLA) entered the hostilities and the battle came to a deadlock. The US, which wanted to move peace negotiations with Japan forward smoothly, agreed in August 1951 to sign the Australia, New Zealand, United States Security Treaty (ANZUS).

Following the conclusion of the Treaty of Peace with Japan in September 1951, Japan-Australia relations developed largely on an economic basis; the security relationship was limited to information exchange. Starting in the late 1960s, Japan grew to become Australia's largest export market, and also gained an important presence as a cooperation partner with Australia in the Asia-Pacific region. For that reason, when Japan began taking a proactive stance on defense policy, Australia reacted positively. In 1980, Japan's Maritime Self-Defense Force (MSDF) participated in the US-led multinational Rim of the Pacific (RIMPAC) maneuvers for the first time, joining with a naval contingent from Australia. The following year, full-scale bilateral joint exercises by the MSDF and the Royal Australian Navy began as Japan-Australia friendship exercises, and have generally been held once every two years ever since. Because these bilateral exercises have been held quietly, they are not well known. Nonetheless, just as economic cooperation between Japan and Australia developed steadily over time once it was initiated, security relations between the two countries progressed in a similar fashion.

Even in the 1980s, however, vague fears about Japan making overseas incursions persisted in Australia. As investment by Japan in visible forms such as real estate suddenly increased, the Returned and Services League (a support organization for active and retired military personnel) and other parties raised warnings that Australian territory, which had been defended from Japanese military invasion during the war, was being bought up with bundles of yen. Moreover, when the Yasuhiro Nakasone administration (1982–1987) announced an increase in defense spending for burden-sharing with the US, the foreign minister of the Labor Party administration of Prime

Minister Bob Hawke expressed concerns about Japan's dramatic increase in military expenditures. Even though Japanese and Australian naval vessels were participating in joint exercises as part of RIMPAC, at this stage, the people of Australia still viewed the Japan-US alliance fundamentally as a restraint mechanism to prevent the remilitarization of Japan.

Japan-Australia Security Cooperation after the Cold War

Around the time the Cold War ended, Australia had to grapple with new diplomatic issues in terms of both the economy and security. In the economic sphere, the Hawke administration—which viewed the advance of economic integration both in Europe and North America as a major challenge to Australia as a maritime trading nation—proposed the creation of the Asia-Pacific Economic Cooperation (APEC) forum based on the concept of "open regionalism." Japan's Ministry of International Trade and Industry offered strong support from the sidelines for Australia's diplomatic initiative. This kind of collaboration between Japan and Australia led to a ministerial meeting being held in the Australian capital of Canberra in 1989, which eventually resulted in the establishment of APEC. Since the mid-1960s, both Japan and Australia had developed a steady track record of working toward regional economic cooperation, and based on this they were able to realize APEC, a major diplomatic achievement.

In the security arena, island nations in the South Pacific region near Australia were facing political unrest, as well as social and economic upheaval, as they negotiated the transition from traditional societal structures some twenty years after gaining colonial independence. In Fiji, a military coup d'état in 1987 toppled the democratically elected government. While the British Commonwealth expelled Fiji and imposed other sanctions in response, the main countries in the region, Australia and New Zealand, had to simply observe the situation, as they were unable to take any action. In Papua New Guinea, which had been an Australian colony, the government was unstable; on Bougainville Island, which had exhibited a strong separatist tendency in the past, demands for independence intensified in reaction to toxic copper pollution by a leading Anglo-Australian mining company. From the end of the 1980s, residents seeking independence took up arms, and the country fell into a civil war as separatists fought government forces trying to quell their resistance. Australia attempted to mediate peace, but the stalemate was not easy to break, and the civil war continued for nearly ten years thereafter.

In response to the instability in neighboring countries, Australia's Labor Party government, which had mostly focused on economic diplomacy in the 1980s, began to also emphasize regional stability starting in the 1990s. As part of this, the administration of Prime Minister Paul Keating, who replaced Hawke in 1991, proactively pursued peace in Cambodia through its minister for foreign affairs, Gareth Evans. When the United Nations Transitional Authority in Cambodia was established through mediation by Evans and others in 1992, an Australian Defence Force (ADF) general was sent to command its military wing and actively lead the peacekeeping operation in Cambodia. In this way, Australia showed the surrounding countries its willingness to contribute to regional stability.

Starting in the 1990s, the Australian Labor Party government, which was then focusing on the stability of the Asia Pacific along with the effetive development of regional economic cooperation, began to have expectations of collaboration with Japan following the successful establishment of APEC. In 1990, the deputy secretary of Australia's Department of Defence and the vice chief of the ADF visited Japan and called for the establishment of a regular security dialogue. Japan agreed, and Australia became Japan's second security-dialogue partner, following the US. Even after Japan was harshly criticized by the international community for failing to play a visible role in the Gulf War, the Australian Labor Party government called on Japan to play a role in the stability of the Asia-Pacific region that was commensurate with its economic strength. Furthermore, even at this early stage, Australia clearly expressed support for making Japan a permanent member of the United Nations Security Council. Thus, when Japan agreed to dispatch its Self-Defense Forces (SDF) to the peacekeeping operation in Cambodia, Australia interpreted this action as an affirmative response to its various requests for Japanese collaboration. This encouraged the Keating administration to move Japan-Australia defense exchange forward, going so far as to mention the possibility of a regional collective defense agreement including Japan and Australia and of joint Japanese-Australian exercises on the Australian mainland. In 1995, Prime Minister Keating and Prime Minister Tomiichi Murayama released the Joint Declaration on the Australia-Japan Partnership, in which the two nations pledge to play important roles as partners to reduce tension and enhance political cooperation in the Asia-Pacific region and the government of Japan "reaffirms that Australia is an indispensable partner in regional affairs."[1]

Japan, however, reacted with caution to Australia's initiative to boost

Japan-Australia security cooperation. Despite the enthusiastic calls from the Australians, Japan-Australia defense exchange was not mentioned in the main text of Japan's Defense White Paper until the 1999 edition. Even though both countries stated their commitment in the Joint Declaration on the Australia-Japan Partnership to "reducing tension and enhancing political cooperation," which are clearly security-related objectives, Japan's Defense White Papers made no mention of this whatsoever. That is because Japan felt that the Australian proposal for security cooperation was so premature at that time that it would cause concerns in domestic public opinion and among neighboring countries about overseas activities by the SDF. Australia's Labor Party government was oriented toward multilateral cooperation in the security arena and promoted a framework similar to Europe's Conference on Security and Cooperation. Japan, however, responded with skepticism, stating that such a framework was not appropriate for the politically and culturally diverse Asia-Pacific region, and might weaken its alliance relations with the US.

This was at a point when the Japan-US alliance was being called an "alliance adrift." If Japan had moved forward with bilateral security cooperation on the timeline desired by the Australian administration, the US might have misinterpreted this as a move by Japan to pursue some option aside from its alliance with the US. From that perspective, it makes sense that the Joint Declaration on the Australia-Japan Partnership released by Prime Minister Murayama, head of Japan's Socialist Party, and Prime Minister Keating, head of Australia's Labor Party, deliberately reconfirmed strong support for the US presence and strategic involvement in the Asia-Pacific region. Australia viewed Japan as a regional cooperation partner on security matters following on their economic collaboration in APEC, but Japan at that time had just begun fulfilling its roles overseas in peacekeeping operations and other duties. Positioning a country other than the US, Japan's ally, as a cooperation partner in the security arena was outside the realm of expectations.

In 1996, John Howard was elected prime minister of Australia, leading the first conservative coalition government in thirteen years, and Japan returned to a Liberal Democratic Party administration. The two countries each made respective joint security declarations with the US that confirmed US commitment to the Asia-Pacific region. Japan and Australia both agreed with the US that their alliance relations would be used to promote the peace and stability of the region. Top officials at the US Department of Defense proclaimed that Japan and Australia formed the "northern and southern anchors" of the Asia-Pacific security network. The Chinese media response was highly critical, protesting that these two anchors were like the pincers of a crab being used by the US to contain China. At any rate, the bilateral security cooperation framework between Japan and Australia that emerged under the Labor Party government seemed to be developing into a trilateral Japan-US-Australia framework under conservative governments in both countries.

However, a rare instance emerged where the Japanese objected to a foreign policy stance by the Howard administration as too hasty. In 1999, following the referendum on independence in East Timor, paramilitary troops backing the existing annexation by Indonesia massacred supporters of independence on repeated occasions, and the public security conditions grew markedly worse. In response to this sudden crisis, the Howard administration decided to dispatch the ADF as the core of the International Force for East Timor to restore peace and order there. This move was backed by Australian public opinion, which had been sympathetic to East Timor since its 1975 occupation and annexation by Indonesia, and by the UN and the US, which were concerned about the civil disorder. Australia was forced to dispatch troops on a scale not seen since the Vietnam War. Moreover, as it was assumed that the Indonesian National Armed Forces were backing the local pro-integration paramilitary forces, there were concerns that if a confrontation were to break out between the Australian and Indonesian militaries, it would result in numerous casualties. While Australia strongly hoped that the US would send ground forces, Washington only provided rear-guard support, and was not willing to dispatch troops.

Driven by anxiety and impatience, the Howard administration made several diplomatic errors related to the East Timor situation. In September 1999, when Australian troops were dispatched to the International Force for East Timor (INTERFET), a magazine quoted Howard as saying that Australia was functioning as a "lieutenant" in the region to the world's policeman, the US. While Howard subsequently denied using the term "lieutenant" that had appeared in the article, the issue took on a life of its own, raising the ire of Indonesia and other Asian countries. Shortly thereafter, Australia's minister for defense stated that if the International Force for East Timor were subjected to hostile attack, they would counterattack and pursue the attacking forces across the border into the territory of West Timor. This statement drew a strong reaction from the Indonesian National Armed Forces. Jakarta protested vehemently, saying that Canberra had damaged bilateral relations in its enthusiasm to intervene in East Timor and admonish Indonesia. Hence it unilaterally repealed the Australian-Indonesian Security Agreement that Keating concluded in 1995 just after Canberra had dispatched the ADF to East Timor.

The Japanese government was deeply concerned about this sudden decline in relations between Australia and Indonesia over East Timor. Japan's year 2000 Diplomatic Bluebook stated that Australia had participated actively in INTERFET. "However," it noted, "the Government of Australia's hard line and the anti-Indonesian tone of Australian public opinion and the media ultimately created friction between Australia and Indonesia, and also alarmed neighboring countries."[2] This was a swipe at the Howard administration's insufficient consideration of Indonesia and the countries nearby. Tokyo also reportedly was disturbed by Canberra's persistent demands for Japan to make financial contributions to support INTERFET, even though Japan's review of its policies toward Indonesia with respect to East Timor was not yet finished. The roles that Japan could play in peace enforcement activities involving the use of force—as opposed to peacekeeping operations—were quite limited. Furthermore, the Japanese and Australian policy approaches to Indonesia diverged significantly, leaving little room for cooperation between the two countries regarding INTERFET.

Thus, from the end of the Cold War through the transition to the new century, Australia attempted to reinforce security cooperation with Japan in response to the dramatic changes in the post–Cold War international environment. While Japan showed some interest in these overtures, it did not emphasize Australia to an extent that would affect the Japan-US alliance as the backbone of Japanese diplomatic and security policy. Consequently, when Australia put itself at the forefront of regional security cooperation and came into conflict with Indonesia on the issue of East Timor's independence, Japan had to pull back. Nonetheless, with the security dialogue and defense exchanges that had begun in the 1990s, routine Japan-Australia security cooperation grew steadily during this period as well.

The Path to the Japan-Australia Joint Declaration on Security Cooperation

As China's rapid military emergence and the development of missiles by North Korea destabilized the security environment in the late 1990s, Japan began proactive efforts to reinforce the Japan-US alliance with the new Guidelines for Japan-US Defense Cooperation and other initiatives. While not conspicuous, Japan-Australia security cooperation also began showing new progress in the twenty-first century. Around this time, the US also began calling for

Australia to contribute to the security of the Asia-Pacific region. In 1999, former assistant secretary of defense Richard Armitage, who later served as deputy secretary of state in the George W. Bush administration, said if a crisis in the Taiwan Strait should develop into war between the US and China, Australia, being an ally, could not sit back and watch, or the US would not provide assistance to Australia when it called for help. High-level Australian foreign affairs and security officials responded to Armitage by arguing that this was seeking too much from Australia. Then, at the press conference following the US-Australia two-plus-two foreign and defense ministerial consultations held in Canberra in July 2001, US Secretary of State Colin Powell voiced interest in a trilateral Japan-US-Australia security dialogue. Being reluctant to irritate China and other Asian countries, Australian Minister for Foreign Affairs Alexander Downer stated in reply that they were not aiming at an Asian version of NATO. From the time it came into power in 1996, the Howard administration had been harshly criticized by China for adopting provocative policies toward China, including recalling Australia's ambassador to China during the Third Taiwan Strait Crisis and strongly opposing demonstrations of military force by the PLA navy. However, the administration subsequently shifted its stance, adopting the position that the Australia-US alliance was not intended to contain China. In the end, the Japan-US-Australia Trilateral Strategic Dialogue was quietly launched at the senior official level in 2002.

Although Australia's conservative coalition government had become sensitive to how the reinforcement of the Australia-US alliance was provoking China, in the wake of the 9/11 terrorist attacks on the US in 2001, Australia began to demonstrate solid support for its alliance with the US. Prime Minister Howard happened to be visiting the US when the World Trade Center towers were destroyed; immediately upon his return home he decided that Australia would invoke the ANZUS treaty for the first time in history, and dispatched troops to Afghanistan. The following year, Australia realized that it was itself a terrorism target when eighty-eight Australians were killed in the 2002 Bali bombings. Australia was drawn deeper and deeper into the US-led war on terrorism. During the Iraq War in 2003, the Australian government dispatched ADF units despite the clear objection of the opposition Labor Party and strongly dissenting public opinion. Through such actions, Australia demonstrated to the world that it was a loyal member of the US-led "coalition of the willing."

For its part, Japan under Prime Minister Jun'ichirō Koizumi (2001–2006) showed a more vigorous response to the war on terrorism than ever before. During the war in Afghanistan, the Japanese government passed the Anti-Terrorism Special Measures Law and dispatched MSDF supply vessels to the Indian Ocean. During the Iraq War, the SDF's Iraq Reconstruction and Support Group was deployed to Iraq under the Iraq Special Measures Law, opening a new path to sending the SDF overseas. In 2003, when the US proposed the Proliferation Security Initiative aimed at preventing the trafficking of weapons of mass destruction, Japan and Australia both actively participated. That same year, the first maritime interdiction exercise was held offshore Queensland in northeastern Australia, and the Japan Coast Guard sent a patrol vessel. Japan hosted the second exercise the next year with the participation of the US, Australia, France and other countries, and Japan-US-Australia trilateral security cooperation gained momentum.

Some analysts say this Japan-US-Australia cooperation developed smoothly because all three countries were under the lead of neoconservatives—Koizumi, Bush, and Howard—and this made it easy to reach agreement on the approach to the war on terrorism. At this time, however, the Howard administration took a complex stance that attenuated its embrace of the US. Just when the US was preoccupied with the war against terrorism in the Middle East, Australian exports of natural resources and energy to China suddenly increased; China's economic importance to Australia was growing year by year. The Howard administration began to make strong overtures to Beijing by emphasizing Australia's relations with China, and in 2003 President Hu Jintao was warmly received with an invitation to speak before Australia's Federal Parliament—the first foreign leader other than the US president ever to address that body. Moreover, the following year in Beijing, Minister for Foreign Affairs Alexander Downer announced that a crisis in the Taiwan Strait would likely fall outside the range of the ANZUS Treaty. The US reacted sharply, and Prime Minister Howard promptly issued a statement apologizing for Downer's words, stating that Australia's policy on its alliance with the US remained unchanged. At that time, however, Howard began discussing a new policy direction under which Australia would utilize its good relations with the two superpowers in the Asia Pacific to serve as a bridge between the US, its long-standing ally, and China, its rapidly growing customer. Some even viewed the Howard administration's diplomacy as intentionally distancing Australia from its alliance with the US.

In the face of China's emergence, Japan began to make diplomatic overtures toward Australia. In 2005, Japan lobbied strongly for Australia, India, and New Zealand to be added to the ASEAN Plus Three framework (consisting of the members of the Association of Southeast Asian Nations plus China, Japan, and South Korea), resulting in the creation of the East Asia Summit (EAS). Prime Minister Howard was invited to the first EAS in Kuala Lumpur that year, realizing a political achievement that the Labor Party government had desired but had been unable to accomplish. At that time, a high-level Japanese foreign ministry official was quoted as saying he had a heartfelt desire for Australia to participate in the EAS—an unusually strong call for Australia's commitment to regional cooperation.

Later in 2005, following a request from the government of Japan, Australia reversed its policy on not sending additional troops to Iraq and dispatched ADF forces to protect the SDF's Reconstruction and Support Group in Iraq. On Anzac Day—which is Australia's war memorial day—of the same year, an SDF Reconstruction and Support Group commander attended the Anzac Day ceremony at the ADF post at Samawah, Iraq; the scene was broadcast throughout Australia by a national network. Up until that time, the Australian government had consistently shown caution in engaging in security cooperation with Japan, downplaying the Japanese military presence out of deference to the Returned and Services League and other groups with deep-rooted anti-Japanese sentiment. The very act of showing citizens top commanders from the ADF and SDF attending the same ceremony on this national day of memorial demonstrated the Australian government's enthusiasm for visible security cooperation with Japan.

In a subsequent recollection, Prime Minister Howard said that the decision to have the ADF guard the SDF at Samawah was important in building strategic ties on top of the long-standing economic exchanges between Australia and Japan, and stated that it opened the door to full-scale Japan-Australia security cooperation.[3] Up to that point, the pattern in moving Japan-Australia relations forward had been for Australia to take the initiative and Japan to respond; this had been true in the diplomatic and security spheres as well as in economic relations. With the Japanese now initiating such actions as providing support for adding Australia to the EAS and requesting that Australia deploy troops to guard the Japanese forces in Iraq, Australia showed an even more positive reaction, generally working to move bilateral relations a step further.

With respect to security, US initiatives moved Australia-Japan relations forward decisively. The first Trilateral Strategic Dialogue (TSD) foreign ministerial meeting was held in Sydney in 2006, and an agreement was reached to seek constructive engagement from China and to work on increasing cooperation with the ASEAN countries, South Korea, and India. The Bush administration, which had up to that point appeared to be wholly engaged with the war on terrorism in the Middle East, began to address the change in the balance of power in the Asia-Pacific region head-on. The Howard administration responded without hesitation. When Minister for Foreign Affairs Downer visited Japan that August, he met with Prime Minister Koizumi and then chief cabinet secretary Shinzō Abe (who succeeded Koizumi as prime minister the following month) to test the waters about concluding a security cooperation agreement with Japan, and received a solid response.

This led to the Japan-Australia Joint Declaration on Security Cooperation, which was issued in March 2007, during the first Abe administration (2006–2007).[4] That declaration simply affirms that Japan and Australia have shared values and interests; that they will move forward with security cooperation regarding anti-terrorism, preventing the proliferation of weapons of mass destruction, peacekeeping operations, and disaster relief; and that they will hold an annual Japan-Australia foreign and defense ministers two-plus-two ministerial dialogue. This was the first time that Japan had exchanged such a security declaration and held a two-plus-two dialogue with any country other than the US. The Howard Administration had signed the Lombok Treaty on security cooperation with Indonesia the year before, repairing the relations that had worsened since the INTERFET incident. Australia was initially looking to sign a similar pact with Japan, but Japan was concerned that this might be held up by deliberations in the Diet, so they settled on a joint declaration. In any case, while the Lombok Treaty was signed by the foreign ministers of both countries, the Japan-Australia Joint Declaration on Security Cooperation was concluded by Prime Minister Abe and Prime Minister Howard, demonstrating the importance both countries placed on this document.

Once the agreement on further cooperation was made in the joint declaration, activities bringing relations closer accelerated. At the first two-plus-two dialogue in June 2007, various areas of cooperation were confirmed. In July, on the occasion of the APEC summit in Sydney, the first TSD summit was held with Prime Minister Abe, President Bush, and Prime Minister Howard, showing an acceleration in Japan-US-Australia security cooperation, along with progress in security cooperation between Japan and Australia. In this way, in supporting Australian security relations with both Japan and the US, the Howard administration abandoned its previous idea of serving as a bridge between the US and China, and solidified its clear commitment to reinforcing relations with allies that shared its values.

At this time, however, it seems that the Japanese government as a whole did not yet recognize the specific significance of Japan-Australia security cooperation. For example, at the joint press conference following the 2005 summit, while Prime Minister Howard spoke about security-related matters ranging from the TSD to the North Korean problem, and stressed the importance of strategic relations between Japan and Australia, Prime Minister Koizumi merely expressed his gratitude to Australia for guarding the SDF at Samawah, and said nothing further.[5] Even Prime Minister Abe—who was more enthusiastic about relations with Australia and proposed Japan-US-Australia-India quadrilateral ties in his book—devoted an entire page of that book to explaining the importance of Japan's relations with India, but just one paragraph regarding Japan's relations with Australia.[6] Until that time, Japan's security cooperation with Australia had been passive, responding to initiatives from the Australian side and joining US efforts to strengthen the TSD. The paucity of words about those bilateral relations from Koizumi and Abe, the two Japanese prime ministers who contributed so much to advance Japan-Australia security cooperation, indicated that the Japanese government did not yet have a clear plan on how to incorporate Australia into the Japan-US alliance that lies at the heart of Japan's national defense.

Japan-Australia Security Relations and the US Rebalance to Asia

By the end of 2007, Abe and Howard had both been replaced in office, and it appeared that Japan-Australia security cooperation would face a setback. In Australia, the conservative coalition lost the election held at the end of 2007, and a Labor Party government, led by Prime Minister Kevin Rudd, took office for the first time in eleven years. Rudd was a politician who had worked as a diplomat and was proficient in Chinese, and the Labor Party had a history of orientation toward an independent diplomacy, so some thought the Rudd administration would change direction from the pro-US orientation of the Howard administration and move closer to China.

In fact, at the joint press conference following the February 2008 Australia-China foreign ministers' dialogue, the new Australian administration made it clear that it would not participate in the Japan-US-Australia-India quadrilateral strategic dialogue that had been proposed by Abe and welcomed by Howard. Around that same time, the Rudd administration took the one-sided action of sending a Customs and Border Protection Service vessel to pursue the Japanese whaling fleet—which was operating in the Antarctic Ocean while under interference from an animal welfare organization—and posted images of copiously bleeding whales being hauled onto the mother ship, transmitting Japan's "barbaric" acts worldwide. Moreover, Rudd included China on his first full-scale trip abroad and bypassed Japan. With numerous measures that apparently reversed the progress of Japan-Australia relations under former prime ministers Abe and Howard, speculation that Rudd was anti-Japan and pro-China suddenly spread.

However, Australia-China relations gradually grew worse under the Rudd administration. In 2009, Aluminum Corporation of China Limited presented a plan to increase the capital of the leading Anglo-Australian metals and mining company Rio Tinto, which was struggling. Australian business leaders were extremely wary of turning over Australian natural resources to a state-owned Chinese company. The Rudd administration put off the approval of the capital increase, and in that interval, Rio Tinto's performance recovered and it rejected the Chinese offer. Furthermore, in that same year Australia published a new version of its Defence White Paper, which provides the guidelines for Australian defense policy. This paper presented military expansion plans, including the acquisition of twelve submarines and 100 F-35 joint strike fighter aircraft, to respond to the rapidly changing international environment, and mentioned restraining China's military expansion. The Chinese media responded to this series of unexpected anti-Chinese moves by the Labor Party government with harsh criticism of Rudd.

In fact, however, this was really a stratagem by Rudd to respond to China's rise by pushing the US into making a greater commitment to the Asia-Pacific region. For example, in 2008 Rudd put forth the Asia-Pacific Community concept and proposed the construction of a regional cooperation framework to handle security issues that would include the US and India. While this concept was ultimately abandoned due to insufficient preparations, the US and Russia were added to the EAS in November 2011, so one might say that it was realized de facto. In addition, just before President Barack Obama attended the 2011 EAS in Bali, Indonesia, he dropped by the northern Australian city of Darwin to announce the rotation deployment of US Marines to that location and the launch of the US "rebalance to Asia" strategy. This can be viewed as consistent with this concept as put forth by Rudd, who had lost the prime minister's position in an intra-party challenge the previous year and was then serving as minister for foreign affairs. In fact, US Secretary of State Hillary Clinton said the US pivot to Asia was largely influenced by Rudd's idea.

Prime Minister Julia Gillard, who took over leadership of the Labor Party government in 2010 after Rudd stepped down, dismissed Rudd, who could not hide his ambition to regain leadership, from his ministerial position in early 2012. Gillard formed a strategic partnership with China, and the two countries agreed to hold annual summit meetings as well as meetings of their foreign ministers and trade ministers. In contrast to her predecessor, Gillard focused on strengthening economic relations with Asia, and with China in particular. Diplomatic documents under the Gillard administration came to use the phrase "China is not an adversary." At the 2012 Australia-US Ministerial Consultations, out of a desire not to provoke China, Australia declined more frequent use of Australian navy and air force bases in the state of Western Australia by US military vessels and aircraft.

Nevertheless, the Gillard administration's emphasis on China did not signify a reversal of Australia's positive stance on the US rebalance to Asia strategy that had been laid out by Rudd. In a speech to a joint session of the US Congress in March 2011, on the sixtieth anniversary of the signing of the ANZUS treaty, Gillard called for the US to continue manifesting strong leadership in the Asia-Pacific region. In 2013, after the warming of Australia's friendly relations with China, even as it repeated that "China is not an adversary," Australia's Defence White Paper introduced the concept of the Indo-Pacific region, posed the outbreak of a conflict in the nearby region as an instance where the ADF would be mobilized for conventional warfare, and placed particular emphasis on closer defense cooperation with Indonesia in order to respond to such a situation. This indicated that the Gillard administration was giving serious consideration to preparations for the contingency of conflict breaking out between China and Indonesia or some other Southeast Asian country over the South China Sea. Furthermore, the 2013 Defence White Paper weakened the national defense self-reliance principle that had been an ADF tradition starting with the first Defence White Paper in 1976 and continuing through the 1987, 1994, 2000, and 2009 editions, and hinted at a movement toward emphasizing Australia's alliance with the US military. One could say that because Rudd lobbied the Obama administration, the US announced the rebalancing strategy, Australia provided the base at Darwin for use by the US Marines, and the Gillard administration also followed this policy direction of strengthening ties between Australian and US military forces.

Over the six years of Australia-Japan relations under the Labor Party government, what drew the most media coverage in Australia was the fuss about Japanese whale hunting each year. Similarly, while Japan had five different prime ministers—including three from the Democratic Party of Japan—who served short terms between the end of first Abe administration in 2007 and the start of the second in 2012, there was little coverage of Australia in the Japanese media. Nevertheless, during this period bilateral security cooperation, which had moved up to a higher level with the 2007 Japan-Australia Joint Declaration on Security Cooperation, steadily became institutionalized despite being conducted without fanfare. The Democratic Party of Japan administration and the Australian Labor Party government came to conclude the Japan-Australia Acquisition and Cross-Servicing Agreement in 2010 and the Japan-Australia Information Security Agreement in May 2012. Following the March 2011 Tōhoku earthquake and tsunami, the ADF sent transport aircraft and cooperated with Japanese and US forces in carrying out extensive disaster relief activities. Just a month later, Prime Minister Gillard personally visited the town of Minamisanriku in Miyagi Prefecture, which had been devastated by the tsunami; she was the first foreign head of state to visit a disaster area following the earthquake.

Furthermore, the fourth Japan-Australia two-plus-two ministerial meeting held in September 2012 adopted the ambitious document, "Australia and Japan—Cooperating for Peace and Stability: Common Vision and Objectives."[7] This paper emphasizes cooperation in the Asia-Pacific region and calls for "working together as active partners to maintain and strengthen comprehensive US engagement in the region . . . to strengthen regional cooperation on issues that have the potential to undermine the stability of the region." The Common Vision also calls for enhancing trilateral cooperation between Australia, Japan, and the US through the TSD, supporting China's constructive participation in the international order, and strengthening cooperation on security issues with other countries in the region, including India, South Korea, and ASEAN countries. While the Japan-Australia Joint Declaration on Security Cooperation called mainly for cooperation in anti-terrorism and other nontraditional aspects of security, the Common Vision stipulates that the rules-based order and response centered on the US alliances with Japan and Australia will be upheld to address the changed balance of power in the region. It can therefore be interpreted as an effort to upgrade security cooperation. Japan-Australia security cooperation was steadily institutionalized through the 2007 Joint Declaration and gained a resilience that was not affected by political shifts. Then, with the momentum from the US rebalance to Asia, the shared Japan-US-Australia goal of expanding security cooperation in the region was expressly recognized by the governments of Japan and Australia in the form of the Common Vision. With the subsequent political developments in both countries, the vision formulated by the Democratic Party of Japan and Labor Party administrations in this inconspicuous document would come to make rapid progress in a more concrete form.

Japan-US-Australia Security Cooperation under the Second Abe Administration

In Japan, the Liberal Democratic Party won an overwhelming victory in the December 2012 elections, and the second Abe administration was formed. Meanwhile, in Australia, Prime Minister Gillard lost an intra-party struggle in June 2013 and former prime minister Rudd regained control. Then, in September 2013, Australian voters turned away from the Labor Party and for the first time in six years voted a conservative coalition government into office, headed by Prime Minister Tony Abbott, the leader of the Liberal Party. The Abbott administration organically incorporated Japan into the foundation of the Australia-US alliance prepared by the Rudd and Gillard administrations, and promptly set out a clear policy of actively reinforcing Japan-Australia security cooperation.

In October 2013, just a month after taking office, Prime Minister Abbott held his first summit meeting with Prime Minister Abe at the APEC Summit in Bali. Just prior to this, the first TSD ministerial meeting since 2009 took place, attended by Australian Minister for Foreign Affairs Julie Bishop. The TSD meeting adopted a joint declaration opposing unilateral changes to the status quo by force in the South China Sea and East China Sea, and clearly supported Japan and the US as opposed to China in the dispute regarding the Senkaku Islands for the first time. Furthermore, at the end of that month, when China unilaterally declared an air defense identification zone (ADIZ) in the East China Sea, Minister for Foreign Affairs Bishop immediately summoned the Chinese ambassador and voiced Australia's strong protest against China's action, stating that this ran counter to the principle of freedom of navigation upheld by Australia. In response to the new Australian administration's resolute opposition to China in the latter's territorial dispute with Japan in the East China Sea, Chinese Foreign Minister Wang Yi stared sullenly into the camera as he was shaking hands with a smiling Bishop when they met for ministerial talks in December 2013. His treatment of Bishop was considered remarkably rude for a diplomatic setting, but Bishop held her ground in asserting her country's position.

Right after coming into power, Australia's conservative coalition government had supported Japan's position regarding the Senkaku Islands at the risk of damaging relations with China, Australia's largest economic partner. Japan responded by launching policies clearly aimed at reinforcing Japan-Australia security relations. The second Abe administration, which had secured a stable majority in the Diet, relaxed Japan's Three Principles on Arms Exports, enacted new security legislation, strengthened Japanese security policy, and greatly expanded the leeway for security cooperation not only with the US but with Australia as well. Prime Minister Abbott, who shares conservative values with Abe, visited Japan in April 2014. Only three years had passed since the visit by former Prime Minister Gillard, who had also come as a guest of state, but Abe received Abbott with exceptional warmth. At their summit, they reached a basic understanding on a defense equipment and technology transfer agreement that would provide Maritime SDF Sōryū-class submarines to the ADF. They also moved forward on the contents of the Japan-Australia Economic Partnership Agreement, which had been pending since 2006, and confirmed that Japan and Australia would develop a "new special relationship." In July 2014, Abe visited Australia and signed the two agreements without delay. He was given the opportunity to address the Australian parliament, making him only the second head of state of a nation other than the UK or the US to do so (after China's President Hu Jintao in 2003).

In parallel with Japan-Australia ties, trilateral ties with the US were also reinforced. At the Brisbane G20 Summit in November 2014, Abe, Obama, and Abbott held the first TSD summit since 2007, and the three countries agreed to move forward with collaboration on issues at both the regional and global levels, and to actively lobby regional partners as well. In the security field, trilateral exercises were stepped up. The ADF joined the US and Japan for the first time in the disaster relief exercise Michinoku ALERT14, which was held in the Tōhoku region of Japan, while the Ground Self-Defense Force (GSDF) joined Australia and the US for the first time in the full-scale joint training exercise Talisman Sabre 15.

On the Japanese side, the development of Japan-Australia relations under the Abe and Abbott administrations was characterized by unprecedented efforts to provide benefit to Australia, and to strengthen bilateral and trilateral relations under the banner of proactive pacifism. For example, the proposed technology transfer of Sōryū-class submarines to Australia would have been out of the question a few years earlier, because it entailed a large risk that state secrets could be leaked. Furthermore, when Australia faced unexpectedly strong calls for domestic production in order to boost employment, Japan even began considering having its Sōryū-class submarines built in Australia. As the April 2014 Japan-Australia Economic Partnership Agreement included beef and other items that were politically sensitive within Japan, the outlook for a deal was quite poor. In spite of this, a basic agreement was suddenly reached just before the summit. For the government of Japan, opening Japan's closely protected agricultural market to highly competitive Australian imports was a bold decision accompanied by great political risk, and a major achievement for Australia. This exhibited an unprecedented level of effort by the Japanese to enhance Japan-Australia relations.

The Australian media, which viewed Prime Minister Abe as a right-wing proponent of nationalist values, responded to the Abbot administration's efforts to strengthen relations with Japan with concern. There were fears that Abe might take a hard-line stance against China over some minor clash regarding the Senkaku Islands, and that this would ultimately drag Australia, willing or not, into a Japan-US confrontation with China in faraway Northeast Asia. Bob Carr, who had served as minister for foreign affairs in the latter half of the Gillard administration, noted that public opinion polls showed the overwhelming majority of Australians were against dispatching the ADF in response to a dispute in the Senkaku Islands. Maintaining that the Senkaku Islands were as distant a concern as the Falklands for Australia, he sounded a warning about the dangers of Abbott's movement toward closer relations with Japan.

Despite Abbott's clear pro-Japan and pro-US stance, China did not criticize him the way it had criticized his predecessor Rudd. Prior to the 2013 election, Abbott's conservative coalition had pledged to conclude free trade agreements (FTAs) with Japan, China, and South Korea, Australia's three major economic partners in Northeast Asia, within one year of taking office. By the middle of 2014, the Abbott administration had concluded its negotiations with South Korea and Japan, and political support emerged for a basic understanding on an FTA between Australia and China when President Xi Jinping attended the November 2014 Brisbane G20 Summit. For China, Australia is not only a supplier of natural resources and agricultural products; its mines and farms are important targets for Chinese investment. For that reason, the Abe administration's concessions on agricultural products and its conclusion of an economic partnership agreement with Australia ahead of China put pressure on China and narrowed its diplomatic leeway with the Abbott administration.

As it happened, Prime Minister Abbott did reach a basic understanding on an Australia-China FTA in his talks with Secretary General Xi, thereby achieving his campaign pledge of concluding FTAs with the three countries of Japan, China, and South Korea, which had been viewed with skepticism prior to the election. In the security sphere, the participation of Australian nationals in the Islamic State (IS) drew attention, and the threat of home-grown terrorism emerged in an incident where a hostage was murdered in downtown Sydney; furthermore, in 2015 the ADF was dispatched to bomb IS targets in Iraq in response to a US request. By sending the second-largest military presence in the field after the US, the Abbott administration demonstrated its reliability as a US ally in the war on terrorism.

However, the Abbott administration suffered a string of policy failures on the domestic front, and Abbott lost support within the ruling Liberal Party because the conservative coalition was falling below the Labor Party in public opinion polls. In September 2015, Abbott lost the office of prime minister to Minister for Communications Malcom Turnbull, who enjoyed strong popularity among the Australian public. Turnbull is a former businessman with deep ties to China; his son's wife is Chinese, and her father is a member of the Communist Party. Long a pro-China politician, Turnbull once said that by fighting the war against Japan, China had saved Australia from the crisis of Japanese invasion. While Turnbull had served as the leader of the Liberal Party, which was then the opposition party, during the Rudd administration, his strong liberalism was unpopular in the party; he subsequently lost the party leadership to Abbott, who was supported by the conservative faction. Even after Turnbull became prime minister, there is no doubt that he still had to pay careful attention to disaffection from the conservative members of his party.

For that reason, although Prime Minister Turnbull comes from the liberal wing, little can be said since these are still the early days of his administration. To date he has basically followed the Abbott administration in the diplomatic and security arenas. His administration has clearly shown its intention to continue with the bombing against IS, and it is strongly supporting freedom of navigation operations by US warships in response to China's construction of man-made islands in the South China Sea. A Royal Australian Air Force patrol plane in flight above the South China Sea was recorded receiving warnings from a PLA Navy warship on November 25, 2015 and sending repeated messages in response that it was implementing freedom of navigation operations. In December, Australia's Department of

Defense acknowledged that this was part of routine maritime surveillance patrol activities by the ADF in the South China Sea.

In Japan-Australia relations, there were rumors of a secret agreement between Prime Minister Abbott and Prime Minister Abe under which Australia would procure submarines from Japan, and criticism spread within the ruling party that Abbott had abandoned his campaign pledge to support domestic production. To address this, the Abbott administration was forced to hold competitive bidding and opened a review of three models from Japan, Germany, and France. Japan, which had no experience building submarines overseas, lost its advantage, and ultimately in April 2016 the Turnbull administration selected the French model for Australia's next-generation submarine.

However, in relation to the matter of submarine selection, it is worth noting that under the second Abe administration, Japan changed its stance from prior administrations to strongly push solidarity with Australia. At the November 2015 two-plus-two ministerial meeting, Japan vigorously advocated the high-level strategic benefits of reinforcing the Japan-US-Australia partnership by adopting the Sōryū design and took a positive stance toward domestic production inside Australia.

As China commits increasingly brazen acts of aggression in the South China Sea not far from Australian territory, support from Japan via the trilateral Japan-US-Australia structure called for in the Common Vision, as opposed to relying solely on the bilateral alliance between Australia and the US, would extend Australia's range of security cooperation to the Indo-Pacific Region. While the diplomatic approach of the Turnbull administration is likely to be more evenhanded than that of the Abbott administration, the basic structure of regional security cooperation involving Japan, the US, and Australia is already deeply established. Regardless of changes of administration, we may assume that Japan and Australia will continue to steadily strengthen bilateral ties. In fact, Australia's Defence White Paper released in February 2016 stresses the importance of the trilateral cooperation between Japan, the US, and Australia more explicitly than ever before.

Conclusion

As outlined above, following the end of the Cold War, Australia overcame its former domestic wariness of Japan and advocated full-scale Japan-Australia security cooperation, looking to Japan as a partner in regional security cooperation. From Japan's perspective, however, Australia was then just one counterpart country in its regular defense exchanges, and the two nations were sometimes at cross-purposes. With the rise of China and other changes in the international environment in the region, however, the US showed strong interest in developing Japan-US-Australia trilateral ties. Japan joined Australia in the war on terrorism and otherwise actively responded, and bilateral relations improved greatly, as shown by the 2007 Japan-Australia Joint Declaration on Security Cooperation. Nevertheless, at that time, Japan did not show clear recognition of Australia's position in its own security policy. Once the US launched its rebalance to Asia, however, Australia's strategic value increased and the significance of the strategic alliance between Japan and Australia emerged. Then, when the Japanese side made positive efforts to reinforce relations with Australia under the second Abe administration, Japan-US-Australia solidarity became much stronger.

Let us reconsider the significance of Japan-Australia security cooperation in the context of this reinforced trilateral Japan-US-Australia cooperation. After the Second World War, Japan and Australia deepened their bilateral relations mainly in the economic sphere; these deepened bilateral ties also became the motive force for economic cooperation across the Asia-Pacific region. With Australia taking the lead and Japan serving as a reliable coordinator, their collaboration resulted in APEC, a significant achievement. Behind this success in regional cooperation lay the two countries' important shared interest as maritime trading nations in securing the open economic system in the region.

Today, while Japan-US-Australia ties are growing deeper, there is still room for greater Japan-Australia security cooperation in areas such as peacekeeping operations, disaster relief, and capacity building. By surely and steadily building a record of cooperation to date, Japan and Australia have realized accomplishments in the economic and security fields. In the Indo-Pacific region, which is diverse in a variety of ways, the strengthening of bilateral cooperation is a shortcut to regional cooperation. From this point on, Japan and Australia should take their steady approach to bilateral cooperation as the model for their efforts to pursue regional cooperation.

1   Ministry of Foreign Affairs of Japan, Joint Declaration on the Australia-Japan Partnership, May 26, 1995, https://www.mofa.go.jp/region/asia-paci/australia/join_au.html.

2   Ministry of Foreign Affairs of Japan, "Chapter III: Regional Developments, Asia and the Pacific

(Oceania)," in Diplomatic Bluebook 2000: Toward the 21st Century–Foreign Policy for a Better Future, https://www.mofa.go.jp/policy/other/bluebook/2000/III-a.html

3   John Howard, *Lazarus Rising: A Personal and Political Autobiography* (Sydney: Harper Collins Publishers, 2010), 458.

4   Ministry of Foreign Affairs of Japan, Japan-Australia Joint Declaration on Security Cooperation, March 13, 2007, https://www.mofa.go.jp/region/asia-paci/australia/joint0703.html.

5   Joint Press Conference after the Japan-Australia Summit Meeting, April 20, 2005, https://japan.kantei.go.jp/koizumispeech/2005/04/20press_e.html.

6   Shinzō Abe, *Utsukushii kuni e* [Towards a beautiful country] (Bunshun Shinsho, 2006), 159–160.

7   Fourth Australia-Japan Foreign and Defence Ministerial Consultations, "Australia and Japan—Cooperating for Peace and Stability: Common Vision and Objectives," September 14, 2012, https://www.mofa.go.jp/files/000034392.pdf.

CHAPTER 11

South Korea's Maritime Strategy and Its Implications for Japan

Narushige Michishita
Vice President, National Graduate Institute for Policy Studies (GRIPS)

South Korea's Maritime and Naval Strategy

Maritime Strategy

The Korean Peninsula has long functioned as a bridge between Japan and China, and has had significant political, military, and cultural importance to Japan. As soon as Korea became independent from Japan in 1945, the US-USSR confrontation caused the division of the peninsula. As a result, the Democratic People's Republic of Korea (North Korea) was established in the north and the Republic of Korea (South Korea) in the south in 1948. South Korea—which was originally a peninsular country—became a de facto maritime state with 11,542 kilometers of coastline and more than 3,000 islands, surrounded on three sides by the Sea of Japan, the Yellow Sea, and the East China Sea.

The economy of South Korea is highly dependent on foreign trade: in 2018, it had a trade-to-GDP ratio of 86.8 percent and an exports-to-GDP ratio of 53.1 percent. Because more than 99 percent of South Korea's import and export freight is shipped by sea, maritime strategy is essential for its economic development.

The South Korean government recognized the importance of maritime development following the rapid economic growth achieved in the 1970s and 1980s, and took several measures to cope with the new development. In 1990, the maritime research center associated with the Republic of Korea Institute of Science and Technology became an independent organization called the Korea Ocean Research and Development Institute. The institute was subsequently renamed the Korean Institute of Ocean Science and Technology in 2012, and expanded into a government-affiliated corporation under the Ministry of Oceans and Fisheries. In 1992, an ocean policy committee established under the South Korean prime minister began to formulate a comprehensive maritime development plan. South Korea ratified the United Nations Convention on the Law of the Sea (UNCLOS) in 1996; in that same year, the Korea Maritime and Port Administration, the Fisheries Agency, and other bodies were merged into a new Ministry of Oceans and Fisheries. The purpose of the new ministry was to develop a framework for creating consistent maritime policy in response to the emergence of a new maritime legal order. Furthermore, the Maritime Police Agency, which had been under the National Police Agency, was restructured as an independent agency affiliated with the Ministry of Oceans and Fisheries. In a speech celebrating Ocean Day (May 31), President Kim Young-sam said that South Korea must first become a maritime state before it could take center stage in world affairs in the twenty-first century.

South Korea addressed several different issues in its efforts to become a full-fledged maritime state. First, for marine environmental protection, the government constructed an integrated coastal management system and addressed marine water quality, recovery of marine debris, wetlands protection, and other issues. Second, for marine resources development, it worked to develop technologies to mine nickel, manganese, and other resources from the deep seabed of the South Pacific. Furthermore, in 2000 the government drafted its first national ocean and fishery development plan, "Ocean Korea 21," a ten-year plan that covers all these issues. The second national ocean and fishery development plan, drafted in 2011, established a strategy for South Korea to become a global maritime state by the year 2020.

Meanwhile, there was some back and forth in the organizational management of the Ministry of Oceans and Fisheries, which implements maritime policy. The Lee Myung-bak administration, which took office in 2008, merged the ministry's maritime division with the Ministry of Construction and Transportation and renamed the latter the Ministry of Land, Transport, and Maritime Affairs. The fisheries division was transferred to the Ministry of Agriculture, Forestry, and Fisheries, and the marine environment division was transferred to the Ministry of Environment. This restructuring divided the various units responsible for maritime policy, making the formulation of comprehensive maritime policy difficult.

To resolve these concerns, the Park Geun-hye administration, which came into office in 2013, reestablished the Ministry of Oceans and Fisheries. However, the researcher appointed to lead the reestablished ministry faced political backlash after an accidental oil spill offshore Yeosu City. She stated that the company whose pipeline was hit by a tanker was the prime victim; this remark drew the anger of local fishermen. The ministry was criticized by the public and in political circles. Furthermore, in the *Sewol* ferry disaster, in which a large passenger ferry sank in April 2014, the Ministry of Oceans and Fisheries was harshly criticized for collusion with the shipping industry, and the Korea Coast Guard was blamed for its ineffective rescue efforts. Meanwhile, the Park administration announced its "Eurasia Initiative" in October 2013, launching a strategy oriented more toward the continent than toward the seas. Regardless, while the confrontation with North Korea remained unresolved, South Korea and ports in the Russian Far East were linked by a sea route from 2014, providing South Korea with access to the Eurasian continent via the ocean.

The Leap to a Blue-Water Navy: The Development of Naval Strategy and Power

As noted above, South Korea is part of what was formerly a single Korean nation, and it is surrounded by the sea on three sides. For those reasons, the seas have significant military strategic importance. The Republic of Korea Navy (ROKN) was officially launched in 1948 based on the naval contingent of the Marine Defense Group founded in November 1945 after Korea was liberated from Japanese colonial rule. Since the most important military threat to South Korea lies across the land border with North Korea, most defense expenditures have gone toward the development of the army. The navy functioned mainly as a coastal force because its most important objective was to prevent intrusions by North Korean agents using small high-speed vessels.

Plans to expand the ROKN into a blue-water maritime force began to emerge in the early 1990s. With South Korea's remarkable economic growth, the navy began working to develop sufficient operational capabilities to protect national interests and support national policies not just along the country's coasts and in adjacent waters, but also in the Pacific Ocean and the Indian Ocean, which encompass critical sea lines of communication. In addition, a debate emerged concerning the development of the naval power required to restrain the navies of nearby countries, due to the belief that a power struggle over the control of the Pacific Ocean was inevitable in the twenty-first century. The navy was already examining the introduction of domestically manufactured Aegis Combat System destroyers in the mid-1980s, although it was only around the mid-1990s, some ten years later, that it moved forward with specific manufacturing plans.

The ROKN began to make a formal appeal for a blue-water navy in 1995, under the Kim Young-sam administration. In a public information pamphlet titled "Toward a Twenty-First-Century Navy," the ROKN stressed the need to build up an "oceangoing navy of the twenty-first century" to prepare for potential maritime disputes in Asia. At the same time, the government launched a construction plan for domestic destroyers (KDX: Korean Destroyer eXperimental). As a first-round project, the government commissioned the domestic construction of three destroyers—*Kwanggaeto*, *Eulji-mundok*, and *Yang Manchoon*—between 1998 and 2000.

In the meantime, the Ministry of National Defense and the Joint Chiefs of Staff were concerned about possible friction with neighboring countries; the army may have also felt concerns about having its resources taken by the navy. Ultimately, the South Korean government decided not to provide strong support to the ROKN's calls for the building of an oceangoing navy. Furthermore, in the Asian financial crisis that broke out in 1997, the currencies of several Asian countries lost value, starting with the Thai baht, and South Korea almost fell into default. As a result, in January 1998, the Kim Young-sam administration cancelled the entire budget for the second-round project construction plan for Korean-made destroyers, which were to be the first to carry fleet air-defense missiles.

The subsequent Kim Dae-jung administration decided to focus once again on the buildup of the ROKN, which had gone stagnant, and resume the second-round project. In his speech at the 1999 naval academy commencement and entrance ceremony, President Kim said he would give positive consideration to an "ocean-going navy of the twenty-first century," and at the 2001 ceremony he called for securing a fleet with strategic mobility. Six Korean-made destroyers were then commissioned for the second-round project from 2003 through 2008: *Chungmugong Yi Sun-sin*, *Munmu the Great*, *Dae Joyoung*, *Wang Geon*, *Gang Gamchan*, and *Choi Young*. These destroyers were dispatched for anti-piracy operations offshore Somalia from 2009. Then, as a third-round project, three Aegis-equipped destroyers were commissioned from 2008 through 2012: *Sejong the Great*, *Yulgok Yi I*, and *Seoae Ryu Seongryong*. In February 2010, the ROKN's first mobile force,

Maritime Task Flotilla Seven, which comprised mobile forces led by an Aegis destroyer, was established at Busan Naval Base. The Maritime Task Flotilla Seven is now home-ported at the Jeju Naval Base.

Furthermore, the Defense Reform Basic Plan 2012–2030 released in 2012 called for adding a total of six next-generation South Korean–made destroyers (5,000-ton class), which are smaller than the existing Aegis destroyers, to the ROKN between 2019 and 2026, and for constructing three more Aegis destroyers as well. The revised Defense Reform Basic Plan 2014–2030, compiled after the Park Geun-hye administration took office, calls for the introduction of these three Aegis destroyers by the mid-2020s.

The Development of Coastal Defense Capabilities

In response to frequent incursions by North Korean high-speed boats crossing the Northern Limit Line in the Yellow Sea and by North Korean special operations units slipping into South Korean territory, the ROKN introduced high-speed boats and patrol vessels in the 1970s and 1980s, and worked to build up its coastal defense capabilities. South Korean–manufactured high-speed Chamsuri-class patrol vessels and the Pohang-class corvettes introduced under the Yulgok defense buildup plan played central roles in the First Battle of Yeonpyeong, which broke out in June 1999. In the Second Battle of Yeonpyeong in June 2002, a North Korean patrol boat launched a surprise attack on one of the Chamsuri-class patrol vessels and sank the ship.

Having learned from this experience, the ROKN launched the PKX (Patrol Killer eXperimental) program for the introduction of vessels with long-distance attack capabilities and air defense capabilities to intercept anti-ship missiles fired from the coast—the PKX-A (400-ton class, missile armed) and the PKX-B (200-ton class, without missiles). These were to serve as a replacement for the Chamsuri-class patrol vessels. In the first phase (2002–2010), the focus was on the PKX-A, and in December 2008, the *Yoon Youngha*, named after a South Korean officer who was killed during the Second Battle of Yeonpyeong, was commissioned as the first Gumdoksuri-class missile patrol ship.

In March 2010, the *Cheonan*, a Pohang-class corvette that had seen action in the First Battle of Yeonpyeong, was hit by a North Korean torpedo in the Yellow Sea and sank, killing forty-six seamen. The ROKN was criticized for its inability to protect South Korean waters, and had to temporarily refrain from using the term "ocean-going navy." In the disputed waters around the Northern Limit Line, the Aegis destroyers and high-speed missile ships gave the ROKN an overwhelming advantage in fighting power against the North Korean navy, which mostly deployed small vessels of 400 tons or less. The ROKN had not given much emphasis to anti-submarine warfare, judging that operations by large North Korean submarines would be difficult in the shallow waters of the Yellow Sea. Following the sinking of the *Cheonan*, the ROKN introduced improved versions of the former US Navy S-3B anti-submarine patrol aircraft and reinforced its anti-submarine warfare capabilities. Admittedly, there is a limit to what these assets can do. These anti-submarine patrol aircraft are vulnerable to attack by surface-to-air missiles from the North Korean coast when they approach the Northern Limit Line.

In accordance with the Defense Reform Basic Plan 2012–2030, the ROKN also established a Submarine Force Command at Jinhae Naval Base in February 2015 to counter North Korea's submarines. The navy presently operates a total of twenty-two submarines, three cruisers, six destroyers, seventeen frigates, and thirty-two corvettes.

The Development and Present State of South Korea's Maritime Security Capabilities

The former Korea Coast Guard, which had been responsible for South Korea's maritime safety, was abolished under orders from President Park Geun-hye after its slipshod efforts at saving lives in the April 2014 *Sewol* ferry disaster brought its accountability into question. Its Maritime Guard Bureau, Maritime Pollution Response Bureau, and Equipment and Technology Bureau were transferred to the new Korea Coast Guard under the new Ministry of Public Safety and Security, which was established under the prime minister in November of that year. Its Investigation and Intelligence Bureau was transferred to the National Police Agency.

The Korea Coast Guard was originally established in 1953 as the Maritime Police Force in the Public Safety Bureau of the Ministry of Home Affairs. Following a series of name changes and organizational restructurings, it became the Maritime Police Agency in 1991, and was affiliated with the National Police Agency. Then, in 1996, the Maritime Police Agency was made an independent government agency affiliated with the newly established Ministry of Oceans and Fisheries. This was in response to the ratification of UNCLOS by the National Assembly and the introduction of the 200-nautical-mile exclusive economic zone (EEZ) system in that year. As a result, the duties of the Maritime Police Agency expanded from guarding the waters within the 12-nautical-mile limit to guarding a wide-ranging ocean area, and the Maritime Police Agency began to conduct operations to maintain order in addition to its pollution control duties.

As part of this organizational expansion, the rank of the head of the Maritime Police Agency was upgraded to the vice-ministerial level, with the head of the agency becoming a commissioner general in 2005. Also, the English-language name used externally was changed from "Maritime Police Agency" to "Korea Coast Guard." In this process, the Korea Coast Guard strengthened its investigative functions more than its maritime safety activities; when it was disbanded in 2014, the Investigation and Intelligence Bureau had three times more personnel than the Rescue and Safety Bureau. It has been noted that these circumstances contributed to the lackluster rescue efforts in response to the *Sewol* ferry disaster.

Today, the Korea Coast Guard has a total of eighty-one patrol and coastal combatants, eight amphibious landing craft, six aircraft, and sixteen helicopters. Since 2004, the number of incidents involving illegal operations by Chinese fishing vessels inside the EEZ have increased rapidly. The Ministry of Public Safety and Security secured 619.6 billion won (US$524 million) as the FY 2015 budget for the Korea Coast Guard, with one-sixth of that allocated for the construction of large vessels. Also, to respond to illegal fishing by Chinese ships, which is growing more prevalent, special teams led by personnel with experience in military special forces units are being formed, and enforcement is being strengthened.

Outstanding Issues Regarding Territorial Seas and Fisheries

Outstanding Issues between China and South Korea

Socotra Rock jurisdiction dispute

Socotra Rock (referred to as Ieodo in South Korea and Suyan Islet in China)[1] is located in the Yellow Sea at the southernmost tip of South Korea, 170 km southwest of Jeju Island (149 km from Marado). South Korea and China are currently in a dispute regarding jurisdiction over its surrounding sea area. Socotra Rock is a submerged rock whose high point lies 4.6 meters below sea level at low tide, and the surrounding sea area has a depth of 50 meters. The South Korean government calls this rock an "island," but legally, it is not recognized as an island or as territory. According to South Korea's claim, if the median line principle based on UNCLOS is applied, the sea area near Socotra Rock is included in South Korea's EEZ. Conversely, China claims, using the continental shelf principle based on the natural extension of land territory, that Socotra Rock lies within China's EEZ. Because of this situation, the median line between China and South Korea has not yet been demarcated.

Nevertheless, based on its own claims, South Korea began building the Ieodo Ocean Research Station on Socotra Rock in 1995; construction was completed in 2003. Although China protested this via diplomatic channels, it did not develop into a major diplomatic issue. In September 2006, China's State Oceanic Administration disclosed that Chinese aircraft had conducted surveillance activities around the research station five times. Moreover, in a regular press conference in October, a Chinese foreign ministry spokesperson stated, "Suyan islet is located in the northern part of East China Sea below the sea level,"[2] implying that it is not an island under international law. The spokesperson also made it clear that China did not approve of the unilateral construction of the research station by South Korea, but stated further that China and South Korea had no territorial dispute. This was the first time that the Chinese government formally repudiated South Korea's jurisdiction over Socotra Rock.

The Fisheries Agreement between China and South Korea, which has been in effect since June 2001, also has no explicit provisions regarding the jurisdiction over Socotra Rock; it simply includes the sea area around Socotra Rock as a joint fishing area for both China and South Korea. Accordingly, as there is no agreement between the countries regarding jurisdiction, it is only natural that the Chinese government should not approve of the ocean research station that South Korea unilaterally constructed on Socotra Rock. Nevertheless, South Koreans were shocked by China's stance on the matter. On Jeju Island, which is geographically close to Socotra Rock, there was a movement in 2008 to establish a "Ieodo Island Day," but that was put off at the request of South Korea's Ministry of Foreign Affairs. The South Korean government views the Socotra Rock issue in a different light from its territorial dispute with Japan regarding Takeshima (disputed islands in the Sea of Japan that the Koreans call Dokdo), positioning the dispute with China as a matter related to the EEZ rather than one of territory, and does not find it necessary to provoke China regarding this issue.

China has maintained its claims. In a March 2012 interview with the Xinhua News Agency, State Oceanic Administration Director Liu Cigui announced that Socotra Rock is located in sea areas under Chinese jurisdiction, and that it is included in the patrol range of Chinese patrol vessels and aircraft. A foreign ministry spokesperson also made clear China's position that while Socotra Rock is not the subject of any territorial dispute, the jurisdiction should be determined by demarcation of the EEZ.

As explained above, China and South Korea disagree about the EEZ boundary between the two countries. Negotiations on the issue were delayed because the responsible authorities in China (the Ministry of Foreign Affairs' Department of Boundary and Ocean Affairs) were giving priority to the South China Sea issue and the Senkaku Islands issue in the East China Sea. In June 2014, however, bureau-head-level discussions took place for the first time in three years, and at the China–South Korea summit held the following month, an agreement was reached to conduct full-scale negotiations on the EEZ boundary demarcation from 2015. A preparatory meeting took place in Shanghai in January 2015.

Illegal operations by Chinese fishing boats

Because the EEZ boundary between China and South Korea has not been demarcated, under the China-Korea fisheries agreement which came into effect in 2001, the sea area where the EEZs overlap in the Yellow Sea is set as a "provisional waters" area where both countries jointly manage the fisheries order. Nevertheless, the perpetual violations of this agreement by Chinese fishing boats in these waters are worrisome for the South Korean side. In particular, there are a very large number of cases where Chinese fishing boats operate illegally inside South Korea's territorial sea or EEZ without permission, or where they receive permission but violate restrictions on fishing equipment or make false reports on the quantities of fish caught. The South Korean enforcement activities are conducted by fishery management organizations and by the Korea Coast Guard. The Korea Coast Guard has dealt with Chinese vessels engaged in illegal fishing activities each year since the time the fisheries agreement came into effect in 2001, with a peak of 584 cases in 2005 and around 500 cases per year since 2011, for a cumulative total of 5,303 cases as of 2013.

As many Chinese fishing boats often engage in illegal fishing operations together, the Chinese fishermen will collectively or systematically resist enforcement. For example, in September 2008, a Korea Coast Guard officer who was trying to board a Chinese boat that was fishing illegally in South Korea's EEZ drowned after being hit with a shovel and knocked into the sea. In December 2011 a Korea Coast Guard officer boarded a Chinese fishing boat for enforcement and was stabbed to death by the ship's captain. In response, the Korea Coast Guard authorized the immediate use of small arms in cases where Korea Coast Guard officers feel that their life is threatened or cannot exercise their duties using other means while conducting enforcement activities against illegal fishing boats. Prior to that time, the use of small arms had only been authorized in cases where enforcement using nonlethal weapons was not possible. As a result, Chinese crew members became victims as well. In October 2012, one Chinese crew member died after being hit by a rubber bullet fired by a Korea Coast Guard officer, and in October 2014 the captain of a Chinese fishing boat was killed in a clash where a Korea Coast Guard officer used a gun to take control of the vessel while the Chinese used weapons to resist.

Outstanding Issues between Japan and South Korea

The fisheries issue and the Takeshima territorial issue

Under the Agreement between Japan and the Republic of Korea Concerning Fisheries concluded when the two countries normalized their diplomatic relations in 1965, Japan had enforcement authority only over the waters within its 12-nautical-mile limit. Outside that area, the "flag state principle," whereby the enforcement authority lies solely with the nation to which the fishing vessel belongs, was observed. From the 1980s, with the development of the South Korean marine products industry, illegal operations and overfishing by South Korean fishing vessels increased. Japan, which could not carry out enforcement against such activities, made appeals to South Korea regarding the preservation of the resources of the Sea of Japan and the establishment of a fisheries order.

The issue of the demarcation of the EEZ boundary between Japan and South Korea arose in 1996, as both countries had ratified UNCLOS. The two countries held working-level negotiations toward revising the 1965 fisheries agreement, including resolution of the outstanding issues presented above. However, there was significant disagreement between Japan and South Korea regarding the demarcation of the EEZ boundary in relation to the disputed islands of Takeshima (Dokdo) and the revision of the 1965 fisheries agreement. The Japanese proposed putting off the EEZ boundary demarcation and giving priority to the conclusion of a new fisheries agreement, while the South Koreans called for both issues to be addressed at the same time; the talks ended with the two sides on separate tracks. After Japan set straight baselines under the provisions of UNCLOS in 1997, it repeatedly seized South Korean fishing vessels operating in sea areas that were now within its territorial waters. For that reason, the Japanese felt pressed to conclude a new fisheries agreement. To create a deadline for negotiations on a new agreement, Japan gave unilateral notice that the 1965 fisheries agreement would terminate in January 1998. South Korea, which had been suffering economically due to the 1997 Asian currency crisis, strongly opposed Japan's unilateral notification of the termination of the 1965 fisheries agreement, viewing it as an intentional strategy to take advantage of South Korea's weakness.

Nevertheless, because President Kim Dae-jung, who took office in February 1998, emphasized improving relations with Japan, he took a positive approach to concluding the negotiations. After various ups and downs, the Agreement between Japan and the Republic of Korea Concerning Fisheries was signed by Japan and South Korea in November and came into effect in January 1999. Under the new agreement, Japan and South Korea agreed to make fisheries issues distinct from territorial issues, and established provisional fishing zones around the median lines claimed by both parties, while ignoring the existence of Takeshima. In setting these median lines, Japan called for a baseline between Takeshima and Ulleungdo, while South Korea proposed a baseline between Ulleungdo and the Oki Islands. South Korea did not use Takeshima as a point of origin for its EEZ; Takeshima is still within South Korea's EEZ even when Utsuryōto is used as the point of origin, so there was no real loss. But mostly, this was to avoid conflict regarding Takeshima, because reaching the new agreement before President Kim's visit to Japan was a high priority. Moreover, these negotiations included the majority of the Yamatotai area, one of Japan's favored fishing grounds, in a provisional fishing zone, effectively winning this concession from Japan.

After this, overfishing by Korean fishing vessels ignoring the fisheries order became an increasingly serious problem in the provisional fishing zones where fishing vessels from both countries were permitted to operate. Opposition from fishermen in the San'in region of Japan, whose main fishing grounds were in the provisional fishing zones, grew stronger. In Shimane Prefecture in particular, there were growing demands for the government of Japan to quickly resolve the Takeshima territorial issue; people noted that the provisional fishing zones had been set without settling the jurisdiction over Takeshima. In March 2005, the Shimane Prefectural Assembly approved by an overwhelming majority an ordinance to declare February 22 "Takeshima Day."

Meanwhile, to sidestep complications in Japan–South Korean relations, the Roh Moo-hyun administration proposed a statement to the effect that both leaders had agreed to refrain from words and actions that would bring up memories of an unfortunate past in the joint statement following the December 2004 Japan–South Korea summit. In the end, however, this was not included, as agreement could not be reached with the Japanese side. Amid these developments, South Korea took the enactment of "Takeshima Day" by the Shimane Prefectural Assembly very seriously. The view of the South Korean government was that Takeshima (Dokdo) had been annexed into Shimane Prefecture while Korea was occupied by the Japanese military in violation of its sovereignty, and that the establishment of "Takeshima Day" by one regional government body was therefore not just a territorial issue but a brazen act that denied history. And with this, the South Korean government shifted to a hard-line policy toward Japan. In April 2006, President Roh Mun-hyun linked the Takeshima territorial issue with the issue of historical awareness, and released a special statement strongly demanding that Japan renounce its territorial rights to Takeshima. Since that time, South Korea has ceased making any compromises with Japan regarding this territorial issue.

In April 2006, the South Korean government declared it would take "stern" measures if Japan Coast Guard ships carried out oceanographic surveys in the region around Takeshima. These surveys were cancelled following bilateral diplomatic negotiations; however, a South Korean survey ship then carried out an oceanographic survey in the seas around Takeshima in July of that same year, and entered waters on the Japanese side of the median line claimed by Japan, despite Japanese requests to cancel or postpone such an action. The EEZ boundary demarcation negotiations that had been suspended since 2000 were resumed in June 2006, but the South Koreans came to the negotiations with an aggressive stance. The Japanese first proposed a compromise of establishing a prior notification system for oceanographic surveys and other activities, rather than addressing the sticky territorial issue right away. South Korea rejected that proposal; it also changed its point of origin for the median line for the EEZ border demarcation negotiations from Ulleungdo to Takeshima and began to insist on a median line between Takeshima and the Oki Islands. For that reason, the boundary demarcation negotiations have remained stalled up to the present day.

Japan and South Korea both worked at reaching a compromise by separating the Takeshima (Dokdo) territorial issue from the fisheries issue and setting it aside. Nevertheless, the South Korean government failed to take effective measures against overfishing by South Korean fishing vessels. Fisheries interests in Shimane Prefecture reacted to this by trying to assert Japanese sovereignty over Takeshima; the Roh Moo-hyun administration responded forcefully, characterizing these efforts as an attempt to deny history, and became unwilling to compromise on this territorial issue.[3] As a result, the dispute became even thornier.

Thereafter, President Lee Myung-bak, who had previously supported good relations with Japan, turned away from Japan over the long-standing issue of the Korean women pressed into service as prostitutes ("comfort women") for Japanese troops prior to Japan's surrender in 1945, along with other historical issues. In August 2012, he became the first sitting South Korean president to set foot on Takeshima, adding further emotional complications to the relations between Japanese and South Korea. The confrontational stance of the South Korean government remains unchanged in the early years of Park Geun-hye's presidency; the South Korean government made an active appeal regarding territorial rights over Takeshima (Dokdo).

---

1   The Korean name is "Ieodo" and the Chinese name is "Suyan Jiao." In this chapter, the English name Socotra Rock is used for convenience. In 1984, Socotra Rock was surveyed by a South Korean joint survey team from Jeju National University and the Korean Broadcasting System station on Jeju Island. This team referred to the rock as "Parangdo," but in 2001 the Korea Geographic Information Institute gave "Ieodo" as its official name.

2   Chinese Foreign Ministry Spokesman Qin Gang's regular press conference, September 14, 2006; http://www.china-un.org/eng/fyrth/t272110.htm.

3   According to Lee Jong-seok, who was responsible for the foreign security policy of the Roh Moo-hyun administration at the time, President Roh's declaration in his March 1, 2005, speech that he would respond assertively to Japan over historical issues was an indication of a shift in the Japan policy of the Roh Moo-hyun government. Lee himself also came to Japan on March 28, 2005, and communicated this to former minister for foreign affairs Yoriko Kawaguchi, who was then serving as a diplomatic aid to Prime Minister Jun'ichirō Koizumi. Prior to that, Lee had visited Japan in strict secrecy in December 2004 to negotiate for the inclusion of words to the effect that Japanese and South Korean leaders would refrain from making statements and actions about the unfortunate past into the joint declaration following the Japan–South Korea summit to be held in Ibusuki City, Kagoshima Prefecture, that month. This proposal received a cold reception, as Lee was told by Chief Cabinet Secretary Hiroyuki Hosoda that visits to Yasukuni Shrine by Prime Minister Koizumi could not be halted, and Lee returned to South Korea disappointed. Lee reports feeling offended when he met with Hosoda, who was originally from Shimane Prefecture, and Hosoda thrust a book about Takeshima at him. Lee recalls that he nonetheless maintained dialogue between Japan and South Korea on a practical level, because President Roh had instructed him to conduct free and unbiased strategic discussions without reacting emotionally.

CHAPTER 12

Russia's Sphere of Influence and the Arctic and Far East Regions

Shinji Hyōdō

Director, Regional Studies Department, National Institute for Defense Studies

Introduction

Who would have predicted that the territory of the Russian Federation would expand today, in the twenty-first century, more than twenty years after the collapse of the Soviet Union? The annexation of Crimea by the Russian Federation in 2014 was a challenge to the established international order, effecting a change in the status quo by the use of force, and it was an event that foreshadowed the end of the post–Cold War era.

While the breakup of the Soviet Union in 1991 caused Russia's national territory to shrink, in 2014 Russian President Vladimir Putin boldly moved ahead with the annexation of Crimea without any concern for potential isolation from the international community or the imposition of sanctions by the United States and Europe. Behind his action lies Russia's unique security perspective on its own "sphere of influence," which might be called Russia's domain. This is a Russian security concept that stands apart from political and economic considerations. It may be said that the Ukraine crisis has shown the international community just how strong this idea of Russia's sphere of influence really is. It is the reason why Russia intervened to an excessive level when Ukraine moved to extricate itself from Russia's orbit.

Based on this understanding of the issues, in this chapter I will first identify the features of Russia's sphere of influence as seen in the Ukraine crisis from a military perspective. I will then present the theory that Russia may be starting to regard the Arctic and Far East regions as a maritime sphere of influence. This is in addition to its land-based sphere of influence, which extends throughout the former territory of the Soviet Union, excluding the three Baltic states.

Russia's "Sphere of Influence" Concept Gains Strength

Within Russia's sphere of influence, it is Ukraine that is the most important. Historically, the Principality of Kiev is viewed as the birthplace of the Russian empire, and it is impossible to speak about Russia's identity without mentioning Ukraine. In his March 18, 2014, speech regarding the annexation of Crimea, Putin said that Crimea has always been an inseparable part of Russia.[1] In fact, the Crimean Peninsula was part of the Russian Soviet Federative Socialist Republic during much of the Soviet era.[2]

Moreover, the Crimean Peninsula is a geopolitically important location, as it holds command over the Black Sea. Following the breakup of the Soviet Union, Russia leased Sevastopol, where its Black Sea Fleet command is located, from Ukraine through the year 2042 at a cost of $98 million per year. Putin rushed to annex Crimea because of the growing likelihood that Ukraine might join the North Atlantic Treaty Organization (NATO) and expel the Black Sea Fleet if a pro-Western administration were chosen in its next presidential election. In his March 18 speech, Putin said that the presence of NATO warships in this city of Russia's military glory would pose a threat to Russia.

After having endured more than two hundred years under the Tatar-Mongol yoke and having been invaded by Napoleon and by Nazi Germany, Russia has become extremely conscious of its national security, and has come to view a buffer zone around its borders as essential for its defense. For the Russian people, the lands of the former Soviet Union, which comprised a single state for nearly seventy years, are simply "lost national territory" rather than a "sphere of influence."

The origin of Russia's "sphere of influence" concept can be found in a strategic military planning document titled "The Military Doctrine of the Russian Federation."[3] The February 2010 version can be characterized by its emphasis on responding to traditional threats of conflict among nations, such as the Russo-Georgian war, rather than addressing terrorism by Islamic extremist groups and other nontraditional threats. When President Putin ordered the revision of the Military Doctrine in 2005, the issue was how to reflect the response to Islamic extremist terrorism, which was considered the most urgent security issue, in the revised version. Nevertheless, given the August 2008 outbreak of military confrontation with Russia's neighbor Georgia and the April 2009 declaration of the end of the Second Chechen War, which had continued for about a decade, the 2010 Military Doctrine continued to emphasize traditional threats, as the prior version had.[4]

Because of this continued emphasis, the mindset of viewing the former Soviet bloc as Russia's traditional sphere of influence gained potency. Russia opposed the "color revolutions," expansion of NATO, and the spread of Western influence to the former Soviet states in other ways, and this led to the outbreak of the Russo-Georgian War. To date, Russia's sphere of influence has only been described phenomenologically to explain Russia's external behavior in reaction to US unilateralism. As presented below, however, by specifying Russia's code of conduct in the Military Doctrine, external behavior based on the sphere of influence concept was formalized in a national strategic document.

There are two main provisions in the new Military Doctrine that demonstrate the sphere of influence concept. The first provision, given in paragraph 19, includes the aim "to strengthen the system of collective security within the framework of the Collective Security Treaty Organization (CSTO)" (which comprises the countries of Russia, Belarus, Armenia, Kazakhstan, Kyrgyzstan, Tajikistan, and Uzbekistan) and asserts, "The Russian Federation regards an armed attack on a CSTO member state as aggression against all CSTO member states, and in that case will implement measures in accordance with the Collective Security Treaty" (paragraph 21). It seems that Russia has been enhancing the cohesive force of its own military among the CSTO member states in recent years by promoting the establishment of the CSTO Collective Rapid Reaction Force.

The second provision refers to the deployment of Russian military forces outside the Russian Federation (paragraph 26).[5] The Federal Law on Defense was revised in November 2009 in light of the 2008 Russo-Georgian War, providing the legal basis for sending Russian armed forces abroad to protect the interests and citizens of the Russian Federation and maintain international peace and security.[6] Following this revision to the Federal Law on Defense, the new version of the Military Doctrine also newly stipulated that Russian forces could be deployed to Georgia and other former Soviet bloc countries that are not CSTO members when certain necessary conditions are met.

According to the revised Federal Law on Defense, Russian armed forces may be deployed outside the Russian Federation in four cases: to repel an armed attack on Russian armed forces deployed beyond the territorial boundaries of the Russian Federation; when so requested by another state; to protect Russian Federation citizens abroad; and to combat piracy and ensure the security of shipping. In fact, in accordance with the provisions of the law, on March 1, 2014, President Putin requested approval from the Council of the Federation (the upper house of the Russian parliament) to send Russian troops into Ukraine. At the time the defense law was revised in 2009, many experts on the Russian military noted that after Georgia, Ukraine, which had the possibility of joining NATO, was the presumed destination for the external deployment of Russian troops. However, gaining the option of deploying Russian troops outside the country was seen not so much as an end in itself but more as a means of exerting military pressure to prevent Ukraine from joining NATO.

The Federal Law on Defense stipulates compliance with the universally recognized principles and norms of international law and the international treaties of the Russian Federation as conditions, and does not recognize unconditional military intervention in other countries. By insisting that it was vigilante groups carrying out the military activities on the Crimean Peninsula, and that this did not constitute an external deployment of Russian military forces, Russia showed its awareness that unilateral external military intervention violates international law and the Charter of the United Nations.

Yuri Baluyevsky, deputy secretary of the National Security Council of the Russian Federation and former chief of staff of Russia's armed forces, had a major impact on the sphere of influence concept and the work of revising the National Security Strategy and the Military Doctrine at the National Security Council secretariat. In his article "Toward a New Military Doctrine," which was published in the March 2007 edition of the Ministry of Defense journal *Military Thought*, Baluyevsky identifies the following threats to Russian security: the expansion of US influence in Russia's traditional sphere of influence; the further expansion of NATO; friction regarding energy supplies; international terrorism; nationalism and separatism; and harmful intelligence activities against Russia and its allies.

Baluyevsky asserts that the expansion of US influence is the greatest threat facing Russia, and that the scope of Russian national defense not only encompasses areas adjacent to national boundaries, but also extends across Russia's traditional sphere of influence. This sphere of influence is considered to include to all the former republics of the Soviet Union except for the three Baltic countries, which are already NATO members. In other words, through the external deployment of Russian military forces, the range over which Russian military influence can be exercised has been expanded to include not only CSTO member states but also non-member states like Georgia and Ukraine.[7] Based on this idea, the Federal Law on Defense was revised to permit the external deployment of Russian troops as noted above. This confirms that the army's conservative faction, which emphasizes traditional security, and which counts Baluyevsky among its members, has gained a greater voice in Russia's strategic military planning since the Russo-Georgian War, and that the conservatives' policy line has come to be strongly reflected in the new Military Doctrine.

NATO and China Advance into Russia's Sphere of Influence

The Military Doctrine views NATO, led by the US, as an intruder into Russia's sphere of influence. NATO was expanded three times after the end of the Cold War. In 2004, NATO admitted the three Baltic states, which were formerly part of the Soviet Union, and the Russian exclave of Kaliningrad Oblast was thus surrounded by NATO members. The Cold War–era Western military alliance continued after the collapse of the Soviet Union, and its expansion into Russia's sphere of influence was seen as a sheer insult by Russia, which had lost the Cold War. Moreover, just before the Cold War ended, Soviet President Mikhail Gorbachev had agreed to NATO membership for a united Germany on the condition that NATO would not expand any further. Putin criticized the West for breaking that promise.

Just after the 9/11 attacks on the US in 2001, Putin himself consented to the stationing of US troops in Central Asia, which is within Russia's sphere of influence, and worked to counter Islamic extremists by borrowing US power. But the US military presence lingered even after the anti-terrorist operations were over, so Russian military and other conservatives criticized Putin's decision. Moreover, the color revolutions, which Russia believed to be backed by the US, resulted in the birth of new, pro-Western administrations in Ukraine and Georgia that sought NATO membership. Putin therefore came to be extremely wary of the spread of Western presence in Russia's sphere of influence.

Conflict then broke out with Georgia, which was aspiring to NATO membership, in August 2008, and Russia unilaterally recognized the independence of South Ossetia and Abkhazia, which are inside Georgia. This created areas that are within Georgia's territory under international law, but outside the rule of Georgia's central government. Because NATO is a military alli-

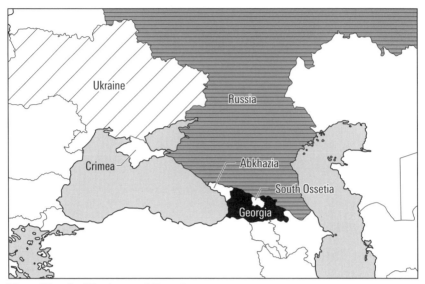

Map of Russia, Ukraine, and Georgia

ance with collective defense functions, this effectively closed Georgia's path to NATO membership, as NATO could not invite and incorporate a country with unrecognized states inside its borders.

It is not only Western powers that Russia views as invading its sphere of influence. One reason Russia decided to annex Crimea was to eliminate the Chinese influence that was spreading in Crimea. Putin was not happy that Ukraine and China were suddenly moving closer in the economic and security spheres.

China's economic advance into the former Soviet bloc spread into Central Asia, and then into Ukraine as well. The Crimean Peninsula, which Russia annexed, was viewed as a base for China's New Silk Road (Belt and Road) initiative linking China with Europe through Central Asia and the Black Sea. This concept was first proposed when President Xi Jinping visited Kazakhstan in September 2013. It is an expansive effort to extend regional economic cooperation from the Asian interior to all of Europe; the goal is the economic development of the western regions of China. Under this initiative, China was to invest $3 billion in ports, highways, airports, and other infrastructure on the Crimean Peninsula, and to build a coal gasification plant and jointly develop aircraft on the Ukrainian mainland. Furthermore, a plan emerged

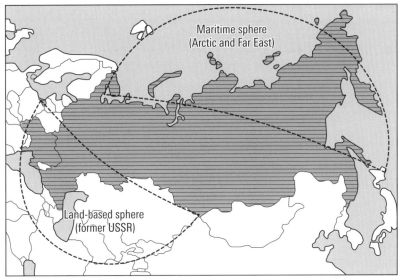

Russia's Spheres of Influence

under which an organization associated with the Chinese People's Liberation Army (PLA) would lease three million hectares of farmland—a territory equivalent to two-thirds of Japan's entire arable land area—in eastern Ukraine for a period of fifty years. If realized, this would constitute one of China's largest leases of land outside its own borders—and its largest farm overseas.

Ukraine, which had huge foreign debt and was facing a default crisis, was weighing its options for accepting economic assistance from China along with support from the West and Russia. In December 2013, Ukrainian President Viktor Yanukovych met with President Xi in Beijing and signed the Treaty on Friendship and Cooperation between Ukraine and the People's Republic of China, which recognizes a mutual strategic partnership between the two countries. This treaty included a provision whereby China would provide appropriate security in cases where Ukraine faces a nuclear threat; the presumption of a Russian nuclear threat angered Russia.

Russia also viewed Ukraine's sales to China of weapons manufactured under the former Soviet Union as problematic. In addition to China's first aircraft carrier, the *Liaoning*, these sales even included a prototype Sukhoi Su-33 fighter aircraft, which Russia had refused to sell to China. China is said to have successfully developed the Shenyang J-15, its first carrier-based fighter aircraft, based on that prototype. According to World Bank statistics, Ukraine was the fourth-largest exporter of arms in the world in 2012, following the US, Russia, and China; from the perspective of Russia's munitions industry, Ukraine is a competitor in the sales of weapons developed by the former Soviet Union. Ukraine recently sold Zubr-class air-cushioned landing craft to China. The world's largest class of military assault hovercrafts, these can carry three tanks at once. At that time, Japanese Minister for Foreign Affairs Fumio Kishida expressed his reservations to the foreign minister of Ukraine regarding the effect of this sale on the security environment of East Asia. Incidentally, these hovercrafts were built at a shipyard on the Crimean Peninsula. China signed a contract to purchase four of the vessels, and apparently two have already been delivered.

According to Russian military sources, Russia's sphere of influence in recent years includes maritime areas in the Arctic Ocean and the Sea of Okhotsk, in addition to the land areas of the former Soviet Union. China is the only other nation advancing into either of these maritime regions. It successfully opened up a northern sea route passing through the Arctic Ocean in the summer of 2012, using the icebreaking vessel *Xue Long* (purchased from Ukraine), and five PLA Navy warships advanced into the Sea of Okhotsk via the Soya Strait in July 2013 for the first time in history.[8] Russia's enhanced military presence in the Arctic[9] and repeated large-scale military exercises in the Sea of Okhotsk in recent years are not unrelated to this Chinese maritime advance into northern sea areas. Russia may be wary of how Ukraine has backed China's enhancement of its maritime military power and its subsequent advance into Russia's maritime sphere of influence.

The Arctic and Far East Regions as a New Sphere of Influence

In recent years, Russia has given greater strategic emphasis to the Arctic region, prepared official documents concerning the Arctic, and worked to bolster its military presence. These developments are linked to the sphere of influence concept presented above.

Viewed geographically, Russia is the largest Arctic Sea coastal nation in terms of its percentage of territory and population within the Arctic Circle, which is located above 66°33' north latitude. Russia's Arctic region plays a significant role in the Russian economy, as it accounts for 11 percent of the country's GDP and 22 percent of its exports.[10] The Arctic seabed contains gold, silver, iron, zinc, tin, nickel, diamond, and other mineral resources, as well as around one-quarter of the world's unconfirmed oil and natural gas reserves, which remain untouched. A large proportion of Russia's natural resources, then, are concentrated in the Arctic region. These resources are strategically important to Russia, and play a leading role in its economic growth and the modernization of its economic structure.

In December 2014, Minister of Natural Resources and Environment Sergey Donskoy announced that by March 25, 2015, Russia would petition the United Nations Commission on the Limits of the Continental Shelf to recognize 1.2 million square kilometers of Arctic Ocean sea area as Russia's continental shelf. According to Donskoy, Russia has discovered 594 oil fields, 159 gas fields, two large nickel deposits, and 350 gold deposits in the Russian Arctic; these are equivalent to about 60 percent of Russia's fossil fuel reserves.

Another reason Russia began to view the Arctic as strategically important was the opening of a shipping lane to the north of Russia's Arctic coast, where permanent sea ice is melting due to global warming. This northern sea route is covered with ice from November through April each year, so passage is only possible during the summer months, but because the range of the ice cover in the Arctic Ocean is rapidly shrinking, the period when navigation is possible is growing longer each year, and year-round passage is expected to become possible in the future. This would cut the length of the sea route connecting Europe with East Asia to two-thirds the length of the present route through the Suez Canal; additionally, there are no piracy problems in the Arctic. Some say this northern sea route could even prompt a maritime transportation revolution that would greatly change global distribution in the future.[11]

The maritime sphere of influence referred to by Russia includes the Arctic and Far East regions. President Putin is referring to the Arctic and Far East regions together on a more frequent basis in all types of speeches and state documents. This is because the Arctic region, which Russia sees as strategically important, is linked to the Far East region via the northern sea route. This phrasing implies that Russia has begun to view both areas as a single unified strategic theater. For example, a presidential decree regarding the modernization of the Russian armed forces and defense industry promulgated on May 7, 2012, the date of Putin's inauguration ceremony, orders reinforcement of the Russian navy in the Arctic and Far East regions. And on December 20, 2013, Putin ordered the Federal Security Service to enhance border security in the Arctic and Far East regions.

Russia is upgrading its military presence in the Arctic with an eye to protecting its national interests in that region. The melting of the sea ice in the Arctic Ocean is also a major issue for Russia from a military and security standpoint. During the Cold War, even though it was a strategic zone where the US and the Soviet Union faced each other head on, the Arctic was not included as an area of military operations, because military deployment was impossible; it was only used as a route for the firing and flight of nuclear missiles. Opening the northern sea route would expand the range of activities of navy warships and offer ocean areas for the possible staging of military landings. Thus, a new strategic zone will emerge not only for Russia, but for all the Arctic Ocean coastal states. As a result, for Russia, the north (the Arctic) has emerged as a fourth strategic zone in addition to the west (Europe), the south (the Caucasus and Central Asia), and the east (the Far East).

Pursuant to an order from President Putin, the Russian government released its "Strategy for the Development of the Arctic Zone of the Russian Federation and National Security up to 2020" on February 20, 2013.[12] This document outlines military readiness to deal with threats in the Arctic region. As a first stage, it recommends establishing the conditions necessary to reinforce national security by 2015. The second-stage strategy, to be realized by 2020, includes the development of an integrated security system for the protection of territory, population, and critical facilities in the Arctic zone of the Russian Federation; maintenance of the necessary level of combat readiness of general-duty troops in the Arctic; and securing necessary and sufficient combat and mobilization readiness to ensure the sovereign rights of Russia in the Arctic, provide strategic deterrence, and repel aggression in the event of armed conflict.

In accordance with these policies, on September 26, 2013, the Northern Fleet, civilian vessels, and icebreakers participated in an Arctic zone safe navigation exercise with practice landing on the Novaya Zemlya archipelago, and the formation of an Arctic army group was announced in December 2013. Russian Ground Forces Arctic Brigade bases are to be established in Murmansk Oblast in 2015 and in the Yamalo-Nenets Autonomous District in 2016; the forces will patrol Arctic Ocean coastal areas and guard Russian facilities and territory along the coast. Also, the Northern Fleet Joint Strategic Command was launched on December 1, 2014, as a fifth military district of the Russian armed forces alongside the western, southern, central, and eastern joint strategic commands. In addition to the Northern Fleet, it includes the Arctic Brigade as well as some air force and air defense force units, and is expected to take unified command of all army, navy, and air force units in the Arctic zone by 2016.

In Russia's maritime sphere of influence, the Far East region primarily refers to the Sea of Okhotsk. These waters were vital for Soviet nuclear submarines carrying submarine-launched ballistic missiles during the Cold War era, and are now being given new strategic value as a choke point to prevent passage to the Arctic Ocean. Chinese icebreakers and warships are constantly passing through the Sōya Strait and the Sea of Okhotsk to the Pacific Ocean; the area around the islands of Japan's Northern Territories (now occupied by Russia) is another route for entry and exit.[13] The Russian armed forces are steadily moving forward with modernization, including plans for military garrisons on two of these islands, Kunashiri and Etorofu, and the deployment of anti-ship missiles. If the importance of the Sea of Okhotsk grows even greater, the relative military value of these two islands will likely increase.

Russia's Sphere of Influence Concept and Japan

As a series of Ukraine crises caused relations between Russia and the West to deteriorate, Western countries, including Japan, strengthened their sanctions against Russia, Putin's visit to Japan originally scheduled for the autumn of 2014 was postponed, and Japan-Russia relations stopped moving forward. As a result, the changing conditions in eastern Ukraine that are influencing the relations between Russia and the West now also have a direct impact on Japan-Russia relations. While Western countries impose harsh countermeasures on a Russia that is increasingly isolated in the international community, the focus is the extent to which Japan can carry out its own independent diplomacy with respect to Russia.

As for Japan-Russia security cooperation, on October 28, 2014, the Maritime Self Defense Force and the Russian navy carried out their annual joint maritime disaster and rescue exercises as usual, offshore Vladivostok. At a time when some Western countries were holding back on summit meetings and military exchange because of the Ukraine crisis, Japan's decision to go ahead with these joint exercises was an indication that it intended to pursue independent diplomacy with Russia; it continued to do so after the Ukraine crisis as well. Thus, even though Japan-Russia relations could not move forward because of the Ukraine crisis, in contrast to other Western countries, Japan maintained its relations in line with its strategic emphasis on Russia.

In April 2013, when Shinzō Abe made the first official visit to the Russian Federation by a Japanese prime minister in ten years, Abe and Putin agreed that both nations would look for a mutually acceptable resolution to the Northern Territories issue, with both sides recognizing that the lack of a peace treaty between the two nations was not normal. Then, in November 2013, the Japan-Russia "two-plus-two" meeting of foreign and defense ministers was launched to conduct a high-level strategic dialogue regarding wide-ranging security issues, establishing a mechanism for the four ministers to hold regular discussions on security topics. Points of contact were also established in December that same year between the two countries' national security councils, and there was movement toward Japan and Russia viewing each other as partners and strategically improving bilateral relations. At the February 2014 summit meeting held at Sochi following the opening of the Winter Olympics, Abe and Putin addressed each other by their first names, their personal relations of trust grew deeper, and expectations rose regarding a resolution of the Northern Territories issue.

Japan's National Security Strategy, formulated in December 2013, officially positions the reinforcement of Japan-Russia relations as part of Japan's approach to national security, as follows: "Under the increasingly severe security environment in East Asia, it is critical for Japan to advance cooperation with Russia in all areas, including security and energy, thereby enhancing bilateral relations as a whole, in order to ensure its security."[14] Moreover, the National Defense Program Guidelines revised at that time declare, "Japan will promote security dialogues with Russia, including the Foreign and Defense Ministerial Consultations ["two-plus-two"], high-level exchanges, and unit-to-unit exchanges in order to deepen understanding about the intention of Russian military activities and develop mutual trust with Russia. In addition, Japan will enhance bilateral training and exercises with Russia to promote regional stability."[15] So, despite the Ukraine crisis, as the security conditions in East Asia continue to deteriorate, the security cooperation between Japan and Russia remains significant.

When considering the outlook for future Japan-Russia relations, it is important to note how China and Russia have been moving closer together since the Ukraine crisis. At the China-Russia summit in Shanghai in May 2014, the two countries agreed to hold joint activities to commemorate the seventieth anniversary of the end of the Second World War in 2015. The Chinese billed this as the "Seventieth Anniversary of China's Victory in the Anti-Japanese War." This joint celebration was proposed by President Xi when he met with Putin in Sochi following the February 2014 Winter Olympics opening ceremonies. The international community has criticized Russia and China—the former for its annexation of Crimea, and the latter for its maritime aggression—and the two appear to be working toward solidarity against the West. Nevertheless, judging by the China-Russia joint naval exercises conducted at the same time that the joint declaration was signed at the summit, there is no evidence that China-Russia strategic cooperation has become qualitatively deeper since the Ukraine crisis.

Although it appears to be moving closer to China to present a united front against the West, Russia's true intent is probably to maintain Japan-Russia relations, which have been expanding in recent years in security, energy, and other areas. In an interview with a news service in May 2014, Putin expressed his displeasure at Japan joining the West in imposing policies against Russia. At the same time, he made it clear that Russia is ready to continue territorial negotiations with Japan, and that the four islands of the disputed Northern Territories are included in the range of those negotiations. The power differential between China and Russia is growing wider, and Russia needs to maintain a diplomatic balance by reinforcing its strategic relations with India, Vietnam, Japan, and other countries in Asia that keep a certain distance from China, so that it will not become China's subordinate. This situation is not likely to change, even if Russia's relations with the West have worsened because of the Ukraine issue. As a result, there is probably no reason for Japan to be excessively concerned about China and Russia working together against Japan, or for Japan to make unnecessary overtures toward Russia.

Conclusion

The Arctic is emerging as a new field for Japan-Russia cooperation, and is not being affected by the Ukraine crisis. Natural resources development and the opening of a northern sea route in the Arctic are expected as sea ice shrinks due to global warming. In 2013, with Russian support, Japan became an observer at the Arctic Council. As the Arctic Ocean becomes a strategic focus of attention, areas for cooperation between Japan and Russia are emerging across a wide range of fields; these include establishing a northern sea route linking Europe and Asia, tapping vast undeveloped natural resources, and securing safe sea lanes.

Russia is showing signs of enhancing its military presence in the Arctic region with an eye toward maintaining its economic interests, securing the safety of the northern sea route, and defending resource extraction facilities, shipping terminals, and transportation pipelines. "The Strategy for the Development of the Arctic Zone of the Russian Federation and National Security up to 2020" was formulated in February 2013; on December 1, 2014, the Northern Fleet Joint Strategic Command was launched, incorporating the Arctic Brigade as well as some air and air defense force units together with the Northern Fleet.

China's advance into the Arctic via the northern sea route is yet another factor influencing Russia's Arctic policy. On July 2, 2012, the Chinese ice-breaking research vessel *Xue Long* departed from Qingdao in Shandong Province on its fifth Arctic exploration mission, and this vessel carried out a sixth such mission in 2014. The most recent Russian military exercises in the Far East region are perceived as being directed toward China's maritime activity. In addition, concerns about China's forays into the Arctic Ocean and the Sea of Okhotsk are apparently motivating Russian expectations for Japan-Russia cooperation in these sea areas, which Russia considers to be within its sphere of influence.

In July 2014, a Japanese commercial shipping company announced it would begin transporting liquefied natural gas (LNG) from the Yamal Peninsula in the Arctic Circle to Europe and Asia in 2018, introducing three ice-breaking LNG carriers as the world's first commercialization of the northern sea route. Because the Sea of Japan and the Sea of Okhotsk are the gateways to the northern sea route from Northeast Asia, in the future, joint anti-terrorism and anti-piracy exercises by the Maritime Self-Defense Force and the Russian navy are expected to expand into the Sea of Okhotsk and the Arctic Ocean. Amid these developments, changes may emerge in the geopolitical importance of the Northern Territories, which have become a pathway to the northern sea route.

From Russia's perspective, the West and China are intruders into Russia's sphere of influence, but Japan does not fall into that category. On the contrary, Russia has recently begun seeking Japanese cooperation in the security and energy fields in the Arctic Ocean and Sea of Okhotsk, which Russia considers part its own sphere of influence. In this way, the more Russia views the Arctic and Far East regions as its maritime sphere of influence, the stronger its emphasis on Japan is likely to become.

1   President's Website, "Address by the President of the Russian Federation," March 18, 2014, http://en.kremlin.ru/events/president/news/20603.

2   Crimea was originally part of the Russian Soviet Federative Republic during the Soviet era, but it was transferred administratively to the Ukrainian Soviet Socialist Republic by Soviet leader Nikita Khrushchev in 1954 to commemorate the three-hundredth anniversary of Ukraine becoming part of the Tsardom of Russia.

3   The Military Doctrine of the Russian Federation, https://carnegieendowment.org/files/2010russia_military_doctrine.pdf

4   For details, refer to Shinji Hyōdō, "Pūchin seiken ni okeru 'kokka anzen hoshō gainen' no kaitei wo meguru ugoki 'kokka anzen hoshō gainen' kara 'kokka anzen hoshō senryaku' e" [Developments in the revision of the national security concept in the Putin administration from the "national security concept" to the "national security strategy"], in *Roshia gaikō no genzai II* [Present Russian diplomacy II], Hokkaido University Slavic-Eurasian Research Center, May 2006.

5   Paragraph 26: "With a view to protecting the interests of the Russian Federation and its citizens and maintaining international peace and security, formations of the Armed Forces of the Russian Federation may be used operationally outside the Russian Federation in accordance with the generally recognized principles and norms of international law, the international treaties of the Russian Federation, and federal legislation."

6   Article 102 of the Constitution of the Russian Federation and Article 5 of the Federal Law on Defense prescribe that the external use of armed forces is under the exclusive jurisdiction of the Federation Council, but in the August 2008 Russo-Georgian War the Federation Council issued its approval for the external use of armed forces after the fact, and other inadequacies of the legal system for the external deployment of troops became an issue. Thus, the dispatch of troops outside the country was permitted for the defense of Russian citizens outside of Russia, and ultimately the authority for the final decision on the dispatch of troops abroad was vested in the president.

7   Ichiu Inui, *Chikara no shinpōsha Roshia* [Devotee of strength: Russia], JCA Shuppan, 2011, 251.

8   *Higashi Ajia senryaku gaikan* 2014 [East Asian strategic review 2014], National Institute for Defense Studies, March 2014, 215.

9   For details, refer to Shinji Hyōdō, "Roshia no hokkyoku seisaku: Roshia ga hokkyoku wo senryakuteki ni jūshi suru riyū" [Russia's Arctic strategy: Reasons for Russia's strategic emphasis on the Arctic], NIDS Journal of Defense and Security, National Institute for Defense Studies, November 2013.

10 Speech delivered by Yevgeny Lukyanov, deputy secretary of the Security Council of the Russian Federation, at "Arctic Frontiers 2013: Geopolitics and Marine Resources in a Changing Arctic," Tromsø, Norway, January 21, 2013.

11 *Nihon Hokkyokukai Kaigi hōkokusho* [Japan Arctic Ocean Council report], Ocean Policy Research Institute, March 2012, 82–98.

12 The Strategy for the Development of the Arctic Zone of the Russian Federation and National Security up to 2020, http://www.research.kobe-u.ac.jp/gsics-pcrc/sympo/20160728/documents/Keynote/Russian%20Arctic%20strategy%202013.pdf.

13 The Northern Territories consist of four islands off the coast of Hokkaidō claimed by Japan but

controlled by Russia. They were occupied by the Soviet Union after the end of the Second World War, and their ownership has been under dispute ever since.

14 Government of Japan, National Defense Program Guidelines for FY 2013 and Beyond, December 17, 2013, p. 11, https://www.mod.go.jp/j/approach/agenda/guideline/2014/pdf/20131217_e2.pdf.

15 Ministry of Defense, National Defense Program Guidelines for 2014 and Beyond, December 17, 2013, https://www.mod.go.jp/j/approach/agenda/guideline/2014/pdf/20131217_e2.pdf.

ADDENDUM TO THE ENGLISH EDITION

Fumiaki Kubo
Professor, Graduate School for Law and Politics, University of Tokyo; Executive Director of Research, Maritime Security in the Asia-Pacific Region and the Japan-US Alliance Project, Nakasone Peace Institute

The 2016 US Presidential Election

The Japanese edition of *The Japan-US Alliance of Hope* was published in April 2016. It was written based on events through around the end of 2015.

The subsequent developments up to the present day can only be called dramatic, as symbolized above all by the advent of the Trump administration in the United States. While this constitutes a massive change for the US, it also has immense implications for Japan, for the Japan-US alliance, and for the maritime security of the Asia-Pacific region.

From the start of his 2016 presidential campaign, under the slogan "America first," Donald Trump gave indications that he might completely revise the internationalist foreign policy and free trade policy long implemented by the US government. In campaigning, Trump called the North Atlantic Treaty Organization (NATO) "obsolete," suggested that Japan and South Korea acquire nuclear armaments and protect themselves, and asserted that the US can no longer defend Japan and South Korea as it could forty years ago, while simultaneously embracing the diplomatic principle of "peace through strength," which has very different implications. His stance was an about-face from America's traditional alliance diplomacy. In foreign trade, as well, Trump expressed opposition to the proposed Trans-Pacific Partnership (TPP) from an early stage, and called for the US to withdraw from or renegotiate the North American Free Trade Agreement (NAFTA). These positions also are, to say the least, inconsistent with the long-standing fundamental policies of the Republican Party.

As a candidate, Trump was also unusual in that, compared with past presidential candidates, he prioritized trade policy while disparaging foreign policy to a considerable degree. Following this logic, Trump might even conclude that China and Japan are America's most pernicious rivals, without distinguishing between the two in some cases. In recent years, influential US diplomacy and security experts have made a sharp distinction between countries that are allies or partners of the US and those that are not, but Trump is at odds on this point. For Trump, the criterion for judging the quality of a country becomes the extent of its trade surplus with the US, with almost no consideration given to shared values or alliance relations. Countries with alliances in which the US bears a disproportionate burden are given a low assessment.

Consequently, as a candidate and even before, Trump perceived Japan as a very troublesome country. Back in the 1980s, he held the view that Japan was making huge profits by exporting automobiles to the US while having the US pay its security costs. This belief is clearly stated in the full-page advertisement he ran in the *New York Times*, the *Washington Post*, and the *Boston Globe* on September 2, 1987. Trump retained this 1980s image of Japan almost unchanged all the way through to the 2016 election.

The statements made by Trump as a candidate were a cause of serious concern for the government of Japan, but the general expectations at that time were that Trump would not be elected. His victory in the election therefore caused enormous surprise and anxiety in Tokyo.

With respect to maritime security, Trump's comments regarding the Senkaku Islands during the 2016 election campaign are worth noting. In an interview in the *Washington Post*, when asked to give his position regarding the Senkaku Islands, Trump said he would prefer not to answer.[1] From the perspective of the government of Japan, that was a very regrettable statement. As noted in this book, during a visit to Tokyo in April 2014, President Obama became the first US president to officially state that the Senkaku Islands are included in the US duty to defend Japan under Article 5 of the Japan-US Security Treaty. It is no exaggeration to say that for the government of Japan, the question of whether or not President Trump would maintain this policy was of the utmost importance. If he did not, it would immediately indicate a rift in the alliance, in which case China's activities in the vicinity of the Senkaku Islands would probably become even more provocative.

Trump's stance on the South China Sea issue was also a cause for worry. During the election campaign, although he criticized China's trade policy, Trump hardly touched on China's military rise and ambitions, including its activities in the South China Sea. From the logic of "America first," it was not clear whether the freedom of navigation operations implemented by the Obama administration from 2015 would be continued under a Trump administration. Toward the end of his campaign, Trump used the slogan "peace through strength" in a speech on foreign affairs, and it became impossible to guess whether this or "America first" would become the basis for his foreign policy. It goes without saying that, as commonly understood, "America first" and "peace through strength" are fundamentally incompatible principles.

In this way, the November 8, 2016, election of Donald Trump as US president caused significant misgivings not only for Japan, but also for Asia and the global order.

The Trump Administration and the Japan-US Alliance

Prime Minister Shinzō Abe quickly took action and met with Trump before his inauguration. Abe then succeeded in holding a summit meeting shortly after Trump came into office on February 10–11, 2017, the outcome of which included a joint statement[2] that mutually confirmed the significance and value of the Japan-US alliance. The two leaders affirmed that Article 5 of the Japan-US Security Treaty covered the Senkaku Islands, and President Trump haltingly read out a text thanking Japan for hosting US forces. Here, President Trump's position on Japan, at least regarding security matters, basically shifted 180 degrees from his stance as a candidate. However, this shift was not consistent. From time to time, he later made comments that contradicted the joint statement.

As one example, in June 2019, there was a media report that Trump had told confidants he was considering the abolition of the Japan-US Security Treaty because it was one-sided and did not require Japan to help defend the US.[3] While the Trump administration has not officially proposed the dissolution of the Japan-US security alliance, this report does suggest that President Trump is not fully convinced of the value of the relationship.

As discussed in chapter 1 of this book, the Japan-US alliance is asymmetrical with respect to the rights and obligations agreed upon by both parties. The greatest weakness of that arrangement is that the average citizens in each country perceive their own country's burdens or obligations to be disproportionately great (for the US, the obligation to defend Japan seems disproportionate; for Japan, the obligation to provide bases for US forces seems disproportionate), so it is difficult to see the overall picture. In some cases, this is not sufficiently understood even by the leaders at the top. What is more, when a leader foments criticism about how the alliance is "one-sided" or "unfair" based on his insufficient understanding, the alliance may face a crisis. In this sense, because of its asymmetry, the Japan-US security alliance is highly vulnerable to populism. While Japan-US relations under the Trump administration, especially with respect to diplomacy and security, appear stable on the surface, these factors have caused a certain amount of uncertainty.

Incidentally, as also pointed out in the original Japanese edition of this book, the package of security legislation enacted in 2015 met with harsh opposition within Japan. Despite the criticism, this legislation permits Japan to engage in combat to support the US military under certain conditions, and it is important to note that it thus eases the asymmetry of rights and obligations under the Japan-US alliance, at least to some small extent. However, President Trump may not fully recognize this point.

In addition, President Trump's focus on the US trade deficit has been even stronger than anticipated. Despite desperate entreaties by Prime Minister Abe, President Trump announced the US withdrawal from the TPP shortly after taking office, as he had pledged during his campaign. In March 2018, Trump imposed sanctions on imports of steel and aluminum, including imports from Japan, and he also announced the start of punitive tariffs against imports of automobiles. Japan and the US subsequently entered into trade negotiations on the condition that the tariffs on automobile imports would not be imposed during the negotiations. This was the first time that serious trade problems had emerged between Japan and the US since the first Clinton administration in the 1990s.

President Trump's attitude toward Russia, and especially toward President Putin, is singular in the US, where both political parties are uncompromising toward Russia, and it continues to be criticized.

President Trump's views on NATO are often negative, and in private conversations he sometimes suggests that the US should withdraw. In particular, Trump is pushing for strict compliance by NATO member countries that are not meeting the 2 percent of GDP defense spending level agreed upon.

Overall, the Trump administration's top officials support "peace through strength," but President Trump's words and actions are inconsistent, and wobble back and forth from "America first" to "peace through strength." In an anonymous opinion piece printed in the *New York Times* in early September 2018,[4] a cabinet-level official in the Trump administration asserted that the administration had become a "two-track presidency" comprising a president who makes impulsive decisions based on ignorance and hunches and a network of "adults" who strive to rectify that to some extent. The trend in the administration's foreign policy seems to be that while the president may act impulsively, those around him generally support peace through strength.

Progress and Limits of Japan-US Cooperation

Despite these kinds of concerns, Japan-US security relations have progressed relatively smoothly under the Trump administration, especially in the field of maritime security.

One reason for this may be that the Trump administration continued the Obama administration's practice of carrying out periodic freedom of navigation operations in the South China Sea. While this has not succeeded in preventing China from constructing military bases, it does indicate the continuation of the US policy not to accept China's land reclamation, construction of bases, militarization, and above all, associated territorial sea claims in the South China Sea. In that sense, the policy of "peace through strength," rather than "America first," is apparent here.

Second, after Prime Minister Abe announced his "free and open Indo-Pacific" concept (the Japanese government initially referred to this as a "strategy" but has been using the term "concept" in recent years) in 2015, the Trump administration also began using this same term in 2017, and adopted it as a diplomatic strategy (the US tends to call it the "Indo-Pacific strategy"). Japan and the US are using the same words, but of course, there is some difference in the content. While the US is keeping a sharp eye on China's activities in the South China Sea and emphasizing the security aspects, Japan is focusing on economic assistance—especially infrastructural aid—as suggested by the fact that Abe initially announced this concept in Kenya. Geographically, the US is addressing the Indian Ocean and Pacific Ocean regions, along with Southeast Asia and the South China Sea, which lie between these two oceans. In contrast, Japan is addressing a vast area ranging from Africa and the Middle East all the way to the Caribbean Sea. For the US, western India is the western edge of its Indo-Pacific strategy. This does not, however, imply that strategy beyond that boundary is lacking; rather, the US addresses areas further west under other categories, such as its Middle East strategy.

Third, and closely related to this, both Japan and the US came to explicitly regard the Indo-Pacific as important in reaction to China's Belt and Road Initiative. The focus on the Indo-Pacific may be viewed as a joint effort by Japan and the US to counter China's global infrastructure development strategy. Japan has long considered foreign aid as a pillar of its diplomacy, while the US had been reducing its aid budget following growing opposition and criticism, especially in the US Congress, from the 1990s. The recent sharp debate in Congress about abolishing the Export-Import Bank may be an indication of how the inward-looking stance in US political circles is growing stronger and stronger. Yet under the Trump administration, as an example, Secretary of State Mike Pompeo proposed providing funding to Southeast Asia in the form of infrastructure assistance, and Congress responded by passing the Better Utilization of Investments Leading to Development (BUILD) Act and the Asia Reassurance Initiative Act in 2018 with bipartisan support. While the amounts of funding pale in comparison with what is provided by China, such legislation marks a noteworthy shift in US policy.

Fourth, Japan and the US, together with Australia, stepped up their vigilance over China, and are implementing strategies that emphasize the Indo-Pacific. China's advance into the South China Sea and Pacific Ocean islands is heightening Australia's concerns. Amid these developments, while firmly maintaining its traditional tendency toward non-alignment, India is definitely growing more wary of China as well. In recent years, the relations between Japan and India and between the US and India have steadily been growing stronger, especially with respect to security. (The Trump administration's trade policy toward India is an exception to this trend.) On the whole, the US has not turned its back on cooperative relations with Japan, Australia, and India in the security field; rather, it is definitely reinforcing those relations.

Incidentally, Southeast Asian countries that claim territorial rights over islands in the South China Sea, such as Vietnam, the Philippines, Malaysia, and Brunei, have a keen interest in the South China Sea problem. The UK and France have shown interest in recent years as well, and have been reinforcing their security cooperation with Japan at the same time.

Conversely, the TPP must be brought up as an example where Japan and the US under the Trump administration chose different paths. As mentioned above, the US withdrew from the TPP talks early in the Trump administration. What is notable here is that after the US withdrawal, the remaining eleven countries, with Japan at the center, then agreed on a revised TPP without the US, renaming it the Comprehensive and Progressive Agreement for Trans-Pacific Partnership (CPTPP); Japan also concluded the Japan-EU Economic Partnership Agreement with the European Union. These agreements are significant in terms of both politics and security, because they kept the initiative for creating a higher-level international trading order from being handed over to China.

The Trump Administration's China Policy

What dramatically changed the security environment of Asia, including maritime security, was the Trump administration's China policy. President Trump himself is obsessed with the massive US trade deficit with China, and in fact the punitive tariffs that the US has unilaterally imposed on China are the most outstanding change in the China policy set forth by his administration. These were to be implemented in four stages, with tariffs on all US imports from China scheduled for implementation in December 2019. While this approach has been harshly criticized both inside and outside the US, domestically, it is being supported not only by Trump backers but also by white labor-union members who had voted for the Democratic Party in the past. On the international front, Japan is critical of the Trump administration's tariff trade policy because it, like China, has been criticized for its large trade surplus with the US and subjected to unilateral sanctions or threats of sanctions. From the Japanese government's perspective, while there are clearly problems with China's trade practices, those should be addressed jointly by coordination among Japan, the US, and the EU. On the other hand, for the US—which had not taken a strong position against China for a long time—to suddenly assume a harsh stance not only against Chinese trade practices but against China's actions and policies overall is basically good news for Japan, which has clashed with China on territorial issues.

Looking at trade policy in the broad sense, while President Trump himself is mainly focused on the US trade deficit, the US government as a whole views a broader range of issues as problematic: China's infringement and theft of intellectual property rights, the existence of Chinese state enterprises, China's disregard or neglect of the principle of equal treatment of domestic and foreign enterprises, and state subsidies and other preferential policies for Chinese domestic companies. The US may also be wary about the "Made in China 2025" project being promoted by the Chinese government, and the competition between the US and China over which country will lead in the development of fifth-generation (5G) mobile telecommunications technology. In that sense, the present US-China trade friction is extremely serious.

In the economic arena, given the president's inclination, the focus is mostly on trade, and punitive tariffs based on investigations by the Office of the United States Trade Representative (USTR) have become the main means of applying pressure. In technology, the National Defense Authorization Act for Fiscal Year 2019 (NDAA2019) passed in August 2018 imposed regulations on inbound investment pertaining to sensitive technology and important infrastructure, and tightened controls and regulations on outbound technology exports. The former reinforced the authority of the Committee on Foreign Investment in the United States (CFIUS) stipulated in the Foreign Investment Risk Review Modernization Act, while the latter strengthened controls over emerging technologies and foundational technologies under the Export Control Reform Act (ECRA). Also, NDAA2019 Section 889 prohibits the US government from purchasing certain telecommunications and video surveillance equipment and services from Chinese companies such as Huawei and ZTE from August 2019, and the US government may not sign or renew contracts with firms using equipment or services provided by those companies after August 2020.

The national security strategy announced by the Trump administration in December 2017 defines China and Russia as US competitors. This marked the first time since the late 1960s that the US government had taken a tough position against both China and Russia at the same time. The Trump administration greatly increased US defense expenditures, reinforcing the space and cyberspace sectors in particular. High-ranking Trump administration officials persistently criticized China for its suppression of human rights in Tibet and in the Xinjiang Uygur Autonomous Region. The administration also stepped up its support for Taiwan, as seen by the enactment of the Taiwan Travel Act and the sale of 108 tanks and 66 F-16V combat aircraft to Taiwan. That sale, which was authorized in 2019, was the first time the US had sold fighter aircraft to Taiwan since 1992. The US also continued its freedom of navigation operations in the South China Sea, as mentioned above.

Inside the US, the Department of Justice launched the "China Initiative" policy in an effort to strengthen prosecution of illegal acts by China, and began full-scale efforts to expose Chinese industrial spies. At the same time, measures were also initiated to counter Chinese efforts to recruit researchers at US research centers, university organs, and defense industry companies. The State Department shortened the length of visas for Chinese studying natural sciences at US universities from five years to one year. In testimony before the US Congress, FBI Director Christopher Wray highlighted the frequent threats from Chinese spies since the Trump administration took office, and gave a strong warning about the naïveté of US universities toward Chinese students engaging in spying.

There was also bipartisan support for a hard-line stance toward China in the US Congress via the passage of the National Defense Authorization Act for Fiscal Year 2018 and the Asia Reassurance Initiative Act.

In 2019, a protest movement broke out in Hong Kong, triggered by government efforts to pass a bill that would have made it possible to turn over accused criminals to the Chinese mainland. The Chinese government hinted that it might intervene, President Trump moved to restrain any effort to do so, and the situation became a new point of conflict between the US and China.

In this sense, the Trump administration's hard-line policies on China represent a pushback by the entire US government, including Congress, despite President Trump's wavering and inconsistencies and the impulsive nature of his decisions. This unified approach, which rallies trade hawks, security hard-liners, and human-rights activists, has combined those who take the toughest stance toward China from both the Democratic Party and the Republican Party.

Of course, as seen in the opinion piece, "China Is Not an Enemy,"[5] which was printed in the *Washington Post* in July 2019, there is opposition to the Trump administration's China policy. This administration's approach does represent a sudden shift from the comparatively generous viewpoint on China maintained over the George W. Bush and Barack Obama administrations.

It would be dangerous to conclude that US policy toward China will continue unchanged into the future. While the view toward China among the Democrats in Congress is presumed to have become more hawkish, the more than twenty Democratic Party candidates presently vying for the 2020 presidential election are focusing almost entirely on domestic issues; they have barely touched on diplomatic issues, including China. Regardless, the shift in the US policy toward China is not caused just by changes in the perceptions of China within the US; it is also deeply rooted in the changes in China itself. Therefore, this shift in US policy may well be a medium- to long-term trend.[6]

Implications for the International Order

The change in America's policy toward China has had a significant impact on international politics. In Asia, for Japan—the country that has confronted China most directly and was increasingly frustrated by the relatively moderate position toward China taken under the Obama administration in particular— the change in US policy should mostly be welcome, despite the many serious problems inherent in the Trump administration. It is a great relief that Japan is no longer obliged to confront China alone, and can now form a united front together with the US. At the same time, this also has the secondary effect of improving Japan-China relations. These bilateral relations have been getting better over the past few years, in part because of factors that are unique to the context of Japan-China relations, and in part because of China's internal affairs. Even so, the influence that the bitter conflict between the US and China has had on Japan-China relations cannot be denied.

While the improved direction of Japan-China relations became clear from 2018, China has continued to make incursions into Japanese territorial waters in the vicinity of the Senkaku Islands. As long as that continues, the situation in the East China Sea will remain unstable, and any improvements in Japan-China relations will remain superficial.

In the South China Sea as well, Chinese moves to construct military bases are ongoing, and remain a destabilizing factor for the region despite measures such as the continued freedom of navigation operations by the US; the 2016 ruling by the Permanent Court of Arbitration in the Hague in favor of the Philippines, denying China's claims; the criticism of nearby countries; and the capacity-building assistance from Japan and the US to the Philippines and Vietnam.

In Asia, the competition in military expansion is intensifying in ways that are qualitatively different from the past, involving the domains of outer space, cyberspace, and electromagnetic waves; this may also be seen as a destabilizing factor.

Developments with South Korea, Australia, and Russia

Now that I have explained the trend toward improved relations between Japan and China, I would like to also briefly touch on the developments in Japan's relations with other countries.

Japan's relations with South Korea suddenly cooled following a 2018 ruling by the Supreme Court of Korea ordering Japanese companies to pay compensation to individual Koreans who were conscripted for forced labor during the Second World War. Furthermore, there was an incident at the end of 2018 in which a South Korean navy vessel locked its fire-control radar onto a Japan Maritime Self-Defense Force aircraft, which brought Japan–South Korean relations to what is considered their worst level in the postwar period. In 2019, Japan imposed restrictions on exports to South Korea, making bilateral relations even more acrimonious.

In August 2019, amid these developments, South Korea gave notice that it would not renew the General Security of Military Information Agreement (GSOMIA), its military intelligence pact with Japan. This action spread the conflict to the security sphere and made it far more serious. To the US, this was a surprise. Secretary of State Pompeo expressed his disappointment; in a second official statement, the Department of Defense also expressed strong concerns and disappointment. Though this decision was reversed just before the pact was due to expire in November, it is noteworthy that South Korea intentionally chose an option that benefited North Korea rather than giving consideration to Japan and the US. While the trilateral security cooperation between Japan, the US, and South Korea in opposition to the North Korean threat did not completely collapse, the worsening of relations between Japan and South Korea saddled it with a serious vulnerability. In the South China Sea problem and other issues, South Korea frequently refrains from taking a critical stance toward China, and the fact that it is heading in a noticeably different direction than Japan and the US in that regard is significant.

In contrast, the cooperation between Japan, the US, and Australia has grown qualitatively deeper. Shortly after taking office, the conservative coalition administration of Malcolm Turnbull, which followed the Tony Abbott administration, discovered in October 2015 that the government of Australia's Northern Territory had signed a 99-year lease on the Port of Darwin to the Chinese company Landbridge Group. The US government expressed strong concerns about this lease. Up until that time, the Australian government had not been forced to choose between the US, its main ally, and China, its largest economic partner, and had been maintaining good relations with both countries. Regarding the lease of the Port of Darwin, the Northern Territory government had reportedly inquired with the central government and particularly with officials at the Department of Defense beforehand, but the office in charge had not realized the magnitude of this decision, and had given routine approval because Australia is open to foreign investment. Thereafter, however, the Australia government established a strict review process for proposed investments from China, especially those related to important infrastructure. In fact, since 2016 Australia's Foreign Investment Review Board has refused approval for the takeover of an Australian electric power transmission company by a Chinese state enterprise and other investments from China, and the framework for review of foreign investment in important infrastructure has become more stringent.

Furthermore, around the middle of 2017, an investigative report found that two wealthy ethnic Chinese Australian businessmen with close relations to the Communist Party of China who made large donations in Australian political circles had arranged for an Australian Labor Party senator to make a speech expressing understanding of China's position on its man-made islands in the South China Sea. The report warned against Chinese interference in Australia's internal affairs. Intelligence sources also warned that the scale of China's involvement in Australian political circles was unprecedented. In response, at the end of that year, the Turnbull administration began to prepare legislation to regulate interference in Australian politics by foreign countries. In August 2018, a decision by the Turnbull administration effectively rejected participation by Huawei, ZTE, and other Chinese enterprises in Australia's 5G mobile telecommunications systems.

While relations between Australia and China worsened in these ways, the Turnbull administration did make delicate adjustments to Australia's foreign and security policies in light of the difficulties of predicting US policy under the Trump administration. The shift in Australia's orientation is presented in Australia's Foreign Policy White Paper, which was published in November 2017.

This was the first foreign policy white paper published by Australia since 2003. To pursue a stable, prosperous Indo-Pacific amid the power shift between the US and China, the white paper calls for Australia to reinforce its own efforts to strengthen national defense capabilities; emphasizes Australia's traditional alliance with the US; seeks to deepen Australia's relations with China, which is Australia's greatest economic partner, through the Comprehensive Strategic Partnership; and calls for Australia to enhance its engagement with the region's major democracies. According to the white paper, Australia can exert the greatest influence through its partnerships with India, Indonesia, South Korea, and other countries with which Australia shares objectives—and Japan is at the top of that list. In fact, after the US withdrawal from the TPP was decided, the Turnbull administration continued to push the remaining eleven countries to quickly conclude the agreement, disregarding the opposition Labor Party, which presumed that the TPP was already dead. As soon as Japan moved to advance negotiations among the TPP 11, the close collaboration between Japan and Australia led to the conclusion of the CPTPP agreement in March 2018. In this manner, Japan and Australia clearly showed they were ready to pave the way for the US to commit to a free and open Indo-Pacific.

The foreign policy white paper also calls for Australia to strengthen ties with Pacific island countries. Prime Minister Scott Morrison, who succeeded Turnbull, is especially keen about stepping up relations in the Pacific, and has visited Vanuatu, Fiji, the Solomon Islands, and other Pacific island nations. While Australia's pursuit of renewed engagement with the island nations of the South Pacific, where China's advance has been conspicuous in recent years, has been noticeable since the Morrison administration took office, the trend toward pursuing cooperation with the US, Japan, and other countries with shared objectives is also evident here. For example, during the November 2018 Asia-Pacific Economic Cooperation (APEC) summit in Papua New Guinea, the US, Japan, Australia, and New Zealand decided to counter China's huge investment of funds for roads and other infrastructural assistance in the capital, Port Moresby, by working together to bring electricity to 70 percent of the residents of Papua New Guinea by 2030. Japan is expected to provide its well-respected capacity-building assistance as well. In the strategic field, Australia agreed to jointly upgrade Lombrum Naval Base on Manus Island, which had been used by the Japanese military during the Second World War, and to make it available for use by the US armed forces.

As demonstrated above, even during the Trump administration, Australia has firmly maintained its traditional alliance with the US even as it pursues a policy of maintaining the benefits of its economic partnership with China while eliminating Chinese interference in its affairs. In this process, Japan—and in particular Prime Minister Abe, who has been pushing the diplomatic ideal of a free and open Indo-Pacific—has been a very reliable presence.

Japan and Russia had been continuing negotiations over the Northern Territories issue into 2019, but there is now a strong sense that these talks have come to a standstill, because Japan can no longer expect even the return of Habomai and Shikotan, the smaller two of the four Russian-occupied islands off Hokkaidō. While the fourth Japan-Russia Foreign and Defense Ministerial Consultation (two-plus-two) took place on May 30, 2019, there are no indications of any major improvement in Japan-Russia relations.

In contrast, US-Russia relations are complex. President Trump himself takes a favorable view of President Putin, and tweeted in support of Russia's return to the Group of Eight in August 2019. On the other hand, the members of the US Congress are critical of Russia, regardless of whether they are Republicans or Democrats. This bipartisan criticism is due to the authoritarian tendencies of the Putin regime, the annexation of Crimea, and also to Russia's pernicious intervention in the 2016 US presidential election. Here, too, President Trump stands alone in viewing the intervention as less than serious. Early in the Trump administration, however, at the end of 2017, the National Security Strategy defined Russia, together with China, as a "revisionist power." Furthermore, because the Trump administration unilaterally withdrew from the Intermediate-Range Nuclear Forces Treaty, relations between Russia and the US became even more tense. Just after that treaty went out of force in August 2019, the US conducted test launches of ground-launched cruise missiles to promote the development of intermediate-range missiles, further increasing the tension. It is worth noting that, in an interview with Fox News on August 21, 2019, Secretary of Defense Mark Esper stressed that the purpose of the test was to restrain China's bad behavior.

Developments in Japan

As explained above, in response to the advent of the Trump administration, Japan has worked to develop closer security relations with the US. Although challenging trade negotiations are taking place between Japan and the US, reaching an agreement should not be all that difficult. While struggling with President Trump's unpredictability, such as his abrupt tweet about abolishing the Japan-US Security Treaty, the government of Japan has been relatively successful in building up relations of trust with the administration's National Security Council staff, cabinet members, and the US military.

In any event, there are apprehensions and uncertainties regarding the future direction of US diplomacy over the medium to long term. In the 2016 presidential election, when Trump was nominated as the Republican Party candidate, he was the first presidential candidate from either of the two main parties since 1945 to have no political or military experience (the last was Wendell Willkie, who won the Republican nomination in 1940). This is a sign of the heightened distrust in the US toward career politicians, incumbents, and the establishment.

Trump was also the first Republican nominee since 1945 to run as an isolationist in his campaign pledges (after he won the election, however, as mentioned above, he turned toward a "peace through strength" stance to some extent). The last comparable candidate in this regard was George McGovern, who won the Democratic Party's nomination in 1972 on the campaign call, "Come home, America."

Furthermore, in the 2016 election, the candidates of both major parties expressed opposition to the TPP; in that sense, both ran their campaigns from a trade protectionist position. This was also a first since the Second World War.

All of these factors suggest that Trump-like presidential candidates may emerge from time to time in the future. There were initially seventeen candidates vying to win the nomination of the Republican Party, which has long adopted internationalism and free trade as its party policy, but it was Trump who took the prize. While there were certainly many variables at play, his nomination was still highly significant. That Trump proved he could win the nomination as the Republican Party presidential candidate despite calling for isolationism and protectionism is no small matter.

Moreover, Trump's rhetoric of combining isolationism and protectionism with fierce attacks against illegal immigrants gained extraordinary popularity among the Republican Party's base, especially among white working-class voters. In the Midwest, in particular, this transcended party lines and eroded the Democratic Party's base of support. When Pat Buchanan challenged the sitting president George H. W. Bush within the Republican Party in 1992 following a similar line, he gained far less support, but the developments in 2016 were entirely different.

Since this has now emerged as a popular policy position in the Republican Party, one may expect many politicians with presidential candidacies based on this stance to appear inside the party in the future as well; that is, in 2024 and for twenty or thirty years thereafter. While they will not all win the party's nomination, or be victorious in the general election, even if such candidates were only elected once in every three or four elections, their impact on the international order would still be enormous. Incidentally, there is every possibility that candidates with a similar stance, minus the hostility toward illegal immigrants, could also emerge from within the Democratic Party.

This is what Japan must prepare for over the medium to long term. Trump may have been helped to some extent by some random coincidences. What is more, he does not possess firm beliefs and principles or an adequate understanding of policy. The situation could become still more forbidding if the person elected pursues this policy line intentionally and also has a strong grasp of policy.

Following President Trump's election, the Institute for International Policy Studies (the present Nakasone Peace Institute) published the Japan-US Alliance Study Group Report "The Trump Administration and Japan: Challenges and Visions for Japan's Foreign and Security Policy in the New Era"[7] in January 2019. Based on the awareness of the issues presented above, the report recommends that Japan become more self-reliant for its security over the medium to long term. As one example, the report proposes that Japan increase its defense spending from the current level of less than 1 percent of gross domestic product to 1.2 percent of GDP in the near future.

The April 2017 report by the Special Task Force of the Mt. Fuji Dialogue, "Toward a Greater Alliance: A Policy Proposal of the Mt. Fuji Dialogue Special Task Force,"[8] also proposes that Japan steadily increase its defense spending during the next medium-term defense program (FY 2019 to 2024). While not presenting specific figures, this report notes that NATO member countries have agreed to spend 2 percent of their gross domestic products on defense.

Both of these proposals place the greatest possible emphasis on the alliance with the US on the one hand, while warning on the other that Japan needs to start preparing for the future based on uncertainty over the outlook for US policy. While neither of these proposals elicited any specific reaction in real-world politics, one can assume that this understanding is being quietly shared among a substantial number of Japanese politicians and policy decision makers. These very issues are the greatest concerns that lie hidden beneath the Japan-US alliance in the Trump administration era, though it appears to be operating smoothly on the surface.

1   The Washington Post, "A transcript of Donald Trump's meeting with The Washington Post editorial board, March 21, 2016, https://www.washingtonpost.com/blogs/post-partisan/wp/2016/03/21/a-transcript-of-donald-trumps-meeting-with-the-washington-post-editorial-board/.

2   The White House, "Joint Statement from President Donald J. Trump and Prime Minister Shinzo Abe," February 10, 2017, https://www.whitehouse.gov/briefings-statements/joint-statement-president-donald-j-trump-prime-minister-shinzo-abe.

3   Jennifer Jacobs, "Trump Muses Privately About Ending Postwar Japan Defense Pact," Bloomberg news service, June 25, 2019, https://www.bloomberg.com/news/articles/2019-06-25/trump-muses-privately-about-ending-postwar-japan-defense-pact.

4   "I am Part of the Resistance Inside the Trump Administration," New York Times, September 5, 2018, https://www.nytimes.com/2018/09/05/opinion/trump-white-house-anonymous-resistance.html.

5   M. Taylor Fravel, J. Stapleton Roy, Michael D. Swaine, Susan A. Thorton, and Ezra Vogel, "China Is Not an Enemy," Washington Post, July 3, 2019, https://www.washingtonpost.com/opinions/making-china-a-us-enemy-is-counterproductive/2019/07/02/647d49d0-9bfa-11e9-b27f-ed2942f73d70_story.html.

6   Fumiaki Kubo, "Reading the Trump Administration's China Policy," Asia-Pacific Review 26, no. 1 (May 2019), 58–76.

7   Institute for International Policy Studies, "The Trump Administration and Japan: Challenges and Visions for Japan's Foreign and Security Policy in the New Era," January 2017, http://www.iips.org/en/research/usjr2017en.pdf.

8   Mt. Fuji Dialogue, "Toward a Greater Alliance: A Policy Proposal of the Mt. Fuji Dialogue Special Task Force," April 2017, https://www.jcer.or.jp/eng/pdf/Mt.FUJI_DIALOGUE20170405report_e.pdf.

About the Authors
(as of March 27, 2020)

Shinichi Kitaoka is president of the Japan International Cooperation Agency. Before assuming this post, he was president of the International University of Japan. In his career he has been a professor at the National Graduate Institute for Policy Studies (GRIPS) (2012–2014); a professor at the University of Tokyo's Graduate School for Law and Politics (1997–2004, 2006–2012); ambassador extraordinary and plenipotentiary, deputy permanent representative of Japan to the United Nations (2004–2006); and a professor at Rikkyō University's College of Law and Politics (1985–1997).

Dr. Kitaoka's specialty is modern Japanese politics and diplomacy. He obtained both his BA (1971) and his PhD (1976) from the University of Tokyo. In addition to being an emeritus professor of the University of Tokyo and of Rikkyō University, he is an adjunct professor at GRIPS. He has received many honors and awards, including the Medal with Purple Ribbon (2011) for his academic achievements.

Fumiaki Kubo has been the A. Barton Hepburn professor of American government and history at the University of Tokyo's Graduate School for Law and Politics since 2003. He is the research director of the Nakasone Peace Institute, a senior visiting scholar at the Japan Institute for International Affairs, and a senior research scholar at the Tokyo Foundation. In 2001 and 2002, Professor Kubo served on the Prime Minister's Commission on the Study of the Direct Election System for Prime Ministers. Since 2007, he has been a member of the U.S.–Japan Conference on Cultural and Educational Interchange (CULCON). In February 2015, he became a member of the Japan–U.S. Educational Commission. He was the president of the Japanese Association for American Studies from 2016 to 2018.

Professor Kubo studied at the University of Tokyo's Faculty of Law, earning his BA from that institution in 1979 and his PhD in 1989. He also studied at Cornell University from 1984 to 1986, at Johns Hopkins University from 1991 to 1993, and at Georgetown University and the University of Maryland from 1998 to 1999. He was an invited professor at Sciences Po (Paris Institute of Political Studies) in 2009, and a Japan scholar at the Woodrow Wilson International Center for Scholars in 2014.

Professor Kubo is the author of many books including *A History of American Politics* and *American Politics and the Public Interest*. He also edited *A Study on the Infrastructure of American Politics*. In 1989, he received the Sakurada-Kai Gold Award for Political Studies and the Keiō Gijuku Award for his book *The New Deal and American Democracy*.

Yūichi Hosoya is a professor of international politics at Keiō University, Tokyo. He is also a senior researcher at the Institute for International Policy Studies, a senior fellow at the Tokyo Foundation, and an adjunct fellow at the Japan Institute of International Affairs. Professor Hosoya was a member of the advisory board of Japan's National Security Council from 2014 to 2016. He was also a member of the Prime Minister's Advisory Panel on Reconstruction of the Legal Basis for Security from 2013 to 2014, and the Prime Minister's Advisory Panel on National Security and Defense Capabilities (2013).

Professor Hosoya studied international politics, earning a bachelor's degree at Rikkyō University, a master's degree in international studies at the University of Birmingham, and a PhD at Keiō University. He was a visiting professor and Japan Chair (2009–2010) at Sciences Po (Paris Institute of Political Studies) and a visiting fellow (Fulbright Fellow, 2008–2009) at Princeton University. His research interests include postwar international history, British diplomatic history, Japanese foreign and security policy, and contemporary East Asian international politics. His most recent publications include *Security Politics: Legislation for a New Security Environment* (JPIC, 2019) and "Japan's Security Policy in East Asia" in *Japan and Asia's Contested Order: The Interplay of Security, Economics, and Identity* (Palgrave, 2018).

Satoru Mori is a professor of international politics and US foreign policy in the Department of Global Politics at Hōsei University's Faculty of Law. Professor Mori, a former Japanese Foreign Ministry official, holds a PhD from the University of Tokyo, LLM degrees from Columbia University Law School and Kyoto University, and an LLB from Kyoto University. During his sabbatical from 2013 to 2015, he was a visiting researcher at Princeton University and George Washington University.

Professor Mori's book on US diplomatic history, *The Vietnam War and Alliance Diplomacy*, published by the University of Tokyo Press in 2009, was awarded the 15th Hiroshi Shimizu Prize for Distinguished Academic Work from the Japanese Association of American Studies. He is also a recipient of the Nakasone Yasuhiro Incentive Award, and is a senior fellow at the Nakasone Peace Institute.

Miyuki Matsuzaki, a captain in the Japan Maritime Self-Defense Force (JMSDF), is currently on secondment as a counselor to the Cabinet Secretariat. Having joined the JMSDF in 1998, she has served as a member of the Maritime Staff Office, the Joint Staff, and the JMSDF Command and Staff College, among other positions.

Captain Matsuzaki holds a bachelor's degree (1996) and a master's degree (1998) from Keiō University, as well as a master's degree from Georgetown University (2006). She was a senior research fellow at the Nakasone Peace Institute from 2014 to 2016.

Shin Kawashima has been a professor of international relations at the Graduate School of Arts and Sciences at the University of Tokyo since 2006. He is a senior researcher at the Nakasone Peace Institute, a senior fellow at the National Security Agency, an associate member of the Science Council of Japan, and has served as an advisor on governmental panels in his field. He is also the editor of *Nippon.com* and of *Gaikō* (Diplomacy) magazine, as well as an academic adviser to the Young Forum in the Mt. Fuji Dialogue.

Professor Kawashima earned a BA from the Tokyo University of Foreign Studies (1992) and a PhD in oriental history from the University of Tokyo (2000). He was a member of the Faculty of Law at Hokkaido University from 1998 to 2006. He has studied and conducted research at the Institute of Modern History, Academia Sinica (Taipei), the Beijing Center for Japanese Studies, Peking University, National Chengchi University (Taipei), and the Woodrow Wilson International Center for Scholars.

Professor Kawashima's work has focused on Chinese and Taiwanese diplomatic history based on Chinese diplomatic archives; he recently began research on contemporary international relations in East Asia. His first book, *Formation of Chinese Modern Diplomacy* (2004), was awarded the Suntory Academic Prize in 2004. He was a contributing author of *Groping for A Modern State: 1894–1925* (2010), *China in the 21st Century* (2016), and *Frontier of China* (2017), and coauthored *Japan-China Relations in the Modern Era* (2017), among other books.

Yōji Kōda, a retired vice admiral of the Japan Maritime Self-Defense Force (JMSDF), is a graduate of the Japan Defense Academy (1972), JMSDF Staff College, and the US Naval War College. As a surface officer, he commanded the JS *Sawayuki* (DD-125), Destroyer Flotilla Three, and the Fleet Escort Force at sea. On shore, he served as director general (DG) for Plans and Operations, as maritime staff, and as DG joint staff, as well as being the commandant of the JMSDF Sasebo District. After retiring from the JMSDF as commander in chief of the Self-Defense Fleet in 2008, Vice Admiral Kōda was invited to Harvard University's Asia Center as a research fellow on Chinese naval strategy from June 2009 to July 2011. He served as an advisor to Japan's National Security Secretariat until March 2015.

Vice Admiral Kōda is a prolific writer on maritime affairs and military history. His recent articles in English include "The Russo-Japanese War: Primary Causes of Japanese Success," *U.S. Naval War College Review* (2005); "Japanese Perspective on China's Rise as a Naval Power," *Harvard Asia Quarterly* (2010); "A New Carrier Race? Strategy, Force Planning, and JS *Hyuga*," in the *Naval War College Review* (2011); "The U.S.-Japan Alliance: Responding to China's A2/AD Threat," *Center for New American Security* (2016); and "Maritime Security in the Region: SCS and ECS as Key Arenas for Converging Political Interests," in the *Asia Pacific Review* (2016). He contributed to *Refighting the Pacific War: An Alternative History of World War II* (Naval Institute Press, 2011) and coauthored *Maritime Strategy and National Security in Japan and Britain* (Global Oriental, 2012).

Futoshi Matsumoto is a career diplomat in Japan's Ministry of Foreign Affairs (MOFA). After graduating from the University of Tokyo and joining MOFA in 1988, he worked in the Peacekeeping Operation Division, the Middle Eastern Bureau and other posts in Tokyo, at the Japanese delegation to the Organization for Economic Cooperation (OECD), and at the Embassy of Japan in Egypt. He went on to serve as director of Non-Proliferation and KEDO affairs, director of the International Department in the Japanese Cabinet Intelligence and Research Office, and director of MOFA's Intelligence and Analysis Service. He was a senior research fellow at the Institute for International Policy Studies under former prime minister Yasuhiro Nakasone on secondment from MOFA. He was named chargé d'affaires at the Embassy of Japan in Syria in 2015 and special coordinator for Syria in 2016. After postings in Amman, Jordan, and Beirut, in 2019 he assumed his current post as deputy chief of mission at the Consulate-General of Japan in New York.

Mr. Matsumoto's publications include *Revenge of World History: The Westphalian Order, the Chinese Order and Daesh* (Kodansha, 2016; in Japanese); "The World Order and a New Behemoth" (*Asia-Pacific Review*, May 2015); and *Missile Nonproliferation* (Bunshun-bunko, 2006; in Japanese). He has also contributed numerous articles to the *Japan Business Press* (jbpress.co.jp) on issues related to the South China Sea and the Middle East.

Kōichi Satō has been a professor of Asian studies at the College of Arts and Sciences at J. F. Oberlin University since 2007. He currently serves as a lecturer at the Japan Maritime Self-Defense Force Staff College, a lecturer at the National Institute for Defense Studies, a policy adviser to the Japan Coast Guard, and a visiting fellow at the Center for Study of the South China Sea at Dōshisha University.

After earning his BA (1983) from the Tokyo Metropolitan University Faculty of Law, Professor Satō studied at the Institute of Southeast Asian Studies in Singapore from 1988 to 1990 and served as a research fellow at the Japan Institute of International Affairs from 1988 to 1993. After receiving his MA from the Tokyo Metropolitan University Faculty of Law in 1993, he served as a lecturer at the Tokyo University of Foreign Studies from 1996 to 2007 and as a professor at the J. F. Oberlin University School of International Studies from 2003 to 2007. He received his PhD in international studies from Waseda University in 2009.

Professor Satō is the author of many books in Japanese, including *The ASEAN Regime* (Keisō Shobō, 2003); *The Lion City and the Wind of the Malacca Straits* (Mekong, 2004); *Japanese Royal Diplomacy in Asia* (Heibonsha, 2007); and *The China Threat and ASEAN Conference Diplomacy* (Keisō Shobō, 2012).

Takako Hirose is an emeritus professor at Daitō Bunka University, Tokyo. Having earned a PhD in international relations from the University of London, she served as Atomic Energy Commissioner of Japan from 2006 to 2009, and in 2010 was appointed by the prime minister as a member of the Council on Security and Defense Capabilities in the New Era.

Professor Hirose's publications in English include "Prospects of Japan-India Nuclear Cooperation," in the inaugural issue of the *East Asia Monitor* (February 2014); "Japanese Emerging Nationalism and Its New Asia Policy" in *Asian Security Dynamic: US, Japan and the Rising Powers* (Promila & Co., 2008); and *Two Asian Democracies: A Comparative Study of the Single Predominant Party Systems of India and Japan* (Konark Publishers, 1994). She has also edited a number of books in Japanese, including *Development and Current Features of Indian Democracy: An Analysis of the 15th Lok Sabha Elections*, (Keisō Shobō, 2011). Her recent works include "India's Nuclear Policy: Promotion of Nuclear Energy Despite Fukushima," in *Political and Legal Analyses of Nuclear Power*, Studies in Political Science, vol. 8 (Center of Legal and Political Studies, Senshū University, 2012).

Teruhiko Fukushima joined the department of international relations at the National Defense Academy of Japan (NDAJ) in March 2009 as a professor specializing in Oceania. Prior to joining NDAJ, Professor Fukushima taught at the School of International Studies at J. F. Oberlin University in Machida, Tokyo. He was a member of the executive board of the Australian Studies Association of Japan from 1992 to 2007, and again from 2010 to 2016. From June 2013 to June 2016, he served as its president.

Professor Fukushima has a PhD in international relations from Australian National University, as well as a master's degree in international relations and a bachelor's degree in the liberal arts from the University of Tokyo. He has written extensively on Australian politics, foreign policy, and diplomatic history, especially on Japan-Australia relations. In recent years, he has written on Australia's response to the rise of China, Australia's links with the Middle East, Australia's maritime security, and Australia's defense legislation.

Narushige Michishita is vice president of the National Graduate Institute for Policy Studies (GRIPS) in Tokyo. He also serves as director of the GRIPS Security and International Studies Program, the Maritime Safety and Security Policy Program, and the Strategic Studies Program. He is a member of the National Security Secretariat Advisory Board and a global fellow at the Woodrow Wilson International Center for Scholars in Washington, DC. He has served as a senior research fellow at the National Institute for Defense Studies of Japan's Ministry of Defense, and as an assistant counselor at the Cabinet Secretariat for Security and Crisis Management.

Professor Michishita earned his PhD from the School of Advanced International Studies at Johns Hopkins University in 2003. A specialist in Japanese security and foreign policy as well as security issues on the Korean Peninsula, he is the author of *North Korea's Military-Diplomatic Campaigns, 1966–2008* (Routledge, 2009) and coauthor (with Peter M. Swartz and David F. Winkler) of *Lessons of the Cold War in*